The
Southeast Asian
Economic Miracle

The
Southeast Asian
Economic Miracle

Edited by
Young C. Kim

Transaction Publishers
New Brunswick (U.S.A.) and London (U.K.)

Copyright © 1995 by Transaction Publishers, New Brunswick, New Jersey 08903.

This book is printed on acid-free paper that meets the American National Standard for Permanence of Paper for Printed Library Materials.

Library of Congress Catalog Number: 94-44021
ISBN: 1-56000-196-8
Printed in the United States of America

Library of Congress Cataloging-in-Publication Data

The Southeast Asian economic miracle / edited by Young C. Kim.
    p.   cm.
    Contains 2 issues of Journal of northeast Asian studies, vol. 12, no. 3–4.
    Includes bibliographical references.
    ISBN 1-56000-196-8 (alk. paper)
    1. Asia, Southeastern—Economic conditions. 2. Asia, Southeastern—Economic policy. I. Kim, Young C. II. Journal of northeast Asian studies.
HC441.S733 1995
338.959—dc20
                          94-44021
                          CIP

Contents

Preface vii
Young C. Kim

1. The Transition in the Political Economy of South Korean Development: Issues and Perspectives 1
Hak K. Pyo

2. Malaysia: The Anxieties of Success 15
Llewellyn D. Howell and Ronald D. F. Palmer

3. Recent Developments and Future Prospects of the Indonesian Economy 47
Anwar Nasution

4. Southeast Asian Economic Experience and Prospects: Myanmar 67
Win Tin

5. The Economic Development of Vietnam, Laos, and Cambodia 85
Frederick Z. Brown

6. The Prospects for Democratization in Southeast Asia: Local Perspectives and International Roles 105
Bruce M. Koppel

7. Government and Business in Thailand 137
Daniel Unger

8. Trade and Investment in Southeast Asian Development 159
Stephen Parker

9. Managing Renewable Resources in Southeast Asia: The Problem of Deforestation 177
Gareth Porter

10. Showtime for Southeast Asia: An Economic and Political Crossroads 207
Bernard K. Gordon

11. The PRC, Taiwan, and the Overseas Chinese
    Ralph N. Clough   227

12. Southeast Asian Economic Experience and Prospects:
    A Summary
    Ben Barber   243

Contributors   257

Index   259

Preface

That the countries comprising the Association of Southeast Asian Nations (ASEAN) and some of their neighbors recorded dramatic increases in key economic, social, and development indicators in the 1980s and early 1990s—the "economic miracle" in the region that is so extensively written about in scholarly and popular media—is of little debate amongst academics, government officials, economists, political scientists, geographers, and others who study the area. There is less agreement, however, about the sources of this growth, and whether the improvements in income, industrial and agricultural production, health, nutrition, and other quality of life measurements are a permanent or transitory feature of the Southeast Asian landscape.

The American Council on Asian and Pacific Affairs (ACAPA) and the Institute of World Economy of Seoul National University convened a conference in November 1993 in Washington, DC, to address these and other questions about the Southeast Asian economic miracle and this book is the product of those discussions. The co-sponsors are grateful to the Jinro Cultural Foundation for generously providing support for this project.

I also would like to acknowledge the valuable contribution made by experts in the field who contributed significantly to the success of the conference as guest speakers, moderators, and discussants. They included, in the order of their appearance, Gaston J. Sigur, ACAPA and The George Washington University; Ezra Vogel, Harvard University; Daniel Lev, University of Washington; John Merrill, Department of State; John Bennet and Alisdair Bowie, both of The George Washington University; Hakchung Choo, Center for Economic Education, Korea Development Institute; Robert Muscat, Institute for Policy Reform; David Steinberg, Georgetown University; Evelyn Colbert, SAIS, Johns Hopkins University; Catherin Dalpino, Department of State; Elaine Grigsby, AID, Department of State; Paul Cleveland, Department of State; Tae Yong Hahm, Korea Long-Term Credit Bank; H. Leedom Lefferts, Jr., Drew University; Danny Leipziger, The World Bank; Robert Sutter, Congressional Research Service; Vance Hyndman, CAPA, The Asia Foundation; and Harry Harding, Brookings Institution.

Young C. Kim

1 THE TRANSITION IN THE POLITICAL ECONOMY OF SOUTH KOREAN DEVELOPMENT: ISSUES AND PERSPECTIVES

Hak K. Pyo

Since after Lipset[1] advanced the proposition that democracy is a product of economic development, there have been voluminous theoretical and empirical studies investigating its validity. The critics of democracy argue that dictatorships can insulate the state from particularistic pressures and, therefore, are better at mobilizing savings. On the other hand, the defenders of democracies argue that only democratic institutions can constrain the state to act in general interest and that dictatorships of any stripe are a source of inefficiency; democracies are better at allocating investment.

After reviewing 18 empirical studies, Przeworski and Limongi[2] conclude that the statistical evidence on the Lipset proposition is inconclusive. Among the 21 findings generated by those studies, eight found that authoritarian regimes grew faster, eight found in favor of democracy, and five discovered no difference.

On the other hand, Lipset's proposition has been examined by a number of comparative historical studies. Moore,[3] for example, has come to skeptical conclusions about the chances of democracy as capitalist economic development spread around the globe. More recently, Huber, Rueschemeyer, and Stephens[4] have examined democratic transition and breakdown in Europe, South and Central America, and the West Indies. They have concluded that the level of economic development is causally related to the development of political democracy. They argue that the underlying reason for the connection is that capitalist development transforms the class structure, enlarging the working and middle classes and facilitating their self-organization, thus making it more difficult for elites to exclude them politically.

The purpose of this chapter is to examine the current democratic transition in South Korea both in an empirical and historical context. The success story of South Korea in development provides us with two edges of the connection between economic development and political regime. On the one hand, as cited by Sah[5] and Bardhan,[6] its development under President Park and President Chun provides a case in favor of an authoritarian regime that fosters economic growth by insulating development-minded decision makers from short-term rent-seeking and distributive politics. On the other hand, it also provides a case for the Lipset proposition in the sense that its economic development invited democratic transition under President Roh and the current President Kim. In this regard, a careful examination of the South Korean case is fully warranted. In my view, South Korea is a perfect example of supporting the view of comparative historical research, advanced by Huber, Rueschemeyer, and Stephens[7] and endorsed by Bardhan,[8] that the level of economic development is causally related to the development of political democracy. In the present chapter, I examine how capitalist development in South Korea has transformed the class structure and the nature of economic dependency.

In the next section, the capitalist development in South Korea under two consecutive authoritarian regimes is analyzed and its dependent nature and limitations are examined. This is followed by a discussion of the transformation of the class structure and the changes in economic dependency that ultimately have brought about a Lipset phenomenon. The final sections discuss the ongoing democratic transition and the conditions for the survival of democracy and reach a contentious conclusion.

ECONOMIC DEVELOPMENT UNDER AUTHORITARIAN REGIMES AND ITS LIMITATIONS

After the independence from Japanese colonial rule, the division of the Korean peninsula, and the subsequent Korean War, South Korea remained a poor underdeveloped country. The Rhee government relied heavily on U.S. military and economic aid. During the period of 1954–1961, the average growth rate of real GNP was about 4.0 percent with an average annual inflation rate of 22.1 percent, as shown in table 1. The balance of payments could be maintained at equilibrium only with U.S. aid.

In a recent article, which refers to South Korean development as an economic miracle, Lucas[9] has compared the country's economic situation in 1960 with the Philippines. Both countries had about the same standard of living with per capita GDP of about 640 U.S. dollars in 1975 prices. The college enrollment rates in South Korea and the Philippines were 5 percent and 13 percent respectively. Only 20 percent of South Korea and the Philippines GDP was generated in industry while the comparable number in the Philippines was 28 percent. Primary commodities made up 86 percent of Korean merchandise exports and 96 percent of Philippine merchandise exports. However, from 1960 to 1988, GDP per capita in the Philippines grew at about 1.8 percent per year, while in Korea it grew at 6.2 percent per year.

President Rhee followed a typical course of development dictatorship, oppressing the opposition party and bribing voters to hold the majority in the assembly. He also alienated himself not only from the public but also from the ruling class. Ultimately, the nationwide voting scandal in the 1960 general election invoked strong opposition by the opposition party and student activists.

The Rhee government was toppled by a student uprising in April 1960 and a cabinet system was formed under the new constitution. Even though the Second Republic under Prime Minister Chang was a seemingly democratic regime, it was too weak to consolidate power and secure both political and economic stability. It could not handle effectively the rampant demands by student activists and the newly formed opposition party.

It was setting up a classic situation for military intervention. While division among elite groups—with no individual group powerful enough to hijack the state by itself—may somewhat enhance the chance of democracy, it should nevertheless be pointed out that in some countries intra-elite conflicts may get out of hand (inviting extra-constitutional interventions, perhaps from the military).[10]

The political instability has provided the military both opportunity and legitimacy to intervene. Following a coup in May 1961, President Park consolidated military power and formed a new government. At the beginning of his rule, he rode on the popular sentiment of suppressing capitalist groups established under the Rhee government. Several well-known businessmen were put into jail and had to surrender their assets to the public. But soon Park realized that he needed their help to restore economic stability and, therefore, released most of them but requested that they come up with development project proposals. He started using the stick and carrot to control the business circle.

President Park was desperate to build the legitimacy of his government against the hesitant U.S. recognition and the vigorous opposition activities. He tried to establish it by making the public concentrate on two issues: national security from the North Korean threat and economic growth to avoid the vicious circle of poverty. The phaseout of U.S. economic aid increased public awareness of economic hardship and, therefore, the slogan for mobilizing national resources for the economic take-off was effectively penetrated into the public's mind.

Throughout the period of Park's presidency (1961–1979), South Korea managed to pass the take-off stage and to achieve a remarkable industrialization. The government drafted successive five-year economic development plans beginning in 1962. However, there was tight security control and political suppression. The political opposition to Park's regime was at its peak in October 1972. After being reelected with a narrow margin against Dae-Jung Kim, President Park declared what is called the "Restoration System" and made himself an almost permanent president by changing presidential election law from direct vote to indirect vote.

However, at the same time, he was able to insulate the development-minded bureaucrats from particularistic pressures and the marauding lobbies of distributive politics.[11] The South Korean economy managed to overcome the first oil crisis in 1974 and to pass the Lewisian turning point in 1975, ending the period of unlimited labor supply. During the 1960s, in order to fill the gap between domestic savings and investment demand, South Korea relied on foreign capital. Foreign capital inflow was made mostly in the form of borrowings from international lending institutions such as the World Bank and bank syndicate loans. The role of foreign direct investment was relatively low. The combination of capital and abundant but well-educated labor made it possible to achieve successful export-led growth.

After 1975, President Park pushed for a second stage of industrialization, focusing on heavy and chemical industries as strategic industries. He became more confident about the country's industrialization after successfully overcoming the first oil crisis. But, pressure from the Carter administration on the human rights issue and the pullout plan of the U.S. forces in South Korea made him obsessed with the goal of self-defense. At the same time, domestic opposition was getting more organized and, consequently, he put more people in jail as the political situation worsened. In addition, a worldwide recession and the second oil crisis was about to come.

As Przeworski and Limongi pointed out,[12] regimes do differ in their probabilities of surviving various economic conditions: authoritarian regimes are less likely than democracies to survive when they perform badly. In 1979, the South Korean economy was heading downward due to sluggish export demand, rampant inflation, and violent labor disputes. The Park regime did not survive: President Park was assassinated on October 26, 1979, by the chief of the Korean Central Intelligence Agency. The downfall of an almost absolute power created a huge vacuum in both political and economic life in Korea. In the following year, the Korean economy recorded a negative growth rate of real GNP (-3.7 percent) and the division of the main opposition party created another classical set-up for military intervention.

In retrospect, no one can deny that President Park became a developmentalist leader[13] and achieved his goal of industrializing the South Korean economy. As summarized in table 1, the economy grew at an average rate of 9.2 percent with inflation averaging 18.5 percent. The economy followed a route of high-pressured extensive export-led growth. Even though the Park government was closely connected with large enterprises and business groups, it promoted competition among them by allocating bank loans through government-controlled banks.

However, the insulation of the development-minded policy elite from politics is only a necessary condition of a developmental state, not a sufficient condition. As Bardhan[14] noted properly, large-scale technocratic development projects directed from above by an insulated modernizing elite were far removed from domestic realities and quickly became white elephants. The downfall of the Park regime was accelerated by inefficient resource allocation. It is evidence for the view that while an authoritarian regime can foster growth, it creates its own limitation. Only democratic institutions can work in the interest of the general public. It is for this reason that we do not observe any single industrial nation with a dictatorship.

In the aftermath of President Park's sudden death, a military group consolidated power and its leader, Mr. Doo-Hwan Chun, became president by another indirect vote after suppressing violent demonstrations in Seoul and Kwangju against the military intervention.

When President Chun began his presidency in 1981, he had to face the same situation President Park had faced two decades ago. The economy was in deep recession with hyperinflation and his regime had to establish political legitimacy. He relied heavily on experienced bureaucrats and supported them in their efforts to carry out a package of stabilization policies. The inflation rate came down and the economy was put back on a sustained growth path. Again the authoritarian regime managed to insulate bureaucrats successfully from politics.

During the Chun regime, the Korean economy went through a significant structural change. A revitalization plan for heavy industries was carried out, streamlining some of the inefficient enterprises. At the same time, major conglomerates started investing in more technology-intensive industries such as semiconductors and automobiles. A series of import liberalization plans were initiated and the industrial policy changed from a direct industry-specific support system to an indirect functional support system (for example, providing tax incentives for investments in energy-saving equipment). In other words, the Korean economy was changing from an extensive growth mode to an intensive growth mode. The latter mode puts more emphasis on productivity growth and quality upgrading of products while the former mode basically depends on the quantitative expansion and accumulation of factors.

Even though President Chun was not popular at all, he must be credited for not exercising further military intervention near the end of his presidency and for ending his single term as he had promised. Somehow he paved the way for the subsequent democratic transition.

President Roh was elected in 1987 by popular vote, taking advantage of divided opposition parties. During his presidency, he was also far from being a popular president but initiated a series of democratic transitions. His military background clouded his image of being a president elected by popular vote. However, his presidency can be viewed as a bridge between the authoritarian regimes of Park and Chun and the current civilian president, Kim. In this regard, economic development and the democratic transition in South Korea during the last three decades seems to have been causally related as Huber, Rueschemeyer, and Stephens[15] argued in the context of endogeneity of democracy.

The macroeconomic performance during the early years of the Roh presidency was quite satisfactory even though it was mainly helped by low oil

TABLE 1

Major Economic Indicators during Authoritarian Regimes: South Korea (1954–1992)

President Period	Rhee 1954–61	Park 1962–79	Chun 1981–87	Roh 1988–92
(1) Growth Rate in Real GNP	4.0 (2.7)	9.2 (3.3)	9.7 (2.9)	8.3 (2.6)
(2) Growth Rate of GNP Deflator	22.1 (19.3)	18.5 (6.2)	6.2 (4.6)	7.9 (2.5)
(3) Balance of Payments: Average Current Account Balance in millions of U.S. dollars	–2.0	–309	473	741

Note: 1) The figures in parenthesis are standard errors of the growth rates.
Source: The Bank of Korea, National Income Account (1988) and National Accounts (1990) (1992).

prices, low international interest rates, and the depreciation of the dollar against the yen. As shown in table 1, the average annual growth rate of real GNP was 8.3 percent with an average inflation rate of 7.9 percent. The current account surplus reached 14.2 billion dollars in 1988 and 5.1 billion dollars in 1989. However, it turned into a deficit from 1990 due to macroeconomic mismanagement.[16]

The significance of the Roh regime in the causal development between economic growth and democracy lies in the fact that economic growth can be sustained under a weaker authoritarian regime or in a period of democratic transition. It survived in the most violent period of wage inflation[17] and labor disputes.

THE LIPSET PHENOMENON IN SOUTH KOREA

The remarkable economic growth in South Korea under the authoritarian regimes brought about a Lipset phenomenon. As a result of late but rapid industrialization, there emerged a balance of class power between the capitalist group and the working and the middle classes that is the core of democratic transition.

The major indicators of structural change between 1965 and 1991 are summarized in table 2. The share of Machinery and Transport Equipment in total merchandise exports increased from 3 percent to 38 percent, which is a clear indication of manufacturing-based export-oriented growth. The secondary school enrollment rate increased from 35 percent to 87 percent, signaling the emergence of the power of the working class and the middle class through dissemination of information and knowledge. As a consequence, the wage differential, measured by the ratio of administrative manager wages and production worker wages, declined from 3.59 in 1971 to 2.58 in 1989.

The emergence of the working class is evident by looking at both urbanization and unionization rates as summarized in table 2. The share of compensation of employees in national income at factor cost increased from 30.1 percent in 1965 to 60.5 percent in 1991, which is further evidence of the emerging working class. The trend in income distribution is mixed. It improved according to data from the urban workers' household income and savings market survey but deteriorated according to data from urban family expenditure. The discrepancy might have been due to the usual omission of capital gains and property income in the family income survey. An improved income distribution indicates the emergence of the middle class. At the same time, a deteriorated distribution of family expenditure also indicates the emergence of the middle class, particularly self-employed professionals and proprietors who tend to report taxable income less than actual income.

Another requisite of democratic transition is the changing nature of economic and geopolitical dependence. Huber, Rueschemeyer, and Stephens[18] regard the transnational structure of power as a relevant element for the chances of democracy. They have argued that the international economy and system of states shape the balance of class power and the balance of power between state and civil society and constrain political decision making. They also have argued that dependency can have long-term effects on the structures of class and that war and geopolitical factors can strengthen the role of the security forces. They expected dependency to be an important factor but one without a clear-cut, unequivocal effect.

The changing nature of dependency in South Korea has been examined by the author.[19] Its economic dependence was examined in the context of trade, technology import, and investment. South Korea has pursued export-led growth by depending on Japan and the United States as both major trading partners and technology suppliers. In particular, it depended on the United States as the largest export market and on Japan as the largest import source of goods and technology. However, the degree of economic dependence has declined significantly over time. As shown in table 3, the share of the U.S. market in total exports has declined from 47.3 percent in 1970 to 23.2 percent in 1991. Over the same period, the share of imports from Japan declined form 41.0 percent to 25.9 percent. The share of the United States and Japan in total technology imports declined from 87.5 percent during the period of 1962–1976 to 75.8 percent during the period of 1977–1991 in terms of number of contracts. The same share in total amount of technology import contracts declined from 82.2 percent to 78.9 percent between 1962 and 1976. It is also noted that the share of U.S. technology in both number and amount has increased while that of Japanese technology has declined between 1977 and

TABLE 2
Major Indicators of Structural Change: South Korea

	1965	1991
1. Industrialization		
Share of Manufacturing in GDP (%)	18	28
Share of Merchandise Exports (%)		
Machinery and Transport Equipment	3	38
Other Manufactures	56	55
2. Education: Enrollment Rate (%)		
Secondary	35	87
Tertiary	6	39
3. Urbanization		
Share of Urban Population (%)	32	73
4. Share of Compensation of Employees to National Income at Factor Cost	30.1	60.5
5. Income Distribution: Gini Coefficient		
Urban Workers' Household Income Savings Market Survey	0.341[1]	0.304[2]
Urban Family Expenditure	0.444[3]	0.297[2]
	0.290[4]	0.333[2]
6. Wage Differential by Occupation Administrative Manager Wages/ Production Worker Wages	3.59[5]	2.58[6]
7. Unionization		
Union Members (1,000 persons)	302	1,803
Total Number of Employees	2,609	11,287
Unionization Rate (%)	11.6	16.0

Notes: 1) For 1963; 2) For 1990; 3) For 1967; 4) For 1966; 5) For 1971; 6) For 1989.
Sources: The World Bank, *World Development Report* (1990), (1993); Economic Plan-ning Board, *Urban Family Expenditure Yearbook* (each year); The Bank of Korea, *Savings Market Survey* (each year); The Bank of Korea, *National Accounts* (1990), (1991); The Ministry of Labor, *Occupational Wage Survey* (each year).

1991. In general, we can argue that South Korea's trade dependence has declined significantly but its technology dependence continues to exist.

On the investment dependence, we may refer to Tharakan[20] who estimated the share of multinational companies' export in total manufacture exports of newly industrializing economies. The share in South Korea (27.8 percent) was lower than Singapore (90 percent), Mexico (45 percent), and Brazil (43 percent). Since the authoritarian regimes allocated credit via state-controlled banks as an important means of controlling the business sector, they preferred syndicated bank loans to foreign direct investment and multinational enter-prises. Therefore, the investment dependence has not been of significant con-cern in South Korea.

While economic dependency has been reduced to a significant extent as a result of export-led growth, geopolitical dependency seems to remain as it did

TABLE 3

Trade and Technology Dependence: South Korea (1971–1991)

%

| | Trade | | | | Technology Import | | | |
| | Export Share | | Import Share | | Share in Number of Contracts | | Share in Amount of Contracts | |
	1970	1991	1970	1991	1962–76	1977–91	1962–76	1977–91
U.S.	47.3	25.8	29.5	23.2	21.8	26.9	26.1	48.1
Japan	28.3	17.2	41.0	25.9	65.7	48.9	56.1	30.8
Others	24.4	57.0	29.5	50.9	12.5	24.2	17.8	21.1
Total	100.0	100.0	100.0	100.0	100.0	100.0	100.0	100.0

Sources: The Bank of Korea, *Economic Statistics Yearbook* (selected years); Korea Industrial Technology Association, *Technology Import Report* (1992).

in the past. It has been the main aspect of dependency that has affected and constrained the political decision making of the past authoritarian regimes. Even with the end of the cold war, geopolitical dependency in South Korea did not change significantly and the nuclear issue with North Korea has constrained domestic policies. While there is increasing demand for welfare and social overhead capital, the defense and security budget has not been reduced. The tension with North Korea and the uncertain prospect for unification will continue to influence the future course of South Korea's democratic transition.

DEMOCRATIC TRANSITION AND SOCIOPOLITICAL REFORM

Even though former President Roh was elected by direct popular vote under a new constitution, his military background and the fact that President Chun hand-picked him as his successor obscured the legitimacy of his government. However, the current President Kim had won last year's presidential election against two prominent candidates, Dae Jung Kim, long-time opposition party leader, and Joo Young Chung, the owner of Hyundai business group who had no military background. Therefore, the current government is called the first civilian government since the Rhee government three decades ago.

In fact, the restored legitimacy seems to have provided President Kim with confidence in carrying out a series of sociopolitical and economic reform since his inauguration in February 1993. He introduced the asset registration system of public officials, including ranking officials in the administration, judicial system, and the assemblymen. A series of investigations led by the Justice Department resulted in the purge of several prominent assemblymen, bureaucrats, and generals who are believed to be beneficiaries of the previous authoritarian regimes.

Even though President Kim's campaign for sociopolitical reform has been quite popular among the public with an approval rating well over 70 percent, he has been confronted by explicit or at time implicit resistance by built-in political interest groups. Even within the ruling party, genuine supporters of his reform campaign belong to a minority group because the majority of assemblymen in the party were hand-picked before, either by President Chun or President Roh. Most ranking bureaucrats and military officers were those who were favored and raised under three decades of authoritarian regimes. Since President Kim had won a power struggle against the majority of Roh followers, his personal popularity does not seem to be well backed up by organized political forces.

Some have argued that his campaign for reform aimed against his political adversaries. Others have argued that his reform is doomed to fail because it is basically a negative campaign, not a positive one. In other words, they have claimed that the new government aims at disabling interest groups with veto powers from doing what they should not but does not enable them to do what they should. However, it must be pointed out that the interests of favored groups under authoritarian regimes of three decades have been rooted so deeply that it seems extremely difficult to pursue both democratic transition and sociopolitical reform simultaneously.

President Kim declared that he would not accept any political contributions from business and that he would pursue revisions of the political funds act and the political party act. In August 1993, he introduced a real-name system in all financial transactions by an emergency presidential order. In the past, anyone could hold an account at banks under a fictitious or borrowed name if he or she wanted to withhold sources of income and maintain confidentiality. Since a combined income tax system has not been introduced yet, interest income has been taxed separately. Even though such a system was not a transparent one, it has helped in channeling funds in the unorganized curb market into savings in financial institutions. The reform of the apparently non-transparent system into a "real-name system" was conceived in the early 1980s during the Chun administration but actual implementation has been delayed due to politicians' and business interest groups' lobbies against it. The Roh administration had once planned to implement it but gave up due to both to intensive lobbies and the uncertainty about its effects on the economy.

At the initial stage, there was much concern about the potential impacts of the real-name system on the economy, which had been already in recession. Quarterly real GNP growth rates during the first two quarters of 1993 (3.4 percent and 4.2 percent) were much lower than those during the corresponding periods of 1992 (7.4 percent and 5.9 percent). Some speculated that there would be a financial crisis in October because medium- and small-scale industries and retail proprietors who relied on the private loan (curb) market would not be able to finance their businesses.

In fact, South Korea is the first developing country that introduced such a system. Knowing that even Japan has not introduced a full real-name financial system yet, such worries could not be ignored. However, as it turned out, there was no financial crisis and, instead, the stock price index has jumped from 650 to 800 since the system was put into effect.

The real-name financial system may not solve all the problems but may facilitate further reform and help democratic transition. The alliance between political power groups and big business has become more difficult to operate and the contribution of political funds will have to be more transparent than before.

The sociopolitical reform initiated by the president has gained overwhelming popularity with the public who have been discontent with the abuse of power and wealth accumulated and exercised by a few beneficiaries of past authoritarian regimes. However, public support will continue if and only if their economic well-being improves. As Bardhan[21] writes, if the rate of economic development in a democracy is too slow to meet the ever-widening circle of democratic awareness and raised aspirations among the people, the resulting demand overload may endanger the survival of democracy. In addition, the organized apparatus of the state is not necessarily for drastic reforms. Therefore, unless there emerge organized political groups and bureaucrats who can actively support the president's campaign, the prospect for the success of reform programs is quite uncertain.

Barro[22] could find in the entire world only three countries, Chile, South Korea, and Singapore, where dictatorships were not hostile to private property. Indeed, the past authoritarian regimes in South Korea have protected capitalist property from private encroachments by organized workers and landless peasants. There was an implicit alliance between the military and the capitalists through the authoritarian regime that somehow promoted economic growth. Now that a democratic transition is settling in, insecure capitalists are hesitant in making investment decisions. The task ahead is to combine capitalism with democracy and safeguard property rights while promoting development against increasing demands for equal distribution and social welfare.

Harberger[23] estimated private after-tax rates of return on capital in selected countries and called South Korea (15.2 percent) an "outlier" in comparison with other countries: the United States (7.6 percent), West Germany (5.6 percent), the U.K. (4.4 percent), and Canada (6.4 percent). However, according to my recent estimate,[24] South Korea is no longer an "outlier." Its private after-tax rate of return had declined from 15 percent in 1971 to 6.3 percent in 1991: a convergence toward the level of industrial nations. Therefore, with rising wages and falling rates of return on capital, South Korea must face slower growth but increasing social demands.

SUMMARY AND PROSPECTS

In the present chapter, I have reviewed economic development in South Korea under authoritarian regimes. The insulation of the development-minded decision makers by the authoritarian regime from the ravages of distributive politics and the inevitable lobbies of group predation has been one of the most important factors for the success of economic development. The protection of property rights by the regime was another contributing factor for sustained private investment. In addition, more egalitarian initial wealth distribution[25] and more mobility of social status by means of education have also provided the state with a conducive environment for rapid development.

However, such authoritarian development lacked autonomy and participation of the people. When things go wrong, authoritarian regimes are less likely than democracies to survive, as noted by Przeworski and Limongi.[26] The downfall of the Park regime occurred not by accident but by the limitations of authoritarian development.

As a result of authoritarian economic development, there appeared a Lipset phenomenon in South Korea. We have examined the phenomenon in the context of the emergence of the working and the middle class and the changing structure of dependency. The democratic transition had been far from smooth, costing the state violent demonstrations and labor disputes. In a genuine sense, the democratic transition has just begun with President Kim who had been a prominent opposition party leader but was elected by last year's popular vote.

Lastly, we have also reviewed President Kim's campaign for sociopolitical reforms and the difficulties with such reform programs. To make these reform programs a success, the current regime needs to provide leadership in resolving collective action problems. Bardhan points out "this leadership has two aspects: formulating cohesive developmental goals in line with a nation's collective aspirations and, more importantly, avoiding prisoners' dilemma-type deadlocks that can occur in the pursuit of even commonly agreed upon goals."[27]

The success of the current democratic transition will depend on two aspects of sociopolitical change. The first is how to reorganize political groups and bureaucrats who have been proponents of democracy and supporters of the sociopolitical reform programs and mobilize them in implementing collective action programs. The second is how to transform the cause of political pluralism and the raised expectations of the working and the middle classes into an engine for renewed growth. In this regard, we are back to a classic proposition of whether democracy fosters or hinders economic growth. If Korean society can endure a slow and at times exasperating process of democracy and constrain itself to act in the general interest, it will succeed in completing the combination of capitalism and democracy. However, it it fails to do so, we will have further evidence to the claim that capitalist democracy was a part of history that may not be repeated.

NOTES

1. S. M. Lipset, "Some Social Requisites of Democracy: Economic Development and Political Legitimacy," *American Political Science Review*, vol. 53 (1959).

2. A. Przeworski and F. Limongi, "Political Regimes and Economic Growth," *The Journal of Economic Perspectives*, vol. 7, no. 3 (1993).

3. B. Moore, Jr., *The Social Origins of Dictatorship and Democracy* (Boston: Beacon Press, 1966).

4. E. Huber, D. Rueschemeyer, and J. Stephens, "The Impact of Economic Development on Democracy," *The Journal of Economic Perspectives*, vol. 7, no. 3 (1993).

5. R. K. Sah, "Fallibility in Human Organizations and Political Systems," *The Journal of Economic Perspectives*, vol. 5, no. 2 (spring 1991).

6. P. Bardhan, "Symposium on Democracy and Development," *The Journal of Economic Perspectives*, vol. 7, no. 3 (1993).

7. Huber, et al., op. cit.

8. Bardhan, op cit.

9. R. E. Lucas, "Making a Miracle," *Econometrica*, vol. 61, no. 2 (1993).

10. Bardhan, p. 49.

11. Ibid, p. 46.

12. Przeworski and Limongi, op. cit.

13. Ibid, p. 65.

14. Bardhan, p. 47.

15. Huber, et al., op. cit.

16. See H. K. Pyo, "Combined Terms-of-Trade Shocks and Structural Adjustments in a Rent-Seeking Economy: Korea, 1985–1989," in Academic Studies Series, *Joint Korea–U.S. Academic Symposium on Impact of Recent Economic Developments of U.S.-Korean Relations and the Pacific Basin*, (Washington, DC: Korea Economic Institute of America, 1991).

17. The average growth rate of monthly earnings in all industries during the period of 1987–1991 was 16.6 percent while that of value-added labor productivity was 10.4 percent.

18. Huber, et al., pp. 73–74.

19. Hak K. Pyo, "The Korean Economy in the World Capitalist System: A Critical Appraisal," *Korean Economic Journal*, vol. 30, no. 3 (1991).

20. P. K. M. Tharakan, *The International Division of Labor and Multinational Companies* (Saxon House, 1979).

21. Bardhan, p. 49.

22. R. J. Barro, "A Cross-Country Study of Growth, Saving, and Government," NBER Working Paper, no. 2855 (1989), p. 22.

23. Arnold C. Harberger, "Perspectives on Capital and Technology in Less Developed Countries," in *Contemporary Economic Analysis*, edited by M. J. Artis and A. R. Nobay (London: Croom Helm, 1978).

24. H. K. Pyo and H. J. Yoo, "A Comparison of Cross-Country Rates of Return and an Indirect Test of the Convergence Hypothesis," mimeograph, 1993.

25. In a cross-country test for dependency-stagnation hypothesis, I found that the countries with more egalitarian income distribution at the beginning of the development process grew faster than those with less egalitarian income distribution. See Hak K. Pyo, "A Cross-Country Test on the Dependency-Stagnation Hypothesis," in Kyong-Dong Kim, ed., *Depen-*

dency Issues in Korean Development: Comparative Perspectives (Seoul: Seoul National University Press, 1987).

26. Przeworski and Limongi, p. 63.
27. Bardhan, p. 4.

2

MALAYSIA: THE ANXIETIES OF SUCCESS

Llewellyn D. Howell and Ronald D. F. Palmer

AN ECONOMY AS PERSPECTIVE

The concept of economics is a prism imposed on the Malay world by the West, an attempt to displace the spectacles of religion and ancient culture that gave breadth and depth to life in those fifteenth century islands. Some in that world shed spectacles for prism, some did not, many kept both. But since some views of the world were changed, all were changed. Westerners—the British in Malaya—reshaped all human relationships in this context. Where the Malay did not fit the Western economic mold, the British simply placed the Chinese or the Indian. For 200 years the British perspective shaped economic policy and structure in Malaya. At the end of the era the Malayan economy was an appendage of the British economy, an outgrowth of the land rather than its people, and ill-prepared for the even newer dreamscape presented by the internal post-Western challenge of Marxism-Leninism. In the years of turmoil after World War II, Malaya remained a soil-based economic entity where prosperity remained directly tied to what Mother Nature had provided.

Emerging from colonial domination as an economic novice along with most of the developing world, Malaya (Malaysia after 1963) made its initial attempts at industrialization only in the late 1950s, after independence in 1957 and following a 1955 World Bank report, which had recommended import substitution as the appropriate tack under mild protection, backed by investment incentives. Heavily reliant on exports of tin, rubber, and other primary commodities, Malaysian GNP growth was 4.8 per annum in the 1960s.

Recognizing early the dependence on primary products, the Pioneer Industries Ordinance of 1958 offered specific incentives to stimulate investments in manufacturing in Malaya. The focus in this initial stage was primarily on the production of consumer goods. A radical shift from an inward-looking defensive industrialization strategy of import substitution to an outward-looking aggressive strategy of export promotion took place after 1968 and the Investment Incentives Act of that year. Export allowances and acceleration of depreciation were a part of the process introduced.

But the muddy economic roads traveled in the heady first decade of independence left what would become a bloody residue of imbalance in wealth and health in Malaysia. While the Chinese population had prospered in the laissez-faire atmosphere of the 1960s, Malays had not. When Chinese political gains in the 1969 West Malaysia election threatened to give Malaysian Chinese dominance in both business and politics, economic frustration was translated into street fighting and then military suppression. Government intervention in halting ethnic conflict was followed by equivalent intervention in social and economic policy.

The establishment of free trade zones beginning in 1971 reflected the onset of the New Economic Policy (NEP), a 20-year plan designed to redistribute equity from primarily foreign hands into *bumiputera* (indigenous peoples, primarily Malays[1]) hands. Under the NEP and in the effort to bring Malays more fully into the mainstream of the economy, manufacturing became the leading sector, growing at an average rate of 12.5 percent a year and commanding 20.5 percent of GDP in 1980.

The generation of employment in manufacturing was impressive, expanding 7.6 percent a year to reach 15.8 percent of all employment by 1988. Employment of Malays in non-agricultural sectors expanded. By 1980 Malay unemployment dropped from 8.1 to 5.1 percent of the Malay workforce. By 1980 the share of agriculture, forestry, and fishery decreased from 30.8 to 22.2 percent of GDP, while the services sector expanded, especially government services. GNP growth averaged 7.8 percent a year in the decade. Its stimulus was public expenditure, investment, and exports (commodities and oil).

In the same period, fixed public investment rose from 6 to 11 percent of GNP; public consumption increased from 16 to 18 percent of GNP; overall government expenditures, including those from public corporations, accounted for nearly one-third of GNP growth. Private investment rose from 13 to 19 percent of GNP. Exports expanded from 45 to 62 percent of GNP, as crude oil, copper, palm oil, and manufactures led this expansion. Manufactures were increasingly important in the last year of the decade. Most importantly, the incidence of poverty fell from 49 to 29 percent of all households. This was a major achievement.

The second oil shock of 1979 and the world recession of 1980–1982 hit Malaysia hard, particularly in exports of commodities. The value of exports dropped below that of imports in 1981. The combined current account deficits for 1981 and 1982 averaged almost 12 percent of GNP. Government budget deficits in 1981 and 1982 were enormous. Austere budgets were imposed in 1982, 1983, and 1984. Per capita real private consumption fell by 9 percent in 1980–1982. Living standards fell but were lower in rural areas because of depressed agricultural prices. The state of the global economy was about to undermine the progress already made for *bumiputera* and negate the impact of the NEP on social reform.

This was the atmosphere in which the Heavy Industrialization Scheme was launched, based on import substitution to develop industries utilizing Malaysian energy and raw material resources. The 1981–1983 period also saw the launching of the "Look East" policy based on selective emulation of the Korean and Japanese models for commercial management and organizational behavior. The target of the policy was the Malays, with a government hope and intention that some of the sense of order and drive found in those models could be imparted to a new Malay entrepreneurial class.

In pursuit of a corrective strategy, Malaysia resorted to fiscal conservatism beginning in 1984. Negative growth occurred in 1985 but GNP growth resumed in 1986, reaching 5.4 percent in 1987, 8.9 percent in 1988, 8.8 percent in 1989, and 10 percent in 1990. Inflation in the second half of the 1980s was also low, ranging from 0.4 to 2.8 percent in 1989. By 1990, real GNP had increased seven-fold since 1960. Ninety-six percent of all children were completing at least six years of schooling. By 1991, agriculture's share of GDP had declined to 20.4 percent (from 30.8 percent in 1970). Manufacturing rose to 25.1 of GDP (from 13.4 percent in 1970). Per capita GDP income was $2,000 in 1990 (from $500 in 1970). Nevertheless, the real mean income of Chinese in 1989 was 65 percent higher than that for Malays.

The economy has been very open and subject to international economic fluctuations. There are structural problems; the base of the economy still is concentrated in a handful of commodities, which exert a powerful influence on it. While the manufacturing sector has grown well it also is focused on only a few products (electronics and textiles). Much manufacturing is in the hands of multinationals, some of which have little local involvement. There is a growing labor shortage. Macroeconomic management is generally sound but there are weaknesses that stem from political interference (such as in protected heavy industry). Budget deficits have been large by Asian standards. External debt is relatively heavy by NIE standards. Ethnic rivalries still color virtually every aspect of national life. But the NEP survived and so did the image of Dr. Mahathir's guiding hand. *Bumiputera* made measurable and visible economic gains.

Communal leaders have behaved in a reasonably pragmatic and responsible fashion to avoid disturbing racial harmony and political stability during this period. Chinese and Malays are determined to avoid race riots such as occurred in 1969. Important structural changes are underway with both the manufacturing and primary sectors being upgraded through R&D efforts. Malaysian palm oil was the savior of the economy in the 1980–1982 recession and it holds a virtually unassailable comparative advantage in upstream production, refining, and downstream manufacture of high-value products. Downstream value-added is the focus of great R&D effort in Malaysia today.

Significant industrial restructuring is taking place in the manufacturing sector. There has been a shift from labor-intensive to capital-intensive industry, both in technology and human capital. Mohamed Ariff, in his book, *The Malaysian Economy: Pacific Connections*, makes some of these same observations and suggests that "(i)n the long run, the Malaysian manufacturing sector may entrench itself in resource-intensive industries which also happen to be capital-intensive, technology-intensive, and skill-intensive as well" (chemicals, tire manufacture, food-processing, and wood-based industries).

Malaysia is likely to join Korea, Taiwan, Hong Kong, and Singapore as an NIE before the year 2000. This does not thrill many Malaysians who fear this may mean the loss of GSP and other trading advantages Malaysia now enjoys. Malaysia is well-placed in the Pacific economy to enjoy the advantages of Pacific Rim growth, while retaining its economic and commercial ties with the West and continuing its ventures in South-South cooperation, particularly in Southern Africa. Most importantly, Malaysia is in a position to divide a growing economic pie among its competing ethnic groups. Political will and political capability, not economic resources, are the issue in determining equity.

INTO THE GLOBAL ECONOMIC COMPLEX

Malaysia has become an example in the political theory literature of the context within which a consociational democracy can serve to stabilize an otherwise conflictual political system that is afflicted by fundamental ethnic differences, which in turn might be exacerbated in a simple majority-rule system.[2] Malaysia's ethnic/economic circumstances are unique and the solutions that have been employed to bring the society through the traumatic years of the 1980s and 1990s, as successful as they have been, probably will not serve as an example to other national social systems. In the face of ready contributions of criticism and complaint, the Malaysian government has adopted an offensive strategy as the best approach to a good defense.

Malaysia has unabashedly taken the lead in what the *Far Eastern Economic Review* has called a "new East-West confrontation"[3] over differing Asian and Western approaches to human rights. Washington and the West have been accused of trying to impose alien values derived from "post-Renaissance liberal western traditions." Prime Minister Mahathir Mohamad has accused the West of seeking to use human rights policy to create dependency, "This is what the West wants—not democracy, not freedom, not human rights," the prime minister said in a recent speech.[4]

Prime Minister Mahathir pointedly did not attend the November 1993 Asia Pacific Economic Cooperation (APEC) Ministerial meeting in Seattle because the United States had previously opposed his concept of a subregional East Asian Economic Caucus. Mahathir and Malaysia were portrayed in the Western press as out of step. Meanwhile, the Kuala Lumpur Stock Exchange continued to soar and Malaysia will apparently register 8 percent or so economic growth again this year. The Malaysian economic example was cited by the Chilean finance minister in a November 24, 1993, *Washington Post* article on the surging Chilean economy. Speaking of the good Chilean record of investing 28 percent of its GDP, the minister stated, "Only China, Singapore and Malaysia have a higher rate of investment."[5]

Malaysia may have slipped a bit from its position as the world's largest producer of rubber as smallholders who account for two-thirds of production are suspending tapping their rubber trees and pursuing other economic opportunities inasmuch as world market prices for natural rubber are low. Smallholders and farmers living on state-sponsored Federal Land Development Authority (FELDA) rural development schemes have turned increasingly to oil palm cultivation since oil palm grows more rapidly than the rubber tree and comes into production sooner. Malaysia remains the world's largest producer of palm oil and has made massive investments in the production of downstream products.

Malaysia remains the leading world producer of saw logs and sawn timber. It is also a leading producer of cocoa, pepper, pineapples, and cut flowers. Malaysia has an important outlet for its fruit and garden produce in the flourishing Singapore market. Tin is no longer a leading Malaysian export but Malaysia remains the fourth largest tin producer. Malaysia pumps over 600,000 barrels of crude oil daily. Oil production providentially came on stream in time for the rise in oil prices in the 1970s and was used in great part to finance the affirmative action policies favoring Malays that were undertaken in the 1971 New Economic Policy (NEP). Large investments were made in infrastructure under the NEP; indeed, Malaysia has had an enviable record of devoting 20 percent or so of development expenditure to infrastructure since independence in 1957.

Malaysia is aggressively moving also to use its abundant endowment of natural gas in its Peninsular Gas Utilization project for energy generation in West Malaysia. PGU I was begun in 1981 and completed in 1985. PGU II was launched in 1989 and involved the laying of a pipeline from Kertih in Trengganu south to Johor Bahru and Singapore, branching to the Klang Valley area in the west coast from Segamat in Johor and was completed in 1992. Bidding is underway on the tender for PGU III, the third phase that will extend the pipeline north from Kertih to Kelantan on the east coast, and north on the west coast up the Klang Valley to the industrial area of Penang Island. Extensive plans are being implemented for the use of natural gas for industrial uses. A methyl tertiary butyl ether (MTBE) project has been completed, making Malaysia the second largest MTBE producer (an octane booster to replace lead) after Saudi Arabia. Ethylene and polyethylene plants located in Kertih are to begin production in 1995 to produce feedstock for a petrochemical industry.

LNG deliveries to Japan began in 1983 from Bintulu in Sarawak from three trains producing six million tons annually. This capacity was later raised to eight million tons annually. Three more trains of 2.5 million tons each are to come into production in 1994, 1995, and 1996. After 1995, Malaysia should be producing 15.5 million tons of LNG a year. Petronas, the national oil company, is purchasing an additional five LNG vessels to transport the product.

Malaysia has made other great strides industrially. It is the largest exporter of air conditioners and semiconductors in the world. It exports a large volume of other electrical and electronic products including color television sets and electric fans. Textiles and other manufactures are important exports. Malaysia is the second largest recipient of GSP benefits in the world.

There are many other positive things to say about Malaysia but the introductory paragraphs of this chapter indicate that there are anxieties that cloud the Malaysian horizon. Perhaps the lessons of the Malaysian experience are that anxieties can be overcome, lived with, and negative energies can be turned into positive synergies. At the base of the phenomenon of Malaysian progress and productivity is profound ethnic rivalry, which has produced sharp competition between the dominant Malays and the Chinese minority. This competition has overtones of ethnic survival and plays an equally important role in the competition between the leading Malay political groups for leadership of the bumiputera community. While knowing the Malaysian circumstance will not necessarily provide opportunities for emulation, the utility (and futility) of Western foreign policy toward Malaysia can be better understood by appreciating the crucible from which emanates the solid success that is modern Malaysia.

A SOURCE IN HISTORY

Histories of Malaysia may begin in a number of places in the context of societal evolution. To fully appreciate the circumstances of today, it is important to begin at a stage far earlier than most political histories even contemplate. There is, unfortunately but expectedly, a "who got here first" argument that enters into the competition between the races.

As is usually the case, this question is not easily answered. It is generally thought that the earliest of the waves of migration brought the peoples that are today known as the "orang Asli," who still populate some of the more secluded and mountainous regions of peninsular Malaysia. The Malays as well as the Chinese themselves trace their origins to the region that today is China. The people who now are known as Malays and the non-Muslim Malay types of Sabah and Sarawak are thought to have begun migration into the region beginning about four to five thousand years ago.[6] Those recognized as modern Chinese filtered into the region over much of the intervening period but their numbers were few and their ability to adapt was great, particularly before the Islamization of the region.

In what came to be known as the "Malay World," several major political units established themselves as significant regional powers. One of the earliest and largest, Srivijaya, can be traced from about 670 AD to about 1365. Encompassing, at its most expansive stage, an influence area the size of the continental United States but composed almost entirely of islands and parts of the peninsula, any political unit to have remained in existence for nearly 700 years certainly requires some measure of recognition and respect. At 700 years, Srivijaya lasted as a recognizable institutional body 500 years longer than the United States has so far. And yet, in the United States, no one recognizes this name.

In addition to its longevity and the extent of its maritime reach, it is important to note that Srivijaya was a Buddhist empire. In those times, and to a certain extent even today, politics and religion were part of a single configuring system. There could only be one apex in religion and politics: the "deva-raj" or god-king. To establish a separate political entity, one also felt compelled to separate oneself in terms of religion—not necessarily out of unhappiness with the religion itself but rather out of political need. A change in religion did not therefore mean an abandonment of the entire creed. New religions assimilated the old.

Madjapahit was a Java-based empire that originated in approximately 1100 and lasted until 1500. This was a Hindu empire. Just as Buddhism did not totally displace the Animism that went before, Hinduism did not totally displace Buddhism as Madjapahit gradually rose to political centrality in the Malay world. Rituals and beliefs were absorbed, albeit in a secondary and unfocused role.

Malacca was the last of the line of major Southeast Asian empires. Based in what is currently Malaysia, Malacca was a set of Islamic sultanates that was begun about 1400 and lasted until conquest by the Portuguese in 1511. Significant here are the facts that an Islamic political system of some importance was established in the region nearly 600 years ago, its location was in modern day Malaysia, and it was a politico-religious system that absorbed elements of previous systems, including their religions, from the region.

Each of the empires is given significant recognition in the Southeast Asia context. The 700-year Srivijayan empire is seen as having equal importance for Southeast Asians to Greece or Rome in the Western context. Most Westerners draw a blank when comparisons like the following are made:

No one nation remains backward forever. And no one nation is progressive always. Empires like those of Greece, Rome, Persia, Srivijaya, Melaka and Britain experience the same phases. At one time they were so advanced and powerful that it was inconceivable they could ever fall. But all of them declined and disintegrated.[7]

Srivijaya, Madjapahit, and Malacca were indigenous Malay empires of significant consequence in Asia. As with most empires, their strengths and successes are remembered more fondly than their weaknesses but it is important to understand that they are remembered. The states of the modern Malay world are built on a base of political and cultural glory that makes pride and identity extremely important in the mechanisms of current competitions.

The Portuguese brought the era to a close with their conquest of Malacca in 1511. Although they were only interested in controlling the Strait of Malacca and therefore disregarded the interior and other sultanates in the region, they ended the period of Malay dominance in the region and began the process of forcible European intrusion into regional governance, economy, and culture.

The Dutch took Malacca in 1641 and began 150 years of Dutch rule in which a European presence and indifference oversaw a continuing disintegration of Malay political culture. The arrival of the British in Penang in 1786 initially produced little change in the relationship between the Europeans and the Malays as they established port facilities and trading connections from bases at Penang, Malacca (1795), and Singapore (1819),[8] However, full-scale political intervention began in the late 1800s on the backs of commercial agreements between the British and Malay royalty. Direct colonial rule expanded throughout the Malayan peninsula through 1909 when a British-Siamese agreement brought about British control of the northern sultanates of Perlis, Kedah, Kelantan, and Terengganu.[9] After 1874 and again after 1909, commercial circumstances changed such that massive Chinese and Indian immigration was encouraged. Their numbers grew at such a rate that by 1911, when censuses were conducted in each of the states, non-Malays comprised almost half of the overall population of Malaya and were a majority in British-dominated west coast states.[10]

A British presence was initiated in what was to become Sarawak in 1839 with the arrival of a former British East India Company officer named James Brooke. Brooke lent the naval guns of his own ship to aid the Sultan of Brunei in suppressing political challenges and later in controlling the piracy that was pervasive in the area. As a reward, the Sultan honored Brooke with grants of territory that he extended into the political unit that was to become Sarawak. Brooke took the title of "raja" and Brooke family rule remained the governing system of Sarawak until after World War II.[11] Under Brooke rule, in a country already divided ethnically between Malays, Ibans, and others, Chinese were brought in as traders and shopkeepers. They grew in numbers during the Brooke period to become an equal in proportion, composing nearly a third of the population, with little of the assimilation that had been the case when the numbers of Chinese were few and a distinct and separate "community" seemed unnecessary.

The current Malaysian state of Sabah, like Sarawak of the early nineteenth century, had a divided ethnic population. Muslim Malays lived along the coastal regions and animist peoples, primarily the Kadazans, populated the interior. Under the control of the British North Borneo Company after 1881, Chinese immigrants were again encouraged to reside in North Borneo and provide commercial services that were otherwise unavailable. The Chinese population grew and absorption became less viable and less likely. A distinct community came into being.

It should be noted that Indian influence and migration were important factors in the region well before the arrival of the Europeans. Royal families were in some cases entirely of Indian origin and other Indians were proponents of the prevailing religion and intermarried with the local population. Depending on both religion and region of origin in India, Indians tended to be less distinct in their communities within Malaya than were the Chinese. Indonesian migration to the area that is now Malaysia has been continuous over the centuries. Many of the peoples who are now classified as Malays, especially in Negeri Sembilan, have their origins in Indonesia. Such migration continues through 1993, with significant labor sources for both peninsular and Kalimantan (eastern) Malaysia being the Indonesians. Both of these groups retain language and cultural identities but have been more easily assimilated than the Chinese. There are approximately 50,000 legal Indonesian workers in Malaysia today and estimates of as high as 100,000 Indonesians working illegally in Malaysia.

If one stands back a bit from the historical Malaysian picture, the period can be seen in five reasonably distinct phases as it relates to the creation of the racial and cultural mosaic that is modern Malaysia: 1) Malay autonomy and empire, 670–1511; 2) European ascendancy, 1511–1874; 3) British mercantile policy, 1874–1909; 4) Communal encouragement, 1909–1957; and 5) Reconfigured independence, 1957–present. The critical turning point was the stage of British mercantile policy, in which not only numbers jumped dramatically but racial communities took on a different level of importance. The population proportions changed very little in the post-1909 period but the decades of consistent emphasis on communal economic specialization and social separation took their toll. The 1920s and 1930s were characterized by a growth in Malay nationalist sentiment, with expressed concern about being inundated—in their own land—by non-Muslim immigrants.

The increasing confirmation of separateness that was fostered by British colonial policy was recognized and utilized by the Japanese during their occupation of Malaya and Borneo during World War II. Prior to their arrival, open conflict was most often between rival economic groups—with Malays and Chinese on both sides—rather than between racial groups. The occupying Japanese encouraged the division between these two groups, with a consequence of interethnic violence in the form of attacks and executions by the predominantly Chinese Malayan Peoples Anti-Japanese Army (MPAJA) against those thought to be collaborating with the Japanese.[12] While the

Japanese themselves were forced to attempt to control this violence, animosity and interethnic fear came to be dominant characteristics of race relations in the postwar period.

This was the environment in which a new political system was to be created under the reluctant sponsorship of the British after the war. Singapore, carved out of Johore by the British East India Company and now populated predominantly by Chinese, was immediately removed from Malayan independence plans. The inclusion of Singapore would have reduced the Malays to a minority and the continued activism of the MPAJA, later as the Malayan Communist party (MCP) but still almost exclusively Chinese, threatened any agreement about Malay dominance under any circumstance.

A POLITICAL CONTRACT: THE RULES OF THE GAME

The post-World War II context of Malayan independence was compelling. The British were rushing to reduce their colonial holdings; Marxist ideology was on the rise everywhere that colonial powers were appearing reluctant or incompetent and posed a religious as well as a political threat in the Malayan context; broadly participatory democracy was also on the rise in the American Rooseveltian era, with concerns about as well as hopes for "majority" rule; the power of nationalism was rising everywhere; the British attitude about preserving a special place for Malays changed as a result of Malay collaboration with the Japanese during World War II. In Malaya, these forces combined to bring about a unique political contract in the form of the Constitution of the Federation of Malaya.

The United Malays National Organization (UMNO) was formed in 1946 in response to a British plan to create a Malayan Union that would drastically reduce the power of the sultans and equalize the participatory political rights of all ethnic groups in Malaya.[13] The Malayan Union proposal divided the population and its leaders clearly along ethnic lines. Malay vehemence, in addition to growing British and American concern about communist influence (the Malayan communists—mainly Chinese—supported the Union concept), led the British to back away from the original plan and propose the Federation of Malaya. The Federation would specifically exclude Singapore and would retain a relatively important role for the sultans. While this was more acceptable to the Malays, it was not acceptable to the communists, who returned to "revolutionary armed struggle" in 1948 and fostered a twelve-year (1948–1960) "Emergency."

Nevertheless, a Malay-dominated Malaya was formed and independence granted in 1957 with the following basic "rules of the game." Between 1948 and 1957 a consensus was worked out whereby the Malays would share political power (in what many contended was still "their country") with the other ethnic groups in exchange for assistance in improving the Malays' economic position in the post-independence society.[14] The sultans would retain important positions (including the election every five years of one of themselves to be the *agong* or king) and special responsibilities for protecting the rights and privileges of each of the ethnic groups, but especially the Malays.

An "Alliance" of race-based political parties (UMNO, the Malayan Chinese Association (MCA), and the Malayan Indian Congress (MIC)) was brought into being to manage political organization and specifically to retain a distribution of political power such that the Malays would continually be in a position of dominance. Two important notes: first, other options were floated and advocated, including the Malayan Union proposal. None were seen as viable in this social and temporal context by any group that could be envisioned as a majority. Second, each of the communities was better off under this arrangement than they might have been under other arrangements or in other circumstances. Members of the Chinese community, in particular, noted the levels of both economic achievement and political participation that were possible in Malaya compared with either China itself or other countries in the region. A bargain was struck and the rules were set.

In the 1980 census, the ethnic background on the peninsula was roughly 56 percent Malay, 33 percent Chinese, and 10 percent Indian. The population of Sabah was 83 percent Pribumis (more or less evenly divided between Malays and Kadazans) and 16 percent Chinese. The Pribumi category incorporates a broad group of indigenous peoples that includes Kadazan, Murut, Bajau, Malays, and Indonesians.[15] In Sarawak, the major groups are Iban (30 percent), Chinese (29 percent), Malays (20 percent), Bidayuh (8 percent), Melanau (6 percent), and other indigenous peoples (5 percent). For the nation as a whole, the Malay proportion of the country has remained fairly constant at about 50 percent since the early 1900s. This marginal percentage is the key to Malay concerns about their role in a democratic political system that is the inheritor of the powerful regional presence that was Srivijaya, Madjapahit, and Malacca.

For anyone addressing the Malaysian racial enigma, it is extremely important to understand the term *bumiputera* and its implications in the politics and economics of modern Malaysia. In the broadest terms, *bumiputera* means "native," implying a racial presence in the country through recent millennia. More specifically, the term is often translated as "sons of the soil." Technically *bumiputera* means "princes of the soil," linking two very important concepts in Malay life and society. *Putera* is a prince, a reflection of the sultanic system that has been in place since the coming of Islam in the thirteenth and fourteenth centuries but that was also present in the prior period in other forms. Today there are 17 formal sultanates still in place and vestiges of others, especially including Malacca and Sarawak. Each has an extensive royal family, providing a very wide base of individuals with some royal blood who can claim the right to a *putera* linkage. Having such a connection makes identity with the society significantly stronger.

The term *bumi* is equally important. Being heretofore an almost exclusively agricultural people, Malays have a very close literal connection to the soil. But the linkage goes beyond that. A very well educated Malay (post masters degree, educated in the West) recently explained why Malays return to Malaysia after study abroad while many non-Malay Malaysians do not. "We cannot stay away," he said. "We belong to the land." In a land and among a people where religions have overlain each other over the last several thousand years, animist beliefs still surface among Muslims whose ancestors were Hindus whose ancestors were Buddhists whose ancestors were animists There is a spiritual relationship between Malays and the soil that does not necessarily exist for others whose citizenship is Malaysian. The relationship is strong and wrought with strong emotion.

While the term *bumiputera* describes accurately the societal and spiritual linkage between a people and their country, it is also a political convenience. The term only came into prevalent use in the wake of racial conflicts between Malays and Chinese in 1969. When the threat of possible Chinese political ascendancy arose, figures cited on Malay numbers in the country were sometimes below 50 percent. That is, if a straight count of Malays were made, Malays might be found to be a minority in "their own country." By counting as *bumiputera* others who were equally (or more) "native," although not Muslim, the percentage was clearly above 50 percent for Malaysia as a whole, giving grounds for "*bumiputera*" control of the democratic political process and "*bumiputera*" priority in the dispersion of economic benefits. But *bumiputera* for all intents and purposes still means Malay. The effort put into the establishment and legitimization of the term is a reflection of the importance of race and racial prerogatives to the Malays. Being cast into a minority status, especially a political minority status, is viewed by the Malay as the beginning of the end of their society. It is a simple formula but an extremely powerful one. Its import can be seen in virtually every aspect of policy and behavior in the Malaysian political system, including today's efforts at environmental control and sustainable economic development.

Historically and geographically, Singapore is a part of the southern peninsular state of Johore. Politically separated by agents of the British East India Trading Company in 1819, depopulated by Malays due to adverse living conditions on the island, and maintained as a distinct entity by the British, Singapore was recreated as a social unit primarily with Chinese immigrants. Its preponderance of Chinese resulted in its explicitly being left out of the Malayan Federation in 1957. But Singapore was still part of Malaya in every other economic and social sense. The interdependence between Malaya and Singapore, and the need for British separation from direct colonial control, led to the proposal for Malaysia in the early 1960s.

Since the population distribution had not changed since 1957, a direct integration of the two units still was not possible. Since the British also intended to depart from control of Sabah, Brunei, and Sarawak, a compromise was put forth that would solve several problems at once. By joining these three other units with Singapore and Malaya, a majority of *bumiputera* could be retained for the new country as a whole—even counting Singapore. The Sultan of Brunei opted not to be absorbed in this scheme but the loss of Brunei did not affect the balance of ethnic groups among the remaining four units.

While the constitutional contract was amended in 1963 to bring in the new units, the basic rules were not. The Alliance would still dominate, Malays would be politically preeminent, and non-Malays could pursue their economic interests with limited but protected political rights. Key to this arrangement was the continuation of political control by the Alliance, with UMNO controlling the Alliance. However, success by Lee Kuan Yew's Singapore People's Action Party (PAP) in the elections of 1964 brought immediately forth a concern that a toppling of the Alliance, and therefore of the contract that was the premise of Malaya and Malaysia was possible. Concern was expressed by both Malays and Chinese. Singapore was asked to leave the federation and did so in 1965.

A new seed of concern, though, had been planted. In the elections of May 1969, opposition gains again induced fears of an Alliance collapse and racial taunting brought fears and animosities to a crest. They took the form of racial fighting, primarily in Kuala Lumpur, that took hundreds of lives and many days to subdue.[16] With the possibility that the non-Malays might have both economic and political dominance, the contract was on the verge of collapse. Democracy, in a sense the source of the problem, was suspended and the Cabinet ruled 1969 to 1971.

ECONOMIC STRATEGY: THE NEW ECONOMIC POLICY, 1971–1990

Parliamentary democracy was restored in 1971 with the imposition of a New Economic Policy (NEP) and a 20-year plan for economic development. The NEP was directed at eradication of poverty but its primary goal was redress of the economic imbalance that had led Malays to fear that both economic and political power would fall into the hands of non-Malays. Concerned that political power could be lost under demands for equal political rights that were evolving elsewhere in the Third World, the Malay leadership decided that changes in the Malay role in the economy were overdue.

The primary objective of the New Economic Policy was Malay politico-economic empowerment, where equity should be redistributed from 1971 levels of 4 percent held by the *bumiputeras*, 34 percent by non-Malays, and 62 percent in the hands of foreigners[17] to a 30–40–30 ratio by 1990. Also a number of economic privileges were granted to the *bumiputera*. These included restricted ownership in a number of important economic areas, such as logging, shipping, petroleum distribution, taxi company ownership, etc.; provision of capital at better than prevailing rates or terms; percentage requirements for the involvement of *bumiputeras* in ownership, management, and employment in certain industries, especially if they are initiated by foreign interests; and rights and support in the educational sector, including higher ratios of entrance to Malaysian universities and financial support for study both at home and abroad.

Early in his tenure as prime minister, Dr. Mahathir bin Mohamad instituted what he termed a "Look East" policy to supplement the NEP equity regulations. This policy encouraged Malays, in particular, to see the Japanese and South Koreans as appropriate examples of a work ethic and a savings and investment style that would help bring Malays into the economic range of the other Malaysians. Only limited numbers of Malays went to Japan to study under this policy. However, in contrast, huge numbers of Malay students went to the United States to study. That number peaked at 25,000 in the 1980s but remains over 10,000. The "Look East" policy was used more as encouragement to Malays to get into the competition with the Chinese and to expect success in business on the basis of hard work and business skill and less on the basis of government support and handouts. It was hortatory but it has had some effect.

As one would expect, there were numerous complaints from Malaysian Chinese and Indians about the *bumiputera* entitlements and economic privileges[18] but the Chinese in particular saw the NEP special considerations as another challenge and most worked to overcome these obstacles. By 1990, the equity ratios had changed to 18 percent in the hands of *bumiputeras*, 55 percent in the hands of other Malaysians (mostly Chinese), and 27 percent remaining to foreigners.[19]

While it may be obvious, several important consequences arise from this particular distribution. First, *bumiputeras* and Malays did not reach their goal and some Malays, particularly in the opposition, have made much of this. On the other hand, *bumiputera* equity was increased by at least 450 percent and this is evident by virtue of the numbers of Malays who were involved in meaningful business and banking activity in 1991. Second, non-*bumiputera* Malaysians do not seem to have been particularly hindered by the NEP restrictions. In fact, they have gone, by anyone's figures, far beyond the NEP goal. Hidden here is the fact that Malaysian Indians do not seem to have shared equally in this expansion and are thought to have become Malaysia's poorest class. Third, foreign-held equity dropped to a point lower than planned, making Malaysia "short" of such equity. The government has recruited new foreign equity widely as a result and has put considerable effort and money into such recruitment.

A review of the 1991 data, despite what some might claim to be obvious unfairness under the NEP and its successor, the New Development Policy (NDP), shows that some economic equilibrium has been brought to Malaysia's racially divided society. While distribution problems remain, and some new ones have arisen (e.g., poverty among the Malaysian Indians), Malaysia has progressed into a reasonably wealthy and stable society. Quotas and "affirmative action" remain integral to the society and many observers classify its political system as "authoritarian," even though its constitutional structure is democratic. But success comes in stages and political equity for the Chinese and Indians will never be available in Malaysia until economic empowerment enables the Malays to bend on the matter of political rights in a context that will not leave them as a political, economic, and social minority in "their own land."[20]

According to World Bank reports, Malaysia has been exceptionally successful in meeting its poverty reduction targets. Early in the NEP, 49.3 percent of the population in Peninsular Malaysia lived below the poverty line and 16 percent had income less than half the poverty level. But with poverty among Malays twice as high as the national average and educational accomplishments well below those of the Indians and the Chinese, the government clearly had to direct its efforts at expanding the income earning opportunities of the Malays. The NEP framed this effort and set the stage for separate policies that would bring the Malays into some reasonable parity with the Chinese.

During the NEP period, Malaysia's poverty indicators have been altered dramatically as a result of government-led programs. The World Bank indicates that poverty incidence in 1990 was estimated at 17.1 percent (4 percent hard core poor), down significantly from 1969. The educational opportunities for Malays and Chinese are now the same. The two races enjoy similarly excellent prospects of finding a modern sector job. Malay achievement has been particularly evident during the Mahathir years. Mahathir's place in history is predicated on continuation and growth of Malay economic success. Mahathir's (and New UMNO's) viability in the face of Islamic and dissident Malay challenges is dependent on growth of the economic pie.

Malaysia has been very successful in attracting direct foreign investment, which has facilitated access to technology and international markets and has introduced modern management practices. Foreign Direct Investment (FDI) in Malaysia increased from M$2.1 billion in 1987 to M$16 billion by 1991. In 1991, the largest national contributor of FDI was Taiwan with M$3.5 billion, surpassing Japan with M$3.2 billion. Korea was next that year with M$1.7 billion, then the United States also with M$1.7 billion, and Indonesia with M$1.2 billion. Significant portions of this investment have been channeled into Malay-owned joint venture operations or government-owned enterprises (with the government acting for the *bumiputera*) and the Malays have reaped many benefits. But for Taiwan investment to continue, it must be clear that the Malaysian-Chinese population continues to benefit from development in the country. Particularly in the timber industry, it is clear that this is the case. This is in part because at least some of the Taiwan-based money that is coming into Malaysia is actually Malaysian-Chinese capital that has been removed from Malaysia and then reinvested under Taiwan corporate auspices to reap the benefits of foreign investment incentives. Investment linkages with Singapore are similarly important and linked with the racial issue in the same way.

Economic and political stability are equally important. The risk of doing business in Malaysia is low because of "consistently good growth performance, low inflation, a stable exchange rate, the development of an efficient and competitive private sector, and a favorable regulatory framework" (World Bank). Comparative analyses have regularly shown that Malaysia's civil service is efficient and relatively free of the corruption that permeates the systems of Indonesia, Thailand, and the Philippines, as well as others in the region. A key to political stability, however, is keeping the Malays and non-Malays in a position of being relatively equal beneficiaries of economic development in the country.

Malaysia's growth performance, following the recovery from the recession of 1985–1986, has been remarkable. The GNP growth rate improved to 5.6 percent in 1987 and then accelerated to an average of 9.8 percent per annum in the four years up to 1991. Led by the exports subsector, the fastest GDP growth was in manufacturing, which has grown by an average of 15.3 percent per annum in the five years since the recession. The pattern and pace of recent growth is helping to shape the structure of the economy. Manufacturing is now the leading sector, accounting for 28.1 percent of GDP, followed by the services sector.

Malay economic empowerment is extremely dependent on there being continued and significant growth in the Malaysian economy. There has been Chinese economic advancement under the NEP and NDP but the relative gains by the Malays have continued and will continue to do so as long as the manufacturing and, particularly, the export sectors continue to grow. The NEP was structured around and totally dependent on the concept of "an expanding pie." If the expanding pie process is threatened, for example by Western demands for greater environmental consciousness and conservation, a threat is posed to the racial stability of Malaysia, to Malaysia's political viability, and to the Malay sense of worth in the global society.

Prime Minister Mahathir is the key to Malay economic empowerment. In addition to Mahathir's sense of history and his sense of responsibility to the Malay people, his personal attributes play a role in his attitudes and behavior on conservation and environmental issues. Mahathir considers himself to be an elder statesman and considers it an affront to have "callow, jejune" foreign policy "experts" telling him what to do, in a society still "capable of blowing up." To the extent that the United States has left single-issue technocrats in charge of developing U.S. policy toward Malaysia, the U.S. government, in particular, has failed to influence Mahathir to move in a constructive direction on almost any issue.

SECULAR POLITICS: UMNO AND THE MALAY THREAT

Malay-Chinese competition is at the source of the state-led modernizing changes that have transformed Malaysian society under UMNO since 1957. The UMNO leadership has adroitly used, even strengthened, the already powerful state apparatus created by the British Raj for the colonial purposes of extraction and police control to implement its political and economic agenda of Malay advancement. This agenda has been nothing less than to steer ethnic competition into economic channels, away from the dangers of overt political competition, in order to promote the development of a powerful capitalist Malay middle class. Jomo Kwame Sundaram criticizes the emergence of these "statist-capitalists" or "bureaucrat-capitalists" in his penetrating class analysis of state economic interventions in pre-independence and post-independence Malaysia.[21] Alasdair Bowie analyzes these interventions in the following framework: a market-led approach in the 1957–1969 period; a mixed market-regulatory policy in the 1970s; and a state-centered strategy in "most of the 1980s."[22] We would add that a state-encouraged private sector-led strategy has been followed in the 1990s.

Generally, the state has sought to provide sufficiently clear regulatory guidelines that the Chinese community could prosper communally, while contributing to national growth, which in turn has provided a buoyant lift to Malay economic power. The Malaysian miracle results from the deft exercise of statecraft by the UMNO leadership to achieve these fundamental objectives.

We describe the exercise of state power by the Malay leadership as secular politics. Secular politics has included a firm commitment to governing through an ethnic coalition of communally based parties. The coalition facilitates vital elite accommodation between Malays and Chinese in both economic and political matters. Secular politics is predicated on Malay political leadership, specifically UMNO leadership. To maintain this leadership, the post-1971 UMNO-led National Front and the pre-1969 UMNO-led Alliance have successfully won each election with a two-thirds majority of the seats in Parliament. Consistently achieving such majorities has had the practical value of enabling the UMNO leadership to amend the Constitution as it deemed necessary. Such amendments have strengthened the already strong state and created concerns about the possible exercise of arbitrary or authoritarian power by the government. The government has defended the strengthening of its constitutional authority by citing the ever present danger of a communal blowup as in 1969. It is clear the UMNO leadership fears such an explosion of communal tensions is more likely to come from disaffected Malays rather than the Chinese. That is why UMNO has sought to lead Malays in secular directions.

Secular politics necessarily is not religiously oriented politics. Secular politics opposes the transformation of Malaysia into an Islamic state. UMNO and the Chinese parties find common cause in pursuit of these objectives.

It should never be forgotten that secular and modernist UMNO seeks to lead a Malay population that includes elements who remain deeply traditional in their "Malayness": the cultural, social, political, economic, historical, and religious world view that makes them "Malay." This outlook has a xenophobic strain that is both anti-Chinese and anti-Western. It fuels a Malay particularism that is reinforced by Islam.

The Malay political alternative to UMNO is PAS, the vehicle of Islamic fundamentalism and ultra Malay communalism. PAS cannot be called a merely religious party but this distinction has little significance since Islam recognizes no separation between church and state. However, PAS is plainly a non-secular party. Equally plainly, if PAS gained political control of the Malay community, the state it would create would be a non-secular state.

Thus, beneath the surface of Malaysian politics and the waves created by Malay-Chinese competition, there has been a deeper continuing struggle between the secular and non-secular tendencies of Malay modernism and traditionalism. While the Malays have been generally sensitive to the danger that a split in their community would enhance Chinese political prospects and threaten Malay political dominance, the UMNO leadership has been under constant pressure to associate itself with and meet evolving Malay demands.

Tunku Abdul Rahman established the UMNO leadership style when he took over as UMNO president from Jaffar Onn in 1950. Jaffar Onn had correctly read Malay political sentiment in 1946 when Malays furiously rejected British efforts to put Chinese on the same political and economic levels as citizens in the Malayan Union scheme. Onn established UMNO and led the campaign that forced the British to maintain Malays in their special and privileged position. Jaffar Onn succumbed to British pressure to attempt to convert UMNO into a multi-ethnic rather than a communal party ("divide et impera"), however, and went into political oblivion when Tunku was selected in keep UMNO Malay. The Tunku also took up the cry for independence of Malay nationalism. The crafty Tunku performed masterfully in balancing mounting Malay demands with the necessity of keeping Chinese support. He was aided mightily in this delicate task by Tan Siew Sin, the leader of the Malayan Chinese Association, who was minister of finance from 1957 until parliamentary government was suspended in the emergency declared after the May 1969 communal riots.

Notwithstanding the careful collaboration of the Tunku and the Chinese leadership, his cultivation of the Chinese was resented by the Malays and cost him their support. Despite the arduous and massive efforts of Tunku's protegee and deputy, Tun Abdul Razak, in Malay-oriented rural development, youthful Malays became estranged from Tunku's conservative leadership. Their demand was for both political and economic Malay dominance even if it meant the suspension of parliamentary government.

Tun Abdul Razak eased Tunku out of the UMNO presidency and led Malaysia away from the racial disaster it had apparently faced in 1969. Aside from further strengthening the Malay constitutional and legal position, Tun Razak attacked the Malay economic problem directly by launching the 1971 New Economic Policy. This was a strategy to co-opt the demands of Malay ultras for economic equity with the Chinese. Simply put, the New Economic Policy was massive "affirmative action" of all types including quotas in business, finance, and higher education. The NEP also stepped up the already substantial investment in rural development and infrastructure. Smallholder agriculture was a particular target of NEP investment. Smallholders now dominate all forms of export-oriented production of commodities such as rubber and palm oil.

Tun Abdul Razak also co-opted the ultra political leadership by bringing the fiery ultra leader Dr. Mahathir Mohamad into the upper ranks of UMNO. Tun Razak and his deputy (and brother-in-law) Hussein Onn also brought PAS into the National Front during most of the 1970s. Perhaps in reaction to his father, Jaffar Onn's, mistakes in political leadership, Hussein Onn was decidedly more sensitive to Malay communalism and nationalism.

Razak died in 1975 and Hussein Onn succeeded him as UMNO president and prime minister. Significantly, UMNO chose the former ultra Dr. Mahathir as UMNO deputy president and deputy prime minister. Dr. Mahathir had won his political spurs in the 1973–1974 period when he was minister of education and took stern action against campus radicals and student disturbances. Islamic youth leader Anwar Ibrahim was put in detention for a year in that period.

Dr. Mahathir became minister of trade and industry in the Hussein Onn government and played a crucial role in promoting Malay entrepreneurship in Malaysia's rousing economic boom of the 1970s alongside his aristocratic political rival, Minister of Finance Tengku Razaleigh. Mahathir was able to turn his nonaristocratic background to political advantage after he was brought to political power by Tun Razak. From that time until 1981 when Hussein Onn retired, Dr. Mahathir outwitted and outmaneuvered all political threats to his position, including those of PAS, Islamic fundamentalists, and Tengku Razaleigh. Mahathir adopted an outflanking strategy toward Islamic fundamentalism after he became prime minister. He successfully asserted his government was itself fundamentalist and all others were "extremists."

Meanwhile, Dr. Mahathir launched an aggressive program of heavy industrialization to propel Malaysia (and Malays) forward. Recession affected Malaysia severely in the mid-1980s and the heavy industrialization faltered. Mahathir did not hesitate to turn away from his program (except for his beloved Malaysian car, the heavily protected Proton Saga). His finance minister, Daim Zainuddin (who had fruitlessly opposed the Proton Saga project), was given free rein to cut off the funding of nonperforming projects and failing Malay entrepreneurs.

From 1986, Daim led an effort to encourage foreign investment as a means of emerging from the recession. Liberalization of such investment fueled renewed buoyant economic growth. The leading source of such investment has been Taiwan. This investment appears to include that of Malaysian Chinese recycling their offshore funds through Taiwan to receive foreign investment benefits. Investments from Taiwan totalled $5.6 billion between 1986 and 1992.

It is of interest that the liberalization of investment, including provisions for foreigners to retain up to 100 percent of equity in projects devoted entirely to exports, took place in an atmosphere of increasing reliance on the private sector. The private sector was the locomotive that pulled Malaysia out of the mid-1980s recession. Chinese businessmen and bankers played leading roles in the private sector-led recovery. The Chinese community's links with Taiwan and the possible problems that might arise from Taiwanese investment were, of course, a source of some concern for the Malay-led government, but as FEER reported, Malaysia "welcomed the men from Taipei because they made a good counterweight to a flood of Japanese investment."[23]

In any case, the Mahathir government had little choice other than to use the recession as a means of changing its economic strategy. The *Financial Times* reported three main tenets of government strategy had been revealed to be faulty.[24] First, there was excessive dependence on commodities: all commodity prices had dropped simultaneously. Second, Mahathir's heavy industrialization strategy of stimulating growth through "substantial foreign borrowing and large scale public sector investment" was flawed. Third, the government was forced "to abandon some of the internationally less attractive aspects of the New Economic Policy." Thus, the government began course corrections including liberalizing foreign investment but also including rolling back "the role of the public sector in industry through a large privatization program and much tighter budgetary controls" and rolling back implementation of the New Economic Policy. It is noteworthy that these dramatic changes took place not just in response to the recession but also at a time of maximum political challenge to the Mahathir government by UMNO dissidents led by Tengku Razaleigh. The UMNO dissidents rejected the leadership of Mahathir who they claimed had demonstrated undemocratic and authoritarian tendencies as well as incompetence in leading the party and the nation. Mahathir faced these problems as well as a crisis in the MCA leadership in Sabah and Sarawak.

The 1986 elections brought Malay dissension to a boil. The Mahathir-led National Front won the elections with the now obligatory two-thirds majority. However, after the August polls, Tengku Razaleigh and adherents of former Deputy Prime Minister Musa Hitam, who had resigned his position in February 1986, joined forces and began mounting a fierce campaign to oust Dr. Mahathir from the UMNO presidency in the upcoming April 1987 UMNO elections.

UMNO became deeply (and dangerously) divided. The Mahathir faction became known as Team A and the Razaleigh-Musa Hitam faction as Team B. New heights or perhaps depths of "money-politics" were reached. Gordon Means comments that both Team A and Team B were seeking to outbid each other in promising the Malay community benefits and the non-Malay community watched the spectacle with a mixture "of hope and trepidation."[25] The factional split perhaps offered new opportunities for cross-ethnic political alliances but could also lead to "more repressive or discriminatory policies directed at non-Malays."

The UMNO elections took place on April 24 in an atmosphere of great excitement and anxiety. Razaleigh's chances of defeating Mahathir from the UMNO presidency seemed good at the outset of the voting. Accusations of skullduggery and corruption have been made against Dr. Mahathir's Team A, but he prevailed as UMNO president (and prime minister) by 43 votes—761 to 718. Dr. Mahathir quickly purged all Team B members from his cabinet. This fact and the post-election rancor over "the questionable validity of the election results"[26] encouraged some Team B members to challenge the election in the courts.

Political anxiety and concern mounted in 1987 over the UMNO issue but the problems of MCA corruption also boiled over. To this witches brew was added the explosive issue of Malay interference in Chinese education. Chinese public rallies ensued, followed by an excited UMNO youth rally on October 17. Communal tensions were building. A giant UMNO youth rally of some 500,000 persons was planned for November 1 that anti-Mahathir elements planned to exploit but that was aimed more generally at intimidating the Chinese. The prime minister invoked his emergency powers to stop the rally and to detain a wide variety of persons of all political stripes.

The unsettled situation continued into 1988 as the suit against the Mahathir election as UMNO president made its way through the courts. The Supreme Court ruled in favor of the dissidents in February, supporting their claim that certain UMNO delegates had been improperly chosen and had voted illegally. UMNO was declared to be an illegal society; however, the Supreme Court did not void the election. Dr. Mahathir refused to resign and set about forming a new UMNO. In response, Tengku Razaleigh established his own version of UMNO called "Semangat 46" ("The Spirit of 46," echoing the formation of UMNO in 1946).

The combative Dr. Mahathir, never one to avoid a fight, fought Semangat 46, fought the judiciary, fought political leaders of Sabah and Sarawak, and demonstrated a bare-knuckled, no-holds-barred proficiency in the political guerilla warfare that ensued in 1988. However, he suffered a heart attack in January 1989 at the age of 64. After bypass surgery, he returned to political combat unrepentant and unmellowed as he led the "New UMNO" (UMNO Bahru) to victory in the October 1990 elections. Semangat 46 had conceded the possibility that Dr. Mahathir's New UMNO would wage a powerful electoral campaign and had set goals of denying the National Front a two-thirds constitution-changing capability and forcing itself into a two-coalition government, but Semangat 46 even in an uneasy coalition with PAS was able only to win 49 of the 180 parliamentary seats contested and 98 of the 351 state assembly seats. However, the National Front did lose Razaleigh's home state of Kelantan, ran weakly in Penang, and was held to a stalemate in Sabah. Nevertheless, Dr. Mahathir clearly won an otherwise unambiguous victory.

Meanwhile, as noted, the economy had been surging. Now, the prime minister turned his attention to codifying the private sector changes that had successfully brought Malaysia out of the recession. The 20-year New Economic Policy had ended in 1990. Mahathir launched its successor, the New Development Policy, in June 1991. Finance Minister Daim had stepped down and had been replaced by Anwar Ibrahim, who had demonstrated his own strong capacities for political warfare during the Team A-Team B conflict. By 1991 Anwar was clearly Dr. Mahathir's heir apparent. His credentials as a former student radical and unquestioned advocate of Islam had proven valuable to Dr. Mahathir in navigating New UMNO through the crisis of Malay disunity.

In announcing the NDP, the prime minister said the basic strategies of the NEP would be maintained (e.g., to eradicate poverty and restructure society to correct social and economic imbalances and "thereby contribute to national unity"). National unity was essential because the goal of the NDP was to "set the pace to enable Malaysia to become a fully developed nation by the year 2020" in every respect. The NDP's "Vision 20/20" would seek to eliminate hard-core poverty and reduce relative poverty. It would focus on the rapid development of "an active Bumiputera Commercial and Industrial Community (BCIC) as an essential strategy to increase and render permanent Bumiputera participation in the economy." The NDP would "rely more on the private sector's involvement in the restructuring process; and focus more on human resource development including moral and ethical values in order to achieve the objectives of growth and redistribution."

Mahathir said less state intervention would be taken to seek poverty eradication and restructuring than had been the case under the NEP. There would no longer be "The indiscriminate distribution of wealth which is immediately frittered away." Amid other vivid statements to the *Bumiputera* community, Dr. Mahathir stated that ethnic quotas for equity ownership for Malays would be replaced with less quantitative standards in an environment of liberalization, deregulation, and privatization. The prime minister called for a growth rate of 7 percent a year to the year 2000 and the transformation of Malaysia from an agricultural to an industrialized nation by 2020. He said the "inefficient smallholder operation" in agriculture would be reformed by shifting land, capital, and labor resources to production by "commercial estates."

The NDP declaration was basically aimed at the *bumiputera* audience but Dr. Mahathir sought to ease Chinese concerns by the hectoring tone he adopted toward his fellow Malays; however, he addressed non-*bumiputera* concerns directly in several places in his speech, especially invoking the need for all communities to participate in the development process. "The New Development Policy takes in account the needs of all Malaysians. There should be no fear or doubts in the minds of any ethnic group that they should lose." Malays must, nevertheless, be brought up to the economic level of the Chinese. "Only by doing this, can we be assured of political and social stability as well as national unity, a prerequisite for national unity."

Under Dr. Mahathir's relentless goading, Malaysia has plunged ahead since 1991 to pursue NDP goals. While PAS continues its assiduous cultivation of rural Malays and those Malays who are urbanized but disoriented by modern life, secular UMNO clearly seems to have the upper hand politically in the overall Malay community under present conditions of economic buoyancy. The prime minister has also apparently stage-managed the ascension of Anwar Ibrahim as his heir-apparent. Anwar demonstrated a Mahathir-like capability to steamroller opposition in the campaign he mounted in 1993 to oust Ghaffar Baba, the incumbent UMNO deputy president, from office in the November 3, 1993, elections.

The forty-something Anwar and his age cohort who rose to UMNO power with him appear to be somewhat incautiously counting the days until they can challenge the deeply Machiavellian Dr. Mahathir for the leadership of UMNO. Dr. Mahathir's mandate runs until 1995 and the interior logic of his NDP speech suggests strongly he has every intention of renewing his electoral mandate and remaining in power, health permitting, until 2000.

Having conquered Malaysian politics and stamped Malaysian history with his own indelible seal, Dr. Mahathir has given every indication that he is seeking world recognition for himself personally and for Malaysia under his leadership. Achieving such international stature, particularly by pugnacious anti-United States and anti-West stances for "bullying" small states,[27] can provide the not inconsiderable benefit of promoting Malaysian South-South trade and investment and political influence, while strengthening Mahathir's position domestically, especially against his Malay opposition. For Dr. Mahathir Mohamad, the issues are as he stated them in his *Malay Dilemma*: the Malays must be modernized and made capable of competing with the Chinese or they run the risk of ending up like the "Red Indians" in America. The issue is and will remain Malay survival.

The World Bank analysis of the "East Asian Miracle" is studied for possible guidance in the pamphlet "The Lessons of East Asia: An Overview of Country Experience" (Leipziger, Thomas) and the common factor in the success of the first round of NIEs (Korea, Singapore, Hong Kong or Taiwan, China) was that economic development "was a matter of survival and therefore of national urgency."[28] Malaysia is grouped with the later East Asian NIEs. However, our analysis indicates that the issue of Malay survival has been a crucial element in creating Malaysian economic competitive conditions (and Malaysian economic success), which have spurred on not only the Malays and the Chinese, but also the factions of the Malay community itself.

Ethnic competition surely has many well-known negative characteristics. However, Dr. Mahathir's statement in his National Development Policy speech deserves respectful attention. Referring to the NEP, Dr. Mahathir said:

We are resolved to undertake this socio-economic engineering exercise within the context of an expanding economy so that in the process of distributing the benefits of development, no ethnic group experiences a sense of absolute deprivation. It is pertinent to mention here that there have been many attempts in other parts of the world at socio-economic engineering. Almost without exception they have failed and they have caused untold misery and dragged down the economy of the nations involved.

As for lessons learned, several are reflected in the "Malaysia" monograph in the World Bank series on "The Lessons of East Asia." These are:

1. Government flexibility in adapting to changing conditions;
2. Factor endowment counts. Malaysia was well-endowed and by and large has used its endowment well;
3. Institutional strength helps. However, a legal and political structure in place has paid high dividends; and
4. "Finally, and most importantly, the Malaysian story highlights the importance of practical sustainability. The country is engaged in a long-range plan, which it is pursuing with flexible short-term objectives." The Malaysian experience seems very relevant to the Balkanized, post-cold war world and the ethnic conflicts that are occurring.

RISK VERSUS OPPORTUNITY

The place for Malaysia in history and global affairs today, the viability of its economy and the standard of living of its people, and certainly race relations within the country all revolve around Malaysia's interaction with the global economy. The national economic pie must grow, Malaysia must forge ahead. It is forging ahead. Symbolic of this is the often heard '80s remark that the Malaysian national bird was the construction crane. The country and society visibly continue to build. To this end Malaysia is especially dependent on foreign investment at this juncture. An investor perspective on Malaysia would be a counterweight to the more societal view that we have provided above.

A structure through which to examine Malaysia's current status and its current standing on these critical issues is sociopolitical risk assessment, a tool for foreign investors who use its outlines to shape investment policy and guard against the liabilities of the social and political environments. There are a number of mechanisms by which sociopolitical risk is currently being forecast in a now firmly established field. We have chosen here a model put forth by *The Economist* [29] as a means of guiding potential investors in examining opportunities and threats in an increasingly competitive world of cross-national investment. Our comments below reflect an assessment from *The Economist* and a 1992 survey of experts on the same issues.[30]

The Economist chose six political variables and four social variables and weighted each by assigning a value. We will use these as a template to examine those societal phenomena that form the network of interdependence between foreign investors and host nations. The first of these variables is one *The Economist* termed *Bad Neighbors*. They assigned three possible negative points to the variable for each country examined. A zero score would have meant no problems in this arena, a three that the situation is as bad as it can get. *The Economist* recognized the situational context as being a critical political variable. They argued that being near any superpower almost automatically meant trouble in that superpowers tend to control their peripheries, often with the use of force. Troublespots are those with a history of being "disturbed" or with historically continuous violence. They cite the Middle East and South Africa as examples. The important implication of the inclusion of this variable is that domestic political environments are inextricably linked with regional and international systems and, no matter what their internal policies or conditions, the success of investments will depend on activities that may be outside the direct control of governments in the investment state.

Malaysia merited a score of one (1) in the 1992 assessment. Several factors account for Malaysia's score, as low as it might be. One is the Spratly Islands problem, where Malaysia is a contender for territorial and offshore mining rights along with five other nations. The Chinese and Vietnamese navies fought a sea battle several years ago and tensions remain high in the area, with each of the contenders except Brunei having troops on some islands. Most of the nations in the area are continuing to develop military facilities and expand air and sea access. Malaysia has always had a concern about the growing strength of China, especially with its own large Chinese population. This is not the case with Japan or the United States. Malaysia also has had minor disputes with Singapore over control of small islands along their common border.

Authoritarianism (7 points): Whether totalitarian or authoritarian, the lack of democracy in a state forebodes ill. The text of *The Economist's* description is somewhat murky on this point, recognizing that totalitarians such as Fidel Castro can use iron-fisted control to maintain a tolerable investment climate, but the data table labels the variable "how authoritarian" and assesses the countries that way. Even rigid totalitarian control is only a temporary holding pattern; disruption and probably violence will seethe underneath.

Prime Minister Mahathir is no Castro. However, Malaysian government control over the society is firm and backed both by existing law (such as in the case of the death penalty for distribution of drugs or possession of illegal firearms) and the capability of adjusting the law constitutionally to maintain control. Malaysia's Internal Security Act (ISA) seems to be an aberration for a democratic society but it is based on similar law in Great Britain. Malaysian government control, it is argued, is needed to prevent a recurrence of racial conflicts such as that which occurred in May of 1969 and resulted in at least hundreds of deaths. Malaysia rates a three (3) under authoritarianism. The prime minister argues that the Western form of democracy is not appropriate for Malaysian circumstances.

Staleness (5 points): The argument is that a leader needs about five years to get his or her bearings and a grip on the situation but that after ten years he begins to get detached and stale. Complacency accompanies entrenchment, along with its siblings: corruption, disdain, and delay.

Staleness refers not just to single leaders but to the administrations that accompany them. Malaysia's administration gets a two (2) under staleness, primarily for this reason. The criterion of most significance with this variable is that of bureaucratic complacency. If administrators have little concern about being thrown out of office by the voters or are firmly ensconced in bureaucratic protectivity, they do not respond to voters (or investors) in a timely fashion. Mahathir has been a vital leader but investors think less of those in the structure below him. The score of two is low considering that Mahathir has been in office for more than twelve years. The score of two is really directed at UMNO.

Illegitimacy (9 points): Legitimacy implies an uncoerced and positive acceptance on the part of the population of a state. Political risk is a function of the gap between acceptability and a government's persistence in power. It is important to note that legitimacy, in the sense used here, is a condition as perceived by those directly ruled, not by outsiders. Singapore's legitimacy is

MALAYSIA: THE ANXIETIES OF SUCCESS   41

a function of how its citizens feel about it, not the way the Western world sees it.

Malaysia's score of two (2) is low but it still registers. The UMNO-led government is still being challenged by some Chinese, particularly through the Democratic Action Party (DAP). It also faces a continuing threat from conservative Muslims in PAS. Both the DAP and PAS would bring about fundamental changes in the political structure and process if they could gain sufficient power. This is particularly true of PAS, which would introduce Islamic law as the standard for all ethnic groups. Investors are particularly sensitive to legal systems since contract repudiation is a primary source of losses by foreign investors.

Another continuing threat exists in both Sabah and Sarawak from sectors unhappy with the federal arrangement that redirects resources to the federal government in Kuala Lumpur from these two very rich and ethnically distinct states, separated by the South China Sea.

Generals in Power (6 points): In response to instability or the lack of competent civilian authority (or the military's perception of competent), military authorities often step in and take control themselves. *The Economist* argues that most military men do not know how to govern nor how to step aside gracefully. Simply as a matter of their own competence, they usually govern like they run their own military establishments. Since there is little in the way of democracy within the military, little shows in military-run regimes and such rigidity tends to breed dissent.

The Malaysian military has been a paragon of virtue. Well trained and respectful of the separation of civil government and military, Malaysia's military leaders have tended to their jobs and kept their distance. It is the other end of the spectrum from the system existing in neighboring Indonesia. Malaysia earned a zero (0) for "generals in power."

War/Armed Insurrection (20 points): War, the most impactful of any of the variables selected, clearly penetrates the investment picture in a number of ways. Apart from the obvious destruction of physical plant, war disrupts the economy and brings about losses in a number of other ways.

A communist rebellion ended finally and officially in 1989 with the surrender of the last of the Malayan Communist party's significant leaders. Despite several territorial confrontations (such as off the north coast of Sabah), there is no war or civil unrest in Malaysia such as that which plagues all its neighbors except Singapore and Brunei. Malaysia gets a zero (0).

Urbanization Pace (3 points): When the urbanization process is too rapid, or is too concentrated on a single city, a number of problems accompany the shift. These include "idleness and crime," an expansion of the drug trade, and economic irregularities, such as in the pricing of food. It is not the fact of urbanization itself but rather the nature of the process and its effect on the society that threatens the foreign investor.

Malaysia rates a one (1) under urbanization, primarily because of unemployment and related problems in Kuala Lumpur. Drugs have been a significant but Malaysia's tough drug laws and recent prosperity have kept the problem under control. Kuala Lumpur remains as one of the best big city residential areas in Asia.

Islamic Fundamentalism (4 points): *The Economist* argues that there was never much political fervor in Hinduism or Buddhism and that Christianity is a spent force. But, they continue, Muslim radicals could still change the world and where they are strong, the risk to investors is high, especially when the investors are foreign and not Muslim. There is certainly something of importance here and many observers focus on Muslim radicals as a key to the nature of the investment climate. But several questions must be dealt with in other studies on the question of political risk. First, does "Islamic Fundamentalism" equal "Muslim radicals"? Many argue that there is more than a finite difference. Second, is it in fact true that other religious fundamentalists are as impotent as *The Economist* claims? Events in November of 1990 in India where Hindu fundamentalists were instrumental in bringing down the government of Prime Minister V. P. Singh would seem to indicate that religious fundamentalists of various types remain potent in political environments.

While Islamic fundamentalism in Malaysia is not the virulent sort that is found in the Middle East, Malaysia still rates a reasonably high three (3) on this variable. Conversations with businessmen in particular have led us to conclude that they are concerned both with PAS activity in Kelantan and, importantly, with Malaysian government reactions to PAS political gains and activities. That is, while the government is opposing PAS, it is also trying to co-opt its followers by implementing some of the rules and norms that PAS is putting forward. Investors feel that government efforts to contain PAS were resulting in actual or potential alterations of operating rules for foreign investors. Some feel that the heightened sense of Islamic religiousness that came out of the UMNO-PAS competition had generated a changing social atmosphere in which non-Muslim business people felt less secure. In surveys over the last few years, Malaysians themselves (including Muslim civil servants) have continually rated Malaysia a two (2) on this variable. In the larger context the score of three seems high but within Malaysia religious tension is kept high by the presence of PAS in the national political picture.

Corruption (6 points): Corruption exists everywhere. U.S. federal department scandals at the end of the Reagan administration and Savings and Loan problems into 1991 reflect its impact in the United States. But in some cases, it has gotten out of hand. Corruption can distort the economy in ways that the best of investor awareness or even power cannot accommodate.

Malaysia earns a two (2) on this factor. It is not nearly as obvious as it is in the other countries of the region (only Singapore and Brunei have lower scores) but necessary "favors" to make things happen exist everywhere.

Ethnic Tension (4 points): Ethnic, religious, and racial tension provide an environment in which simple industry does not suffice. It may redirect government attention, invoke restrictions on investors (hire this group and not that one), restrict labor resources, or result in open conflict. Its presence detracts from normal functioning of political processes, which are almost always necessary for normal economic processes.

The New Economic Policy (NEP) and, now, the National Development Policy (NDP) have done much to mitigate the tension that reached its peak in 1969. But national policy has been directed at appeasing the Malays and to some extent other *bumiputeras*. The Chinese, in particular, strongly resent the favoritism that is granted to the Malays under these policies. Malaysia therefore rates a three (3) under "Ethnic Tension." But in Malaysia, it is only tension. The growing economic pie over the last decade has been able to accommodate both significant economic growth for the Malay community and similar growth for the Chinese.

However, the two communities have not mixed and still stand apart despite their common economic interest. As long as Malaysia's economy continues to grow as it has, the tension will remain just that. But it is important that the government continue to forge ahead strongly on this count (and be seen doing it) to keep these domestic forces at bay. Aggressive national economic and trade policies are critical in this effort. This explains Dr. Mahathir's lonely but often gallant struggle to bring Malaysia to the forefront of global as well as regional issues. Mahathir's fight for the East Asian Economic Caucus (EAEC) is not just an economic effort; it is fraught with political and nationalistic symbolism—David against Goliath.

CONCLUSION

Malaysia's 17 "risk" points generated by employing this model can be seen two ways. Microcosmically, authoritarianism, Islamic fundamentalism, and ethnic tension show up as key areas through which the much needed investment could be discouraged. The ethnic situation has settled somewhat in recent years but Mahathir's extended stay in the prime ministership encourages certain concerns about staleness. Staleness, despite the literal limits specified by *The Economist* (eight to 10 years as the limit), was seen as less of a problem for the specialists resident in Southeast Asia than for those who were abroad and looking at the situation more abstractly. The reverse was true for the problem of Islamic fundamentalism in Malaysia, where the resident specialist scores raised the assigned value from two to three out of a possible four.

At the macro level, Malaysia has lost nothing in sociopolitical attractiveness over the six year period since *The Economist* conducted its survey and gains have been registered in perception of its decreased levels of authoritarianism and increased legitimacy. The picture is considerably more positive when seen as a whole. Among the 10 Southeast Asian states, Malaysia's 17 points are the second lowest, only after Singapore as a nation with low risk for outside investors. Strong attributes of low regional conflict and lack of superpower interference, an established and accepted political process, a non-political military, a lack of domestic or international conflict, and a reduced poverty level and related problems all present precisely the image that investors seek. It must be recognized, or at least argued, that Prime Minister Mahathir's policies and personal political actions have contributed to this positive picture.

Looking at any country as closely as a political risk perspective would have one do will undoubtedly allow the pores to be seen all too clearly. When standing back at a reasonable distance, one sees a country with great potential for conflict but also for tremendous success. The fact that Malaysia is so clearly on the success side of the equation should bring recognition to the political and economic management that has brought it about but is not so readily seen through the international media. Outside of the rhetoric and the perceived affronts of great powers, the leadership capability and administrative accomplishments of Dr. Mahathir should be recognized. A nation that could be in ashes is not. Instead, it is one of the great commercial successes of the free market and democratic world. In the context of Malaysia's political, colonial, cultural, and economic history, it is unlikely that this is an accident.

NOTES

1. As will be more fully discussed below, the term *bumiputera* literally means "princes of the soil." More loosely, it is often translated as "sons of the soil" and substitutes for "native" or "indigenous" in English. Both main elements of the term are significant: royalty/maleness and attachment to the land.

2. Donald Rothchild, "Power-sharing in Africa: Elite Versus Majoritarian Regimes," unpublished paper, prepared for Department of State Conference, 1992, p. 1.

3. *Far Eastern Economic Review*, June 17, 1993, p. 16.

4. *Far Eastern Economic Review*, June 17, 1993, p. 20.

5. *Washington Post*, November 24, 1993.

6. Stanley S. Bedlington, *Malaysia and Singapore: The Building of New States* (Ithaca: Cornell University Press, 1978), p. 21.

7. Mahathir Mohamed, *The Challenge* (Petaling Jaya: Pelanduk Publications, 1986), p. 3.

8. Charles Hirshman, "The Society and Its Environment," in Frederica M. Bunge, ed., *Malaysia: A Country Study*, (Washington, DC: U.S. Government Printing Office, 1984), p. 91.

9. Donald M. Seekins, "Historical Setting," in Bunge, ed., *Malaysia*, p. 28.

10. Hirschman, "The Society and Its Environment," p. 90.

11. For an enlightening and intimate look into the Brooke family politics that underlay the governance of Sarawak for a full century, see R. H. W. Reece, *The Name of Brooke: The End of White Rajah Rule in Sarawak* (Kuala Lumpur: Oxford University Press, 1982).

12. See John H. Esterline and Mac H. Esterline, "*How The Dominos Fell*": *Southeast Asia in Perspective* (Lanham, MD: Hamilton Press, 1986), pp. 152–153; and Hirschman, "The Society and Its Environment," pp. 94–95.

13. David Joel Steinberg, et al., *In Search of Southeast Asia: A History*, revised edition (Honolulu: University of Hawaii Press, 1987), pp. 407–408.

14. Seekins, "Historical Setting," p. 52.

15. Hirschman, "The Society and Its Environment," p. 69.

16. More details and a description of the historical and social context can be found in Margaret Scott, "Where the Quota is King," *New York Times Magazine*, November 17, 1991, p. 66.

17. These figures, and the current figures as well, vary slightly depending on the accounting system applied and a variety of means of determining corporate ownership. Clark D. Neher provides the figures 3 percent, 34 percent, and 63 percent in *Southeast Asia and the New International Era* (Boulder, CO: Westview Press, 1991), p. 114.

18. The complaints were almost uniformly addressed to each other or to foreigners since Malaysian law was also changed to make such complaints tantamount to sedition. Those who criticized Malay rights could be arrested and held without trial, potentially for life.

19. Neher provides the figures 29 percent, 47 percent, and 33 percent, respectively. See Neher, 1991, p. 115.

20. As one Malay noted to Margaret Scott, "This is our country." This sentiment is constantly expressed by Malays and has deep roots in the Malay sense of community and history. See Scott, p. 63.

21. Jomo Kwame Sundaram, *A Question of Class: Capital, the State, and Uneven Development in Malaysia* (Singapore: Oxford University Press, 1986).

22. Alasdair Bowie, *Crossing the Industrial Divide: State, Society, and the Politics of Economic Transformation in Malaysia* (New York: Columbia University Press, 1991).

23. *Far Eastern Economic Review*, March 18, 1993.

24. *Financial Times*, August 24, 1990.

25. Gordon P. Means, *Malaysian Politics: The Second Generation* (Singapore: Oxford University Press, 1991), p. 202.

26. Ibid., p. 205.

27. Malaysia's aggressive position shows clearly in systematic analyses of its foreign policy behavior. See Llewellyn D. Howell, "Event Data for Area Studies Applications: Behavioral Patterns and Issue Domains for Malaysian Foreign Policy Behavior," *International Studies Notes*, vol. 18, no. 2 (spring 1993), pp. 21–33.

28. Thomas Leipziger, "The Lessons of East Asia: An Overview of Country Experience," The World Bank, pamphlet, 1993, p. 4.

29. Countries in Trouble, *The Economist*, December 20, 1986, pp. 25–28.

30. The scores reported here are those generated by business and area specialists in 1992. The full survey by the experts is reported in Llewellyn D. Howell, Syed Rizvi, and Chris Cogswell, "Political Risk in Southeast Asia: A Perspective through the Economist Model," *Journal of Asian Business*, vol. 9, no. 2 (spring 1993), pp. 19–36. The *Economist* model was put forth in 1986 and their 1986 scores are reported in "Countries in Trouble" (see above).

3

RECENT DEVELOPMENTS AND FUTURE PROSPECTS OF THE INDONESIAN ECONOMY

Anwar Nasution

PAST PERFORMANCES

Indonesia, over the past 25 years, has been hailed as one of the dynamic countries and, together with ASEAN and ANIEs, the shining lights of the international economy (World Bank, 1993). Despite various commodity "boom" and "bust," the rise in international interest rates and currency realignments in the mid 1980s, the average annual inflation rate has been controlled at 17.5 percent in the 1970s and 8.6 percent in the 1980s. In terms of GDP, annually, the economy grew by an average of 7.7 percent in the 1970s and 5.5 percent in the 1980s (see table 1).

As a result of the successful implementation of substantial adjustment programs since the mid-1980s, the productive base of the economy has been diversified, the role of the private sector has been expanding and the reliance on oil is decreasing. The annual rate of growth during Pelita V (the Fifth Five Year Development Plan), 1989/90-1993/94, seems certain to exceed the target of 5 percent.

The rapid rate of growth, combined with gradual declining population growth (from 2.2 percent in 1980-1985 to 1.8 percent in 1985-1990), resulted in rising annual average income per capita by 5.5 percent in the 1970s and 3.3 percent in the 1980s. This was accompanied by what appeared to be some steady improvements in the eradication of poverty, with the percentage of population living below the official poverty line falling from 40 percent in 1976 to 20 percent in 1987 and to 15 percent in 1990. The World Bank's *World Development Report 1990* found that, in the past two decades, Indonesia achieved the highest annual average reduction in the incidence of poverty among all the countries studied. With the level of income per capita at US$650 (1992), however, Indonesia remains a poor country.

As a stronger foundation was laid, the government contemplated an economic strategy for the Sixth Five-Year Development Plan (Repelita VI) and the Second Long Term (25-year) Development Program, both of which started on April 1, 1994. Economic development strategy and policy in Indonesia, since 1966, has been formulated for achieving three macroeconomic objectives, namely, maintaining internal and external balances, rapid economic growth, and equitable distribution of development benefits.

TABLE 1

Rate of Growth and Structural Changes of the Economy, 1975–1992

	1975–83 (Avg)	1983–87 (Avg)	1988	1989	1990	1991	1992
1. Aggregate growth rates:							
GDP	6.5	5.0	5.7	7.4	7.3	6.6	6.3
Non-oil GDP	7.0	5.7	7.4	8.2	7.8	6.5	8.1
Agriculture	3.5	3.3	4.7	4.3	2.5	0.9	5.9
Manufacturing	10.6	12.0	12.8	11.6	13.0	10.2	10.7
Mining	6.8	3.4	4.8	11.0	14.6	8.9	24.6
Construction	10.8	1.1	9.5	11.8	13.6	11.5	9.3
Other Services	8.6	6.0	6.9	8.5	7.6	6.6	7.3
(Financial Sector)	19.4 a)	11.8	2.5	14.4	14.1	12.7	12.5
GNY	8.5	3.4	6.2	7.7	8.5	5.6	5.5
Consumption	8.9	4.0	4.3	5.9	7.5	5.2	3.9
Fixed Investment	10.7	10.3	10.3	13.0	19.7	10.7	5.0
Public	12.6	-9.8	11.4	6.8	11.9	11.2	7.0
Private	9.1	0.9	9.7	16.8	24.4	10.4	3.7
2. Structure of the Economy:							
Oil GDP		21.8	19.3	18.6	18.3	18.3	17.3
Non Oil GDP		78.2	80.7	81.4	81.7	81.7	82.7
Agriculture		21.9	21.2	20.4	19.4	18.5	18.3
Manufacturing		11.4	13.6	14.1	14.9	15.5	16.1
Mining		1.2	1.2	1.2	1.3	1.4	1.7
Construction		5.3	5.3	5.5	5.8	6.0	6.2
Other Services		38.5	39.4	40.0	40.1	40.1	40.3
(Financial Sector)		3.6	3.8	4.0	4.3	4.5	4.8
3. Macroeconomic Balances:							
Deficit Current Account/ GNP	2.5	2.3	2.0	2.0	3.8	4.3	2.4
Non-interest Current Acc./ GNP	2.0	2.1	2.2	2.2	0.3	0.1	1.4
Overall Public Sector Balance/ GDP	-2.7	-3.1	-3.1	-1.3	0.2	-0.7	-1.4
Medium & Long Term Debt Service/ Exports		34.8	34.4	31.6	27.8	30.1	30
Medium & Long Term Debt/ GDP		65.5	60.3	54.6	58.6	61.1	57.9
4. Money and Prices:							
Inflation rate,		8.5	5.5	6.0	9.5	9.5	4.9
Interest rate, a)		13.8	18.5	18.6	18.5	22.8	18.9
Narrow money growth (M1)		13.8	13.5	39.8	18.4	22.8	8.4
Broad money growth (M2)		23.3	23.9	39.8	44.2	15.5	9.3
Reserve money growth		12.1	-5.4	23.3	19.0	2.9	19.3
M1/ GDP		10.3	10.1	12.0	12.0	11.2	11.3
M2/ GDP		23.8	29.6	35.0	42.8	42.5	46.7

Note: a) Weighted average interest rates on 12 months time deposits.

Sources: Central Bureau of Statistics, National Income of Indonesia 1985–90
Bank Indonesia, Indonesian Financial Statistics, various issues.

The target and the actual average annual rates of growth and structural change of GDP for fifth Five-Year Development Plan (Repelita V) are summarized in table 2.

STRUCTURAL CHANGES

There have also been some important structural changes in the Indonesian economy. Consistent with the general pattern of development elsewhere, the share of agriculture has gradually declined, even with modernization and a relatively good performance both in the food sector as well as in cash crops. Having been the biggest importer of rice in the world in the early 1970s, Indonesia entered the stage of self-sufficiency in rice in 1985. The share of agriculture in GDP has fallen from 31 percent in 1980 to 24 percent in 1985 and to 18 percent in 1992. Although the share is declining, the agricultural sector remains the biggest employer of Indonesia's work force. The share of employment in this sector has gradually declined from 54.8 percent in 1980 to 54.6 percent in 1985 and to 50.1 percent in 1990 (see table 3).

The most notable feature of sectoral growth has been the rapid rate of growth in the modern industrial sector, including manufacturing, which grew by 11 percent per annum in the 1970s. The import-substitution-industrial (ISI) policy, carried out in the 1960s and 1970s, reached its limits in the early 1980s. To revitalize economic growth the government has gradually changed its development strategy to export-oriented-industrial (EOI) policy. In 1980, manufacturing accounted for 11 percent of GDP, 16 percent in 1985 and 21 percent in 1992. The financial service sector grew comfortably at 12.1 percent per annum in the 1980s. Its contribution to GDP was 3.5 percent in 1985 and 4.2 percent in 1992.

STABILIZATION AND ADJUSTMENT PROGRAMS

The fast growth of the Indonesian economy has been the result of successful implementations of stabilization cum adjustment programs adopted since the early 1980s. The latest package of deregulation measures was announced on October 23, 1993. The coverage and aspects of the adjustment program are depicted in table 4.

The adjustment programs in Indonesia were adopted voluntarily by using various less restrictive sectoral program loans from the World Bank. The objective of the stabilization program has been to restore macroeconomic stability through fiscal and monetary restraints, supported by improvement of external competitiveness through a responsive exchange rate policy.[1] The availability of fast-disbursing loans since 1987, mainly from Japan, the World Bank, and ADB, has indirectly restructured Indonesia's external debt. Such a sound macroeconomic policy has corrected the internal and external

TABLE 2
Target and Actual Rates of Growth and the Structural Change of GDP for Repelita V, FY 1989/90–FY 1993/94

I. Growth Rates (in percent per annum):

	Target	Actual 1989–1992
Gross Domestic Products:	5.0	6.9
Agriculture:	3.6	3.1
Mining:	0.4	4.2
Manufacturing:	8.5	9.9
Construction:	6.0	12.0
Trade:	6.0	7.2
Transportation and Communication:	6.4	10.1
Nominal value of Non-Oil Exports:	16.0	over 20

II. Composition of GDP at the end of Repelita V (at constant 1983 market prices, in percent):

	Target	Actual (1993) (1992)
Agriculture:	21.6	18.4
Mining:	12.6	14.3
Manufacturing Industry:	16.9	20.8
Construction:	5.8	5.9
Trade:	16.9	16.6
Transportation and Communication:	6.0	6.3
Other Services:	20.4	18.0

Sources: The Republic of Indonesia, *Repelita V*, Book I and Central Bureau of Statistics, *National Accounts*, various years.

imbalances.

The adjustment program covers nearly all aspects of the economy: trade, investment, taxation, financial sector, labor market, and public administration. The program has encouraged market competition and promoted the private sector by relaxing barriers to market entry, reducing government controls on the economy and corporatization or privatization of the state-owned enterprises. The second thrust of the program has been to replace the development strategy with an export-oriented policy. In order to improve efficiency and productivity and reduce transaction costs, a competitive market requires improvements in market infrastructure. Because of this, deregulation is also accompanied by re-regulation. Along this line, gradually the authorities have begun to improve legal and accounting systems. The former includes protection of intellectual property rights. The Copyright Law of 1982, the Trademark Law of 1991, and the Patent Law of 1991 protect the copyright, rights of trademarks, and patent respectively. A series of industrial standards were introduced in the 1980s. Re-regulation in the financial sector is taken in the forms of stricter prudential regulatory framework and supervi-

TABLE 3

Employment by Main Industry, 1980–1990

Main Industry	1980		1985		1990	
	million	%	million	%	million	%
Agriculture	28.0	54.8	34.1	54.6	35.5	50.1
Mining and Quarrying	0.4	0.7	0.4	0.7	0.7	1.0
Manufacturing	4.4	8.5	5.8	9.3	8.2	11.6
Electricity	0.1	0.2	0.1	0.1	0.1	0.1
Construction	1.6	3.1	2.1	3.4	2.8	4.0
Trade	6.6	12.9	9.4	15.0	10.6	15.0
Financial and Other Services	0.2	0.4	0.3	0.4	0.5	0.7
Public Services	7.7	15.1	8.3	13.3	9.7	13.7
Other	0.7	1.4	0.1	0.1	0.0	0.0
Total	51.2	100.0	62.5	100.0	70.8	100.0

Sources: Central Bureau of Statistics, Statistical Yearbook of Indonesia, various years.

sion. These include higher capital requirements for banks, insurance companies, and securities firms. In addition, capital requirements of banks and insurance companies are directly linked to the qualities of their assets.

The direction of trade policy reforms in general has been to replace nontariff barriers with tariff as a means of protection. The level of tariff itself has also been reduced gradually (table 5). Indonesia, however, is not a laissez-faire country. Despite deregulation, the government retains some forms of industrial policy and control on the prices of state-vended products.[2] Some sectors of the economy, such as automotive and "strategic" industries, are shielded from internal and external competition by layers of protective measures. These include high import tariffs and sales taxes, a license system, local content programs, and a negative investment list. Deregulation has not covered the 184 state-owned enterprises. In some other sectors of the economy, deregulation is not synonymous with strengthening market competition. It is merely the transfer of monopoly rights from the state to the well-connected private enterprises.

Industrial policies are, among others, reflected in "the 10 strategic industries" (covering aircraft; oceangoing ships; some heavy machineries; explosives; steel products; armaments; some electronics and telecommunications equipment; and railway components, coaches, and cars) under the control of the minister of research and technology. A number of resources-based industries, such as wood-based industries and petrochemical industries, are protected and reserved for Indonesian companies. Bulog (the Logistic Agency) has monopoly rights on the export and import of foodstuffs. Dairy, animal feed, and automotive industries are subject to local content programs. Cartels and price controls are not the only obstacles to strengthening market competition and efficiency in some sectors of the economy. Utilities, such as electric-

TABLE 4
Chronology of the Adjustment Program, 1983–1993

Policy Instrument	
Exchange Rate	1. Rupiah was devalued by 28% against U.S. dollar on March 30, 1983, from Rp. 703 to Rp. 907 per U.S. dollar; since then the exchange rate has been made more flexible.
	2. Rupiah was devalued by 31% against the U.S. dollar on September 12, 1986 from Rp. 1,134 to Rp. 1,644 per U.S. dollar.
Fiscal Policy	1. Tight fiscal policy, since 1983, marked by:
	a. large capital and import intensive projects (particularly investment in manufacturing, petro-chemicals and mining) rephased in May 1983;
	b. major cutback in public real capital spending;
	c. more resources for social programs;
	d. restraints on civil service employment and salaries.
	2. Tax reform enacted in 1983–1985, involving simplifications of both tax structure and tax administration of all tax sources, excluding taxes on foreign trade.
Monetary and Financial Policy	1. Financial reform, initiated on June 1, 1983, involving removal of credit and rate ceilings for state bank's operations, a reduction in the scope of credit programs and introducing of new market-oriented instruments of monetary control.
	2. New deregulation measures introduced in December 1987, October and December 1988, March 1989, February 1991 and May 1993 aimed at enhancing financial sector prudential standards and efficiency, and developing the capital market by, among others, removing barriers to entry.
	3. Improved monetary management to control inflation and to curb exchange rate speculation.
	4. Removal of central bank's direct credits ("liquidity credits") and major reduction of economic sectors covered by subsidized "priority credits" in January 1990 to curb inflationary pressures and credit fungibility.
	5. New regulations introduced on March 14, 1991, which are aimed at strengthening the capital base of banks and tightening supervision over financial institutions. The new measures require the banking system to meet the BIS guidelines on capital adequacy ratio of 8% of the bank assets by December 1993.
	6. Relaxation of prudential standards introduced in May 29, 1993, and the deadline to meet the CAR of 8% was extended to December 1994.
Trade Policy	1. Across-the-board July 1993 and October 23, 1993, reductions in nominal tariffs introduced in April 1995, October 1986 and May 28, 1990.
	2. Measures to provide internationally priced inputs to exporters announced on May 6, 1986, and May 28, 1990, July 1993, and October 23, 1993. This scheme permits exporters and suppliers of input for exporters to bypass the import licensing system and import tariff or, if they cannot bypass the system, to reclaim import duties, although the cost imposed by the NTBs cannot be rebated.

TABLE 4 (Continued)

The import bias of the protective system had been lessened but not uniformly.

3. Major deregulation of import licencing system announced in December 25, 1986, January 15, 1987, May 28, 1990, July 1992, and October 1993.

4. Additional measures to reduce anti-export bias announced in December 1987 by reducing regulatory framework for exporters.

5. Major removal of non tariff barriers, switch from non-tariff to tariff barriers, and general reduction of tariff rates on May 28, 1990, July 1992, and October 1993. Also covering simplification of lisencing procedures in trade, manufacturing, health, and agricultural business, the policy package is aimed at reducing high cost economy.

6. Further removal of non-tariff barriers, general reduction of import tariffs and reopening of several business fields to new domestic and foreign investors was announced in June 2, 1991, July 1992, and October 23, 1993. Several major features of the reform cover outright import bans of cold-rolled steel coils, and other steel products, abolition of the export quota system for palm oil and copra, introduction of an import quota system on built up commercial vehicles and reopening of car component manufacture to new investors.

7. In June 1993, for the first time after 23 years, import ban built up passenger cars was replaced by prohibitive 300% tariff rate, further reduction in tariff for other commodities, and realization of regulations in trade in agriculture products. Domestic automotive industry is, however, remained subject layers of protective measures.

Other Regulatory Framework

1. Reorganization of customs, shipping and ports operations announced in April 1985 to reduce handling and transport cost for exports and to simplify the administrative procedures governing inter island and foreign trade. Further deregulation of maritime activities announced on November 21, 1988, to reduce cost and encourage private sector participation, including foreign capital and foreign shipping companies.

2. Measures to reduce the investment and capacity lisencing requirements, relax foreign investment regulation and reduce the local content program.

3. Measures announced July 6, 1992, to allow joint venture firms to hold right to use the land and use them for credit collateral, liberalized import of used machinery, plant equipment and other capital goods, and liberalize expatriate works permits.

4. On June 10, 1993, the number of investment negative list reduced from 51 to 34.

ity, the oil sector, and telecommunications, are practically monopolized by state-owned enterprises. Their role is still dominant in the financial sector for large plantation and "strategic" and "upstream" industries. In general, these companies operate as an arm-length extension of government bureaucracy. Even the publicly traded private firms typically list only a small fraction of their shares, retaining real control in the hands of a single family. In addition,

TABLE 5
Nominal and Effective Rates of Protection, 1987–1991
(in percent)

	1987	1989	1991*
Nominal rate of protection of:			
Non-oil manufacturing	21.9	17.9	12.8
All tradables	11.8	9.3	7.5
Effective rate of protection of all non-oil manufacturing	72.3	63.6	56.7
Production coverage of non-tariff barriers for:			
Non-oil manufacturing	57.1	38.1	31.8
All Tradables	40.6	27.9	22.3

Note: *)   After June 1, 1991 deregulation package.
Source: P. S. J. Wymenga, "Industrial Development in Indonesia in the 1970s" in P. S. J. Wymenga (ed.), *Prospects of Industrial Development in Indonesia*, Final Report of the Industrial Analysis Project DTA-256, the Ministry of Industry and Netherlands Economic Institute, July 1991, table 1.7, p. 12.

most of them belong to the well-connected conglomerates that have subsidiary companies in many sectors of the economy and operate in various countries. Partly because of the past inward-looking development and high-leveraged financing strategies, rarely is it possible to keep the operations of all subsidiaries up to world standards. In many cases, the less efficient subsidiaries are carried along by sales to other companies within the group. These avoid the stock-market pressures for cutting costs.

In general, the now unprotected ISI projects could quickly adjust to an export-oriented-industrialization (EOI) strategy partly because of a good exchange rate management of Indonesia.[3] To avoid "the Dutch disease," because of "the oil boom" during 1973/74-1982, the authorities devalued the rupiah in November 1978. Concurrently, the external anchor of the rupiah was changed from the U.S. dollar to an undisclosed basket of major currencies. Since then, Indonesia has adopted a managed floating rate system. The rising trend of the real effective exchange rate (see figure 1) provides a competitive edge for Indonesia's products in international markets.

DEVELOPMENT FINANCING

Financing of economic development has strongly depended on development in the petroleum sector, concessionary foreign aid and loans, and foreign direct investment. The financing of Indonesia's twin deficits in the government budget and the balance of payments has depended upon these three sources. To reduce dependency on external resources, in the mid-1980s the authorities reformed the tax system and promoted non-oil exports.

FIGURE 1
Real EFF Exchange Rate Index, 1979–92

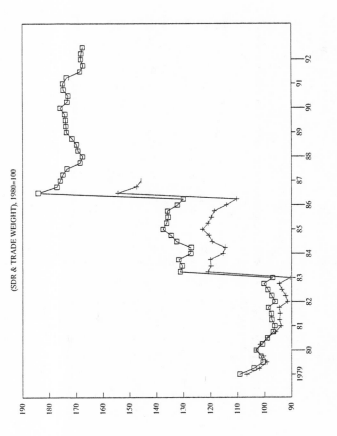

(SDR & TRADE WEIGHT, 1980=100)

Gradually, these efforts began to bear results. In 1980, about two-thirds of government's domestic revenue and nearly 80 percent of export proceeds were generated from oil and gas. In FY 1992–1993, contribution of tax on oil and gas to government domestic revenue was reduced to 36 percent and the 74 percent was generated from taxes on non-oil activities (see table 6). In 1992, contribution of oil and gas to export proceeds fell to 36 percent and the other 64 percent was generated from non-oil products (see table 7). In 1992, over 40 percent of non-oil exports was generated from textiles and garments and wood-based products (see table 8).

Investment-Savings and Resource Gap

The rapid rate of economic growth was made possible because over the past 25 years, Indonesia, annually, invested more than a quarter of its GDP, and the bulk of the resources required came from domestic savings, particu-

TABLE 6
Revenue Structure of Central Government of Indonesia, Selected Years
(Rp billion)

	1973/74	1978/79	1983/84	1988/89	1993/94
Domestic Revenue	997	4266	14433	23005	52769
Oil revenue	347	2309	9520	9527	15128
Non-oil revenue	630	1957	4913	13478	37641
Income tax a)	164	688	2085	4374	16169
Tax on domestic consumption b)	168	491	1392	6187	14755
Tax on int'l trade c)	254	587	916	1348	3136
Non-tax revenue	44	191	520	1569	3583
Development Revenue	208	1036	3882	9991	9553
Project aid	114	987	3868	7950	9126
Programed Aid	94	48	15	2041	427
Total Revenue	1185	5302	18316	32996	62322
As percentage of total revenue:					
Domestic Revenue	82.5	80.5	78.8	69.7	84.7
Oil revenue	29.3	43.5	52.0	28.9	24.3
Non-oil revenue	53.2	36.9	26.8	40.8	60.4
Income tax a)	13.9	13.0	11.4	13.3	25.9
Tax on domestic consumption b)	14.2	9.3	7.6	18.8	23.7
Tax on int'l trade c)	21.4	11.1	5.0	4.1	5.0
Non-tax revenue	3.7	3.6	2.8	4.8	5.7
Development Revenue	17.5	19.5	21.2	30.3	15.3
Project aid	9.6	18.6	21.1	24.1	14.6
Programed Aid	7.9	0.9	0.1	6.2	0.7
Total Revenue	100.0	100.0	100.0	100.0	100.0
As percentage of GDP:					
Domestic Revenue	14.5	18.8	18.6	16.2	18.2
Oil revenue	5.1	10.1	12.3	6.7	5.2
Non-oil revenue	9.3	8.6	6.3	9.5	13.0
Income tax a)	2.4	3.0	2.7	3.1	5.6
Tax on domestic consumption	2.5	2.2	1.8	4.4	5.1
Tax on int'l trade	3.8	2.6	1.2	0.9	1.1
Non-tax revenue	0.7	0.8	0.7	1.1	1.2
Development Revenue	3.1	4.6	5.0	7.0	3.3
Project aid	1.7	4.3	5.0	5.6	3.1
Programed Aid	1.4	0.2	0.0	1.4	0.1
Total Revenue	17.5	23.3	23.6	23.2	21.5
Memo item: Price of Oil (US$ per barrel)	3.73	13.6	29.53	16.04	18.42 d)

Notes: a) Non-oil corporate income tax, personal income tax and land tax; b) sales
tax, exices and other taxes and levies; c) import duties and export tax; d)
March 1993

Source: Department of Finance, *Financial Notes*, various issues.

TABLE 7
Exports by Major Product 1981–1992 (US $ Million)

	1981	1983	1986	1988	1989	1990	1991	1992
Petroleum and Gas	20663	16141	8277	7681	8679	11071	10895	10671
Non-Oil/LNG	4501	5005	6528	11537	13480	14604	18247	23296
Agriculture	1570	1373	1754	1909	1943	2083	2282	2212
Manufactured Goods	2667	3220	4508	9262	11028	11879	15068	19613
Wood Products	417	801	1418	2884	3441	3327	3660	4180
Basic Metals	604	577	445	862	946	624	595	586
Garments	95	156	519	796	1172	1657	2290	3189
Textiles	31	112	279	583	860	1260	1785	2872
Other Manufactured	1519	1575	1848	4138	4609	5010	6738	8786
Mining Products	203	170	247	349	503	636	889	1453
Total	25165	21146	14805	19219	22159	25675	29142	33967
Petroleum and Gas	82.1	76.3	55.9	40.0	39.2	43.1	37.4	31.4
Non-Oil/LNG	17.9	23.7	44.1	60.0	60.8	56.9	62.6	68.6
Agriculture	6.2	6.5	11.8	9.9	8.8	8.1	7.8	6.5
Manufactured Goods	10.6	15.2	30.5	48.2	49.8	46.3	51.7	57.7
Wood Products	1.7	3.8	9.6	15.0	15.5	13.0	12.6	12.3
Basic Metals	2.4	2.7	3.0	4.5	4.3	2.4	2.0	1.7
Garments	0.4	0.7	3.5	4.1	5.3	6.5	7.9	9.4
Textiles	0.1	0.5	1.9	3.0	3.9	4.9	6.1	8.5
Other Manufactured	6.0	7.4	12.5	21.5	20.8	19.5	23.1	25.9
Mining Products	0.8	0.8	1.7	1.8	2.3	2.5	3.1	4.3
Total	100.0	100.0	100.0	100.0	100.0	100.0	100.0	100.0

Source: Central Bureau of Statistic, Monthly Bulletin, various issues.

larly from tax on oil-related activities. In contrast to other oil-producing countries, Indonesia has used its oil windfall effectively to broaden the productive base of its economy. As a percentage of GDP, the annual average investment-savings (I-S) gap in Indonesia was minus 2.3 percent in the 1980s and minus 1.6 percent in the 1980s (see table 9). The negative sign of the I-S gap indicates that Indonesia used part of its revenues from the "oil boom" in 1973/74-1982 to accumulate external reserves, mainly secondary reserves at state-owned commercial banks, and to repay maturing debt, such as Pertamina's (the National Oil Company) debt in 1975.

As a percentage of GDP, Indonesia's resource gap amounted to 2.5 percent in 1988, 0.5 percent in 1990, and 2 percent in 1992.

Foreign Exchange Gap

The current account on the balance of payments represents the foreign exchange gap. As a percentage of GDP, the average annual current account deficit of Indonesia was 1.7 percent in the 1970s, increased to 3.4 percent in the 1980s, and fell to 2.4 percent in 1992. It was projected to reach 2.2

TABLE 8
Non-Oil & Gas Exports

	1983	1988	1989	1990	1991	1992
			US $ million			
Agriculture	1373	1901	1943	2083	2282	2212
Fish & Shrimp	229	597	677	877	1047	1122
Manufactured Goods	3220	9262	11028	11879	15068	19613
Wood Products	801	2884	3441	3327	3660	4180
Garments	156	796	1172	1657	2290	3189
Textiles	112	583	860	1260	1785	2872
Other Manufactured Goods	2151	5000	5555	5634	7333	9372
Others	413	366	509	642	898	1471
Total	5005	11537	13480	14604	18247	23296
			as percentage of total			
Agriculture	27.4	16.5	14.4	14.3	12.5	9.5
Fish & Shrimp	4.6	5.2	5.0	6.0	5.7	4.8
Manufactured Goods	64.3	80.3	81.8	81.3	82.6	84.2
Wood Products	16.0	25.0	25.5	22.8	20.1	17.9
Garments	3.1	6.9	8.7	11.3	12.5	13.7
Textiles	2.2	5.0	6.4	8.6	9.8	12.3
Other Manufactured Goods	43.0	43.3	41.2	38.6	40.2	40.2
Others	8.2	3.2	3.8	4.4	4.9	6.3
Total	100	100	100	100	100	100
			annual growth rates			
Agriculture		—a)	1.8	7.2	9.5	−3.1
Fish & Shrimp		6.8	13.5	29.4	19.4	7.1
Manufactured Goods		21.1	19.1	7.7	26.8	30.2
Wood Products		23.5	19.3	−3.3	10.0	14.2
Garments		29.2	47.3	41.4	38.2	39.2
Textiles		38.6	47.6	46.5	41.7	60.9
Other Manufactured Goods		39.0	11.1	1.4	30.1	27.8
Others		18.4	39.1	26.2	39.8	63.9
Total		−2.4	16.8	8.3	24.9	27.7

Note: a) Average 1984–1988.
Source: Central Bureau of Statistics, Monthly Bulletin, various issues.

percent in 1993. The current account deficits were extremely high in 1982 and 1983 as oil prices began to fall, and again in 1986. Because a substantial portion of Indonesia's external debt is denominated in Japanese yen, a sharp appreciation of the yen, following the Plaza Accord in the fall of 1985, raised Indonesia's debt repayments, measured in the U.S. dollar, its export currency.

TABLE 9
Financing of Investment-Savings Gap, 1986–1990 (Rp Billion)

	1986	1987	1988	1989	1990
Gross National Savings	20296	27212	33732	42704	52829
Private National Savings	16782	22375	27420	35034	42024
Government Savings	3514	4837	6312	7670	10805
Gross Domestic Investment	24782	30980	36802	45649	60206
Private Domestic Investment	15387	21411	26463	35104	50376
Government Investment	9395	9569	10339	10545	9830
Investment-Savings Gap	4486	3768	3070	2945	7377
Private	-1395	-964	-957	70	8352
Government	5881	4732	4027	2875	-975
Financing:					
Government	-5881	-4732	-4027	-2875	975
External Financing	3790	3256	4215	3679	2404
Changes in Reserves a)	2091	1476	-188	-804	-3379
Private	1395	964	957	-70	-8352
External Financing	2566	2956	-1694	-325	267
Changes in Reserves a)	-3961	-3920	737	395	8085
Total I - S Gap	-4486	-3768	-3070	-2945	-7377
External Financing	6356	6212	2521	3354	2671
Changes in Reserves a)	1870	2444	-549	409	-4706
Current Account (Foreign Savings)	4486	3768	3070	2945	7377
National Saving Ratio, (%)	23.2	28.1	29.1	32.8	34.7

Note: a) A negative value represents an increase in reserves.
Source: Central Bureau of Statistics, *National Income of Indonesia*, various issues,
The Public Sector Accounts, various issues.

Financing of I-S and Foreign Exchange Gaps

To finance I-S and foreign exchange gaps, Indonesia has relied on inflows of external resources, both development aid and foreign direct investment. The Indonesian government's external borrowing strategy, since 1966, has been to consistently maximize inflows of development aid, preferably concessional Official Development Assistance (ODA) from its Western creditors. The "oil boom" during 1973–1982 simply caused Indonesia to receive less concessional ODA.[4] Because of this cautious external borrowing strategy, despite its large debt, Indonesia retained access to voluntary market finance throughout the adjustment period in the 1980s.

As a donor country, the share of Japanese aid to Indonesia has accelerated since the mid 1980s. The Japanese percentage of bilateral ODA to Indonesia has increased from 23 percent in the 1970s to 64 percent in 1988-1989 and 55 percent in 1990-1991. On the other hand, the contribution of the United States has sharply dropped from 46 percent in 1970–1971 to 4 percent in 1988-1989 and 5 percent in 1990-1991 (see table 10). Most of the Japanese

TABLE 10
Sources of Bilateral ODA to Indonesia, 1970–91 (US$ million)

	1970–71	1980–81	1987–88	1988–89	1990–91
Japan	127	402	1107	1335	1130
United States	260	146	92	87	96
Others	176	413	565	657	840
Total	563	962	1763	2079	2066
As % of total:					
Japan	23	42	63	64	55
United States	46	15	5	4	5
Others	31	43	32	32	41

Source: OECD, *Development Co-operation Report*, various issues.

ODA has been used for financing of economic infrastructure, environmental management, and human resources development. Massive external borrowings of the private sector occurred in 1989–1991, following the relaxation of financial institutions to international capital markets. To cool down the overheated economy due to this private capital inflow, the authorities adopted a tight credit policy in 1990. To supplement this policy, the authorities postponed unaffordable public investment projects and reinstituted ceilings on foreign borrowings of public sector in November 1991.

Foreign Direct Investment

The broad-based deregulation program carried out since the mid-1980s that improves market competition and market infrastructure has encouraged a rapid inflow of private foreign direct investment (FDI). The value of approved domestic investment, outside of the oil and gas and financial sectors, rose from Rp14.2 trillion in 1988 to Rp19.4 trillion in 1989 and further to Rp55.3 trillion in 1990. During the same years and in the same sectors, the value of foreign direct investment rose from US$4.5 billion in 1988 to $4.7 billion in 1989 and to $8.7 billion in 1990. Since the mid-1980s, the bulk of new private investment approvals, outside the oil-related industries, has been directed towards export activities, particularly in labor-intensive and resource-based manufacturing industries, where Indonesia has a comparative advantage.

Some of the investment projects represent a relocation to Indonesia because of industrial restructuring in Japan and Asian NIEs. Increasing labor costs, higher land prices, heightened concern about the environment, and appreciation of their currencies have led these countries to relocate labor-intensive and resource-based industries offshore. Those countries are now concentrating on high-tech and knowledge-based activities that produce high value-added products. The countries of origin of FDI in Indonesia are de-

FIGURE 2

CUMM. Foreign Investment Approvals

BY COUNTRY, 1967-SEPT 1993 (%)

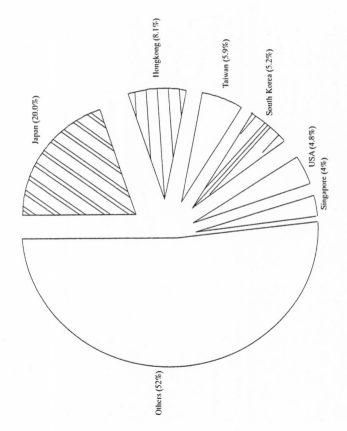

Japan (20.0%)

Hongkong (8.1%)

Taiwan (5.9%)

South Korea (5.2%)

USA (4.8%)

Singapore (4%)

Others (52%)

picted in figure 2.

In the early 1990s, however, the inflow of FDI has been slowed down, partly because of the scarcity in economic infrastructure such as electricity, telecommunications, and industrial water. The other part of the problems are due to the slow pace of deregulation of the real sector of the economy. On the external side, the problems in the financial sector in Japan have reduced its capital outflow.

DIRECTION OF PUBLIC INVESTMENT

Over 60 percent of government development expenditures has been used for investment in infrastructure and human resources (see table 11). When the government cut its expenditures during the stabilization periods, the main victims usually have been subsidy expenditures, civil servants' salaries, and

TABLE 11
Structure of Development Expenditures

	Actual						Budget
	1984/85	1988/89	1989/90	1990/91	1991/92	1992/93	1993/94
	Rp billion						
General public services a)	927	733	909	1247	1345	1606	1580
Education	1231	1606	1507	2052	2417	3147	3565
Population and health	320	339	470	723	891	957	1087
Housing and water supply	224	481	495	677	802	1053	972
Economic services	4877	6145	6872	7854	9722	10873	11564
Agriculture and irrigation	1699	1614	2049	2308	2713	3240	3082
Electric power	911	1955	1397	1707	2286	3042	2993
Transportation and tourism	1428	2011	3006	3743	3910	4537	4667
Other ec. services	839	565	420	96	813	54	822
Other community & Soc. serv.							
Manpower and transmigration	422	266	281	580	718	897	954
Unallocable							
Regional development	791	1137	1369	1938	2478	2920	3562
Government capital participation	292	238	625	335	411	409	394
Others b)	1599	1305	1306	1429	1572	1466	1551
Development Budget Reserve				2000	1500		
Total	10683	12250	13834	19452	21764	24135	25227
	as % of total						
General public services a)	8.7	6.0	6.6	6.4	6.2	6.7	6.3
Education	11.5	13.1	10.9	10.5	11.1	13.0	14.1
Population and health	3.0	2.8	3.4	3.7	4.1	4.0	4.3
Housing and water supply	2.1	3.9	3.6	3.5	3.7	4.4	3.9
Economic services	45.7	50.2	49.7	40.4	44.7	45.1	45.8
Agriculture and irrigation	15.9	13.2	14.8	11.9	12.5	13.4	12.2
Electric power	8.5	16.0	10.1	8.8	10.5	12.6	11.9
Transportation and tourism	13.4	16.4	21.7	19.2	18.0	18.8	18.5
Other ec. services	7.9	4.6	3.0	0.5	3.7	0.2	3.3

Source: Department of Finance, *Financial Notes*, various issues.
Notes: a)   Law and order, defence & security, government apparatus.
       b)   Trade and cooperative, religion, information and science.
            From 1979/80 includes natural resource development and environment.

unaffordable projects, but not investment. Investment in economic infrastructure and human resources has not been affected much by the expenditure cut. This indicates that most of the "oil money" and foreign aid and loans have been used for investment projects that are crucial for a sustained and broad-based long-term growth.

Between 24 percent and nearly 40 percent of public expenditures between 1985 and 1990 have been mainly allocated for economic services, and the bulk was for economic infrastructure. Public investment in this sector has also been directed towards poverty alleviation. Most of the economic infrastructure projects were dams and irrigations and roads in rural areas that are essential for improving productivity in agriculture.

The second priority in the public expenditure was investment in human resources development, which includes education and health programs. In the 1970s until the mid–1980s, over 80 percent of the education budget was devoted to primary and basic education. In the early 1970s, primary school was made compulsory. The health program, which included family planning, was mainly available for the masses, including those who lived in remote areas. Indicators of demography and education are presented in table 11. Investment in human resources improves labor productivity. In contrast to a once and for all increase in production because of an accumulation of physical capital stock, an increase in labor productivity assures continuous growth rate.

FUTURE PROSPECTS

In his Independence Day speech, President Soeharto outlined the focus of the Sixth Five-Year Development Plan (Repelita VI), which started on April 1, 1994, as follows:

1. to promote the manufacturing industry as the main producer of value added and absorber of work force;
2. to improve industrial productivity and efficiency through human resource development by improving skills, creativity, discipline, technology, and managerial skills of the Indonesian work force;
3. to continue the deregulation process of the economy, introduce bureaucratic reforms, rationalize protections, and reduce subsidies;
4. to encourage development of small- and medium-scale businesses;
5. to promote agro-based industries;
6. to continue development of physical infrastructure, such as roads, telecommunications, and energy; and
7. to intensify programs for the eradication of poverty. A new Inpres program has been introduced for poverty alleviation programs in the poor regions and villages, particularly in the eastern part of Indonesia.

During a hearing with the Commission X of the House of Representatives (DPR), the chairman of the National Development Planning Board (Bappenas) highlighted the targets and plans for the Sixth Five-Year Development Plan (Repelita VI) as follows:

I. Rates of Growth in the Sixth Development Plan (percent, per annum):

	Scenario I	Scenario II
GDP	6.5	6.0
Agriculture sector	3.5	3.5
Manufacturing industry	10.0	8.8
Non-oil manufacturing	11.3	9.9
Others	6.1	5.8

II. Sectoral Distribution of GDP (at 1989 market prices, end of the plan period):

GDP	100.0	100.0
Agriculture	17.1	17.8
Manufacturing industry	25.0	24.1
Non-oil manufacturing	22.2	21.3
Others	57.6	58.0

III. Income per capita (Nominal US$, Year: 2000):

847　　847　　769

The investment requirement for implementation of the plan is estimated at Rp704.9 trillion for Scenario I and Rp744.5 for Scenario II, 70 percent of both of which is expected from the private sector. The nominal value of non-oil exports is projected to increase by 19 percent for Scenario I and 16 percent for Scenario II.

THE CHALLENGES AHEAD

Whether Indonesia can implement its national plan is dependent upon international markets and its response to external developments. In the short- and medium-run the Indonesian economy is facing a number of delicate internal and external problems.

The first problem is the financial fragility of the Indonesian banking system, particularly the state-owned banks and some of the domestic private banks. Following the financial sector reforms of October 1988, the balance sheets of these groups of banks have deteriorated as a result of low quality assets and declining profitability. As the state-owned banks group still hold a dominant position in the Indonesian financial system, the financial problems have a great impact on the economy. To ease the financial problem of its banks, the government has strengthened their capital bases by borrowing (US$307) from the World Bank, in November 1992, converting part of Bank Indonesia's outstanding liquidity credits to the capital of these banks, and assuming part of their bad debts. On May 29, 1993, the authorities relaxed some the prudential regulations. Given the size of their loans, however, these measures may not be enough. The financial fragility of the banking sector would constrain economic growth as it drives up interest rates and slows down credit expansion.

The second major problem is caused by the stop-go and slow pace of deregulation in the real sector economy. This creates uncertainty, retains economic distortions, and, along with the shortage in physical infrastructure, retards private sector investment and economic growth. Deregulation programs also have not covered the state-owned enterprises. The next round of deregulation, therefore, should also cover measures to commercialize the state-owned enterprises providing public goods and services. This will make their operations more transparent and accountable, and will contribute to domestic savings mobilizations.

The third problem is how to improve market infrastructure in order to make the market work better and equitable, with low transaction costs. This requires improvements in the legal and accounting systems as well as decentralization of decision making.

The fourth problem is how to distribute the benefits of development equitably. Undoubtedly, Indonesia's record is quite impressive in reducing the number of people living below the absolute poverty line. But an equal distribution in consumption may not necessarily mean equal distribution of wealth and income. Embarrassingly, alleged reports indicate that most of the state-owned banks' bad loans are concentrated amongst a limited number of well-connected conglomerates who have exclusive access to government procurement, cheap natural resources, and high market protection. Industrial Surveys and Censuses indicate high market concentrations enjoyed by these groups.

The fifth (potential) problem is rooted in the Law of Nr. 3 of February 17, 1992, on Workers Social Security (Jamsostek). The program promoted by this law covers four separate programs: worker's compensation insurance, health insurance, life insurance, and pension benefits. The programs are mandated for all workers, both in formal and informal sectors of the economy. The first potential problem created by this law is the fact that the program is exclusively administered by PT Astek, a state-owned worker insurance company under the control of the Ministry of Labor. The mandatory principle and the exclusiveness of PT Astek are against competition and market-based principles of the deregulation programs. Second, it is too administratively burdensome for a single entity. Third, the potential costs are frighteningly high. Fourth, employers' contributions to the program are equivalent to taxes for employing workers. This drives up the costs of production simply because of hiring workers. Fifth, if it turns out that the benefits of the program were below the expectations, the workers' contributions to the programs would be similar to embezzlement of workers' income. This will ignite labor unrests.

On the external sector, new conditionalities imposed by the OECD countries, since the early 1990s, have begun to limit Indonesia's access to concessionary ODA and trade such as GSP. Because of the bloody Timor incident in November 1990, for the first time in history the commitments made by the consortium of Indonesia's donors, in early June 1993, to extend US$5.1 billion in loans, was tied to Indonesia's record on human rights. In the summer of 1993, the United States threatened to stop Indonesia's access to its GSP for alleged violation of labor rights. Wood- and marine-based products are now subject to various national eco-labeling requirements, which are different in various countries. An eco-label is granted to products whose raw materials, manufacturing processes, and waste have a less negative impact on the environment. Exports of textile and garments are subject to quota and to the future of MFA in the Uruguay Round.

REFERENCES

Booth, Anne, ed. (1992). *The Oil Boom and After: Indonesian Economic Policy and Performance in the Soeharto Era.* Singapore: Oxford University Press.

McLeod, Ross. (1993). "Labour: Sharing the Benefits of Growth?" A paper presented at the Conference on Indonesia Update 1993, Indonesia Project-Research School of Pacific Studies, Australian National University, Canberra, August 27.

Nasution, Anwar. (1992). "The Years of Living Dangerously: The Impacts of Financial Sector Policy Reforms and Increasing Private Sector External Indebtedness in Indonesia, 1983-92." A paper presented at the Third Convention of the East Asian Economic Association (EAEA), Seoul, August 20-21.

——. (1993) *Reforms of the Financial Sector in Indonesia, 1983-1991.* PITO Business Environment in Asean. Nr. 7. Honolulu: East-West Centre.

——. (1993). "Financial Sector Policies in Indonesia, 1980-1993." A research report submitted to Asian Development Bank, Manila, Philippines, November.

Ravallion, Martin, and Monica Huppi. (1991). "Measuring Changes in Poverty: A Methodological Case Study of Indonesia During an Adjustment Period." *The World Bank Economic Review* 5, no. 1 (January): 57-82.

Woo, W. T., and Anwar Nasution. (1989). "Indonesian Economic Policies and Their Relation to External Debt Management." In *Developing Country Debt and Economic Performance,* vol. 3, ed. J. D. Sachs and Susan M. Collins. Chicago: Chicago University Press.

Woo, W. T., Bruce Glassburner, and Anwar Nasution. (Forthcoming). *Macroeconomic Policies, Crises and Long-run Growth: The Case of Indonesia, 1965-1990.* Washington DC: The World Bank.

The World Bank. (1990). *World Development Report.* Washington, DC: The World Bank.

——. (1993). *The East Asian Miracle: Economic Growth and Public Policy.* New York: Oxford University Press.

NOTES

1. Since 1968, Indonesia has imposed fiscal discipline by adopting a "balanced budget" principle. In this principle, the budget deficit is financed by foreign aid and loans. These external resources are classified as "development revenues" in the budget and earmarked for financing "development expenditures."

2. The government, for example, sets prices of foodstuffs, agriculture inputs, oil products, and portland cement.

3. Along with the unification of the multiple exchange rate, in April 1971, Indonesia adopted an open foreign exchange rate system. Indonesian citizens and foreigners are free to hold, buy, and sell foreign currencies. Banks licensed in dealing foreign exchange transactions are allowed to accept deposits or extend loans in foreign exchange. Except for a 15 percent withholding tax on interest rates there is neither tax nor subsidy on foreign exchange transactions.

4. Foreign borrowings of public sector, including state-owned enterprises, since 1966, have been centralized at the Ministry of Finance. When Indonesia encountered problems of rising debt repayment, following the currency realignment in 1985-1986, Indonesia, again, turned to its "Western" creditors.

4

SOUTHEAST ASIAN ECONOMIC EXPERIENCE AND PROSPECTS: MYANMAR

Win Tin

The Union of Myanmar, the largest country in mainland Southeast Asia, has a total land area of 676,577 square kilometers and an estimated population of about 42 million. Myanmar is endowed with rich natural resources and cultivable land, which remains largely untapped.

Since Myanmar gained independence in 1948 the country was managed basically along the principles of a market economy with the private sector occupying an important role. However, with the assumption of power by the revolutionary government in 1962, a centrally planned economic system was adopted and continued to be used for about two and one half decades until 1988, during which the economy did not show marked improvement. Nevertheless, following the assumption of state power by the State Law and Order Restoration Council (SLORC) in September 1988, the socialist economic system was officially abandoned and Myanmar was redirected towards a market-oriented economic system, allowing the private sector to flourish once again alongside the state sector.

INTRODUCTION OF ECONOMIC AND FINANCIAL REFORMS

With a view to achieve economic recovery in the short run and to lay down a firm foundation for sustained growth in the long run, a series of economic and financial reforms have been announced and implemented by the government since late 1988. Major reform measures include the following:

1. Enact Foreign Investment Law and allow direct foreign Investment.
2. Enact the state-owned Economic Enterprises Law.
3. Enact new banking laws and allow the establishment of private banks, including foreign banks, for the first time since 1963.
4. Initiate the new financial management system.
5. Allow farmers to cultivate crops of their choice and to freely process transport and trade agricultural products they then produce.
6. Decentralize the industrial sector by allowing the managing directors of the State Economic Enterprises (SEEs) more autonomy in management and initiatives.
7. Encourage private sector development.
8. Abolish price controls and reduce subsidies granted to state agencies.
9. Initiate institutional changes.
10. Enact new taxation law and streamline taxes and duties;

11. Improve infrastructure support.
12. Restructure wages and prices.
13. Allow state enterprises, cooperatives, joint ventures, and private entrepreneurs to claim and utilize fallow and culturable waste land up to 5,000 acres for the enhancement of agriculture, livestock, and fishery production.
14. Promote exports by streamlining existing export and import procedures; encourage the diversification of exports through introduction of new products.

A BRIEF REVIEW OF ECONOMIC PERFORMANCE SINCE 1988

Owing to failures of the centrally planned economic system, GDP suffered a negative growth of about 5.5 percent on annual average between 1986–1987 through 1988–1989. However, due to drastic reform measures undertaken since late 1988, the Myanmar economy recovered immediately from 1988–1989, which registered a positive GDP growth of 3.7 percent, and from 1988–1989 through 1992–1993 GDP, which achieved a growth rate of about 4.1 percent on annual average. A slight decline in GDP growth of one percent in 1991–1992 was basically due to severe damage to crop because of widespread flooding in lower Myanmar rather than to other factors. As a result of all out efforts made to increase production in 1992–1993, which had been designated as the "Economic Year," GDP on provisional basis increased dramatically by 10.9 percent, indicating better performances in almost all sectors of the economy. A brief review of sectoral performance during recent years is related below.

FINANCIAL SECTOR

Financial reform has been initiated in accordance with the market-oriented economic system introduced in late 1988. The new banking laws were enacted in July 1990, the Savings Bank Law in July 1992, and the Myanmar Insurance Law in 1993.

Myanmar's financial structure is comprised of the Central Bank of Myanmar, four state-owned banks, a state-owned finance company, a state-owned insurance institution, and private domestic banks.

Reforms of the Financial Sector

With a view to generate increased revenue, various changes have been made: including the promulgation of the Commercial Tax Law in 1990 to broaden the tax base and a new Tariff Law enacted in 1992 to replace the Tariff Act of 1953; at the same time the Harmonized System of import classification was introduced. As a result of these developments, tax revenue had increased from K 4,373 million in 1987–1988 to K 10,480 million and K 10,321 million in 1991–1992 and 1992–1993 respectively.

On the fiscal front, as a result of various revenue measures that included the expansion of the tax base and tougher enforcement of tax collection, the overall budget deficit as a percent of GDP declined to 6 percent in 1992–1993 from 8 percent in 1990–1991.

On the banking side, the Central Bank of Myanmar Law, the Financial Institution of Myanmar Law, and the Myanmar Agricultural and Rural Development Bank Law were enacted in July 1990 with a view to developing the financial system and improving efficiency of financial activities in harmony with the new economic policy. This was followed by prescription of their rules and regulations.

In accordance with the new banking laws, the Central Bank had already granted operating licenses to eight private domestic banks to provide banking services. The Small Loans Department was separated from the Myanmar Economic Bank in 1992 and set up as a finance company, namely, the Myanmar Small Loans Enterprise.

Interest rates on savings deposits and savings certificates were raised from 8 percent to 10 percent and from 10.9 percent to 12 percent respectively in July 1992. Due to these measures savings increased substantially in 1991–1992 and in 1992–1993.

Expansion of Credit Facility

As the banks have been encouraged to expand their credit facilities to the private sector in support of its increased economic activities there has been a significant increase in bank credits to the private and cooperative sectors.

Despite strong credit requirements of the private sector, the growth of money supply slowed down to 34.4 percent and about 31 percent in 1991–1992 and 1992–1993 respectively, due to improvement in the fiscal situation and a substantial increase in savings.

Regarding insurance, the Myanmar Insurance Law was enacted in July 1993 and new types of insurance such as oil and gas insurance, education insurance, and health insurance have been introduced. Due to these measures its income increased substantially.

Foreign Exchange Liberalization

Regarding foreign exchange a series of exchange liberalization measures have been taken gradually during the transition to the market-oriented economy. For the convenience of foreigners visiting Myanmar, Foreign Exchange Certificates (FECs) have been issued. Myanmar nationals and foreigners who own legitimate foreign exchange earnings are allowed to exchange with FECs.

TABLE 1
Myanmar: Selected Interest Rates, 1987–1992
(in percent per annum)

End of Period	1987	1989	1992
Central Bank Rate	4.00	11.00	11.00
Treasury Bills and Bonds			
Three-month Treasury Bills	1.00	4.00	4.00
Three-year Treasury Bonds	2.50	10.00	10.00
Five-year Treasury Bonds	3.00	10.50	10.50
Deposit Rates			
Call Deposits	0.25	3.00	3.00
Fixed Deposits			
Three Months	1.00	8.50	8.50
Six Months	1.50	9.00	9.00
Nine Months	2.00	9.50	9.50
Savings Bank Accounts			
Basic Rate	8.00	8.00	10.00
Premium on Three-year			
Minimum Balance	2.00	2.00	
Savings Certificates			
Twelve-year Maturity	10.90	10.90	12.00
Lending Rates			
Working Capital Loans 1)	8.00	15.00	16.50
Medium Term Loans			
(up to 5 years)	9.00	12.00	15.00
Long Term Loans			
(5–10 years)	9.00	12.00	14.50
Agricultural Loans			
To Village Banks 2)	8.00	13.00	13.00
To Farmers 3)	12.00	18.00	18.00

Source: Central Bank of Myanmar.

Notes: 1) Overdrafts are charged 0.5 percent above loan rates.
2) Lending rate of the Myanmar Agricultural and Rural Development Bank.
3) Relending rate of village banks.

Foreign currency account holders can use their foreign exchange to buy imported goods and to make payments for import of goods and other services. Due to these measures the number and amount of foreign currency deposits have risen in recent years.

Balance of Payments

With respect to the development in balance of payments, export volume grew by nearly 20 percent in recent years due to measures promoting foreign trade. Large increases have been recorded in receipts from services and private transfers. Therefore, the external current account deficit narrowed to

TABLE 2

Myanmar: Bank Deposits and Loans
1987/88–1992/93 (End of March)
(in millions of kyat)

	1987/ 88	1988/ 89	1989/ 90	1990/ 91	1991/ 92	1992/93 (Prov.)
Deposits						
Demand deposits	1502	1207	2082	3778	5723	5831
Savings	8411	7557	9718	12084	14481	17450
Loans						
Cooperative	1273	1554	2068	4432	5886	7703
Private commercial	78	76	164	2689	4253	9584
Agriculture	668	505	438	455	759	1385

Source: Central Bank of Myanmar.

US$187 million in 1992–1993 from deficits of US$305 million in 1991–1992 and US$457 million in 1990–1991.

Future Prospects

The objective for the 1993–1994 budget is to reduce the public sector budget deficit to about 4 percent of GDP, with further declines anticipated in future years. Revenue would be increased by improved tax administration and by broadening the tax base without increasing tax rates. Defining priorities, unproductive expenditures will be reduced and control of expenditures strengthened.

Moreover, significant progress would be achieved due to new banking laws in banking competition and expanding the financial system through operation of private banks. Issuance of treasury bonds is being processed and the preparation for the establishment of stock market has been continued. In October 1993, the Rural Savings Scheme was introduced to enable farmers to save their earnings as well as to use them for lending as an initial step in the direction of developing rural banking.

Continued efforts are also being made for export promotion and diversification and attracting foreign investment on a large scale, particularly in the energy sector. The foreign capital inflow of US$909 million for 75 enterprises had been successfully induced up to August 1993 and additional foreign exchange earnings are expected to be generated from services, particularly by a strong growth in the tourist industry.

Progress in fiscal and monetary areas is expected to help achieve the targeted real growth rate of 5.8 percent in 1993–1994 and to ease pressure on prices and balance of payments.

AGRICULTURE SECTOR

The Union of Myanmar is basically an agricultural country with about 76 percent of its population residing in rural areas. The agriculture sector, being the life and blood of the country, provides about 65 percent of the total working population and contributes about 40 percent of GDP and 35 percent of Myanmar's external trade.

Objectives and Strategies for Agricultural Development

As a crucial sector of the economy, the agriculture sector has laid down three basic objectives, namely,

- to promote increased cereal production with emphasis on paddy;
- to promote increased production of industrial crops; and
- to generate increased agricultural exports.

Under the market environment since late 1988, reforms were introduced in the agricultural sector, including: freedom of choice for farmers to cultivate, produce, process, and market their crops; introduction of scientific agricultural techniques, which received a positive response; encouragement to reinvest in agriculture, which also received positive response; encouragement to develop new land for agricultural expansion; and increasing engagement in double and multiple cropping.

To further enhance agricultural development the following five principles have been officially adopted:

- the development of new agricultural land;
- the provision of adequate irrigation water;
- the provision and support for increased agriculture mechanization;
- the acceleration of technology transfer; and
- the development and utilization of high yielding quality seeds.

The Development of New Agricultural Land

The present net sown area of the country amounts to 21 million acres, but a further 24 million acres in the form of fallow, culturable, and waste land still exists. Accordingly, the government has been making an all-out effort to develop this new agricultural land and a total of 2.5 million acres have been reclaimed from 1988–1989 through 1992–1993.

Provision of Adequate Irrigation Water

Out of a net sown area of 21 million acres, irrigated land area includes only 12.4 percent and in order for year-round cropping programs to be suc-

TABLE 3
Production of Agricultural Crops

Crop Grouping	1988-89 Area (acres)	Production (MT)	1992-93 Area (acres)	Production (MT)
1. Cereals	13210	13598	14100	15414
Paddy	11800	13162	12603	14913
Others	1403	436	1497	501
2. Oil Crops	5034	720	5310	856
3. Peas & Beans	1802	409	3172	904
4. Industrial Crops	999	2469	1072	3524
5. Culinary Crops	697	418	789	427
6. Plantation Crops	1004	173	1070	198
7. Others	1053	63	1165	63
Total	23802	17850	26678	21386

Source: Ministry of Agriculture.

cessful, irrigation facilities need to be expanded considerably. To fulfill this need the government made intensive efforts to speed up completion of large-scale irrigation works under process and construction of small-scale irrigation dams with local community participation. As such from 1990–1991 through 1992–1993 a total of about half a million acres was added to irrigable land, while about 1.1 million acres of land is expected to be put under irrigation in the near future by construction of dams and land reclamation.

Increased Agriculture Mechanization

As agricultural expansion and multiple cropping continue, farm mechanization becomes indispensable. However, only 1 million acres is at present mechanized and efforts are being made to import tractors and other agricultural machinery. Steps are now being taken to provide incentives to the private sector for participation in farm mechanization. Moreover, the government has encouraged and provided assistance to the state-owned Mechanization Department, industrial cooperatives, and small-scale private work shops for the production of farm machinery and implements.

Transfer of Technology

The extension services of the Central Agricultural Research Institute are mainly responsible for transfer of technology to the farmers by way of introduction of appropriate crop pattern, crop varieties, and cultivation techniques.

Development and Utilization of High Yield Quality Seeds

The quest for high yielding and quality seeds to achieve higher agricultural production has been consistently undertaken. Measures are being taken to develop new varieties to suit different ecological zones and cropping patterns with emphasis on requirements by the export markets.

Prospects

Due to encouragements given by the government to the farmers and the private sector, agricultural production had increased by 19.8 percent (with annual increases of about 5 percent) during the period from 1988–1989 to 1992–1993.

Similarly net sown area increased by 7 percent and multiple cropping area by 38.5 percent, while the volume of agricultural exports increased about 15 times during the same period. As all-out efforts have been made to increase agricultural production, fertilizer utilization is expected to increase about 300 percent in 1993–1994 as compared to 1992–1993. With active participation of both the cooperative and the private sectors, the pace of agricultural production would be further enhanced.

FORESTRY SECTOR

On a regional and global basis, Myanmar still enjoys a substantially high forest and woodland cover of about 74 percent of land area. According to the FAO estimates of 1992 Myanmar closed forest cover is stable at 32.2 to 32.4 million hectares in contrast to dwindling forest resources in most of the other countries in the region.

Although the forestry sector contributes only about 2 percent of GDP, it is the second largest earner of foreign exchange. Teak production and export is prominent among forest products but that of hardwood is also becoming important. Teak production and export is the monopoly of the government for the sole reason of conservation of this product. Due to a change in the economic system in 1988, the private sector is permitted to produce, market, and export hardwood and hardwood products.

Production and Export of Teak and Hardwood

Teak production reached its peak in 1990–1991 and since then has been declining basically because of the policy to conserve for environmental consideration. On the other hand, hardwood production has expanded considerably as the private sector has been allowed to export this product. While teak production increased by only 13.4 percent in 1992–1993 (to 330,000 tons) as compared to 1988–1989, hardwood production has increased by 78.6 percent (to 1,061,000 tons) during the same period.

Similarly, export of teak increased from about 148,000 tons in 1988–1989 to about 172,000 tons in 1992–1993 (16.2 percent increase) while export of hardwood increased from about 72,000 tons to 309,000 tons during the same period (429.1 percent increase).

Counter-Trade in Timber Products

With the objective of enhancing the production of value-added products the government now employs a buy-back system in which the foreign partners supply the machinery and equipment relating to the timber industry and buy back the finished products in return.

Privatization

Since the adoption of a market-oriented economic system in 1988, the government has returned 12 hardwood sawmills to their former owners, whose mills were nationalized in the late 1960s by the former government. This is part of the privatization process pursued by the government.

Foreign Investment

In order to improve its wood-based industry, the government has entered into joint ventures with two foreign companies in timber harvesting, manufacturing, and marketing of plywood. At present more than 33 foreign firms from various countries have submitted their investment proposals, which are now under evaluation by the government.

Forest Conservation

In order to protect endangered wildlife, threatened ecosystems, and biodiversity considerations, the government has instituted the Protected Area System (PAS), which includes natural parks, wildlife sanctuaries, and climatic reserves. The present PAS is about 1 percent of total land area and it is projected to increase to 5 percent of the land area of the country. Myanmar hosts a large variety of wildlife species, including as many as 300 mammals, 360 reptiles, and over 1,000 bird species. For forest conservation Myanmar has received assistance from UNDP and FAO. Moreover, the government has also given emphasis to planting the depleted and degraded natural forest. From 1988–1989 through 1991–1992 a total of 110,170 hectares were planted with teak, hardwood, and other species; and since 1960 a total of 425,219 hectares have been planted to date.

Future Prospects

To develop a sound management of forest resources, the government, inter-alia, envisages increasing the Protected Area System, preventing forest offenses under the new forest law, encouraging forest plantation with citizen participation, raising fuelwood plantation in abundance to address the energy crisis, promoting export of value-added timber products by terminating log exports completely in the not distant future, and according top priority to conservation of environment and biological diversity.

LIVESTOCK, BREEDING, AND FISHERIES SECTOR

Myanmar has a long coastline of 2,832 kilometers with a continental shelf area of 228,781 square kilometers, which is rich in both marine and fresh water fisheries resources. In marine fisheries the maximum sustainable yield is estimated at 1.05 million metric tons out of which only 0.6 million metric tons was exploited as of last year. On the other hand, fresh water fisheries are exploited mainly from 8.2 million hectares of natural lakes, reservoirs, river systems, and ponds, in addition to 25,920 hectares (64,051 acres) of fish culture ponds.

Regarding livestock sector development, the present national livestock production is not sufficient to meet domestic demand but encouragement is being made to increase it.

Performance of Fisheries and Livestock

On a national basis, the total fish production amounted to 733,800 tons in 1992–1993 compared to that of 709,900 tons in 1987–1988, an increase of only 3.4 percent over the period of five years. This calls for efforts to achieve a satisfactory level of production. Similarly, the production of meat, eggs, and milk are not sufficient to meet domestic demand. In order to carry out an integrated farming system Myanmar has formed a joint venture company with a Thai company.

Prospects

National fish production is projected to increase by 6.3 percent in 1995–1996 as compared to 1991–1992, while meat production is projected to increase by 24.7 percent, milk production by 9.1 percent, and egg production by 31.6 percent during the same period.

INDUSTRIAL SECTOR

Myanmar industry consists of many factories that produce the general consumer goods for the country. They include: textile mills; sugar mills; cement factories; steel mills; car tire factories; factories producing trucks and passenger cars; factories producing agricultural machinery and equipment (such as tractors, pumps, and reapers, etc.); factories producing radios, television sets, air conditioners, refrigerators, and some electronic components; bicycle plants; the pharmaceutical industry; battery factories; garment factories; cigarette factories; glass factories; canning factories; and so forth.

Presently, the seven categories of industries that altogether manage 122 factories are given greater autonomy to make changes so as not to sustain any financial loss since the financial year 1989–1990 in accordance with the market-oriented economy. After raising the purchase price of industrial crops, the procurement of industrial crops has considerably improved, leading to greater utilization of the factories concerned.

Another method used to raise the capacity for utilization of the factories is to produce the finished goods on contract for both the local and foreign private businessmen with the raw materials and accessories supplied by them. Various methods adopted by the factories for receiving the processing charges under the contract manufacturing or consignment system are: (1) production sharing of finished products instead of receiving the processing charge in cash; (2) receipt of a combination of a certain proportion of finished products and cash; (3) receipt of a certain proportion of raw materials and cash; and (4) receipt of a certain proportion of raw materials only.

In addition to the consignment system, the other two ways are the formation of joint venture enterprises and buy-back arrangement with foreign entrepreneurs.

Current Arrangements to Promote Production

With a view to raising production, the following measures have been undertaken:

1. Joint venture companies have been formed with foreign firms for the production and export of garments, knitted garments, export-quality cigarettes, wooden products, and Aluzine roofing sheets and steel rods.
2. Arrangements have been made to lease a plot of land to a foreign company to set up wholly owned factories by paying rent in foreign currency.
3. Some factories are leased to local entrepreneurs.
4. Two garment factories have been established with a buy-back arrangement with foreign suppliers of machinery and equipment.

Due to the above measures, annual production value has risen during the last four years. The growth rate of industrial production was 16 percent in

1992–1993 compared to the previous year and was four percent more than the planned target.

In order to raise the productivity of labor, the industries have managed to trim down the size of manpower from 1988–1989 to 1992–1993 but annual production has increased by nearly K 4,500 million within the same period. The financial positions of the industries have also improved by achieving higher profits during 1989–1990 to 1992–1993.

Prospects

Structural changes have been made by transferring some factories to other ministries and by amalgamating some industrial plants. Plans have also been made to form more mutually beneficial joint ventures with foreign firms and widen the scope for other forms of economic collaboration, especially contract manufacturing and buy-back arrangements. Plans are also being made to lease more factories and to enlarge mutual cooperation for contract manufacturing of more items of consumer goods with local entrepreneurs.

MINING SECTOR

The government is inviting foreign investors to enter into joint ventures with mining enterprises to produce metallic minerals, industrial minerals, precious stones, pearls, salt, and marine chemical products. The main activities of the mining sector include the following:

1. Encouragement, giving assistance and services for the successful implementation of the annual production of state enterprises.
2. Cooperation and coordination for the successful implementation of Kyaukpahtoe Gold Project.
3. Signing of joint venture agreements with foreign investors.
4. Participating in Border Trade activities.
5. Formation of Joint Venture Gems and Jade mining units between Myanmar nationals and Myanmar Gems Enterprise.
6. Exploration and exploitation of new precious stones deposit and also declaration of a new stone-tract area in the northern part of Shan State.
7. Authorization of supervision and control by the government upon prospecting, exploration, and mining of minerals, industrial minerals, and various stones.

Future Prospects

To achieve maximum yield the mining enterprises have made projections as follows:

No. 1 Mining Enterprise: To boost production of copper concentrate, zinc, and silver by applying advance technology in Namtu Bawdwin Mine, explore the deposit, and produce zinc metal at Laungkeng Project.

No. 2 Mining Enterprise: To develop the one deposit in Payoungtoung Gold Mine Project, to undertake systematic exploration of diamonds in Diamond Mining Project (Theindaw), to extract tin as well as Tantalum/Niobium, and to explore gold deposits.

No. 3 Mining Enterprise: To produce finished granite, marble blocks, and slabs, to expand No. 1 Iron and Steel Plant, and to develop nickel deposits.

Myanmar Pearls Enterprise: To establish new pearl culturing farms in Tanintharyi Archipelago and breed mother-of-pearl oysters.

Myanmar Salt and Marine Chemical Enterprise: To establish an automatic salt grinding and refining plant and to produce iodine from local resources such as sea weeds from coastal regime.

Department of Geological Survey and Mineral Exploration: To enhance the gold Exploration Project, Platinum Group Exploration Project, and Uranium and Diamond Project.

TRADE SECTOR

The government believes that the economic development of a country can be achieved by foreign capital investment and technology together with joint efforts of the public and private sectors. As such, sufficient legal protection and incentives have been given to foreign investors by the foreign investment law of 1988. As the government has given full encouragement to develop the private sector, the number of private enterprises, including foreign companies, registered totaled 10,489 at the end of August 1993.

External Trade

Like most developing countries, Myanmar is mainly an exporter of agricultural and other primary products while its imports consist largely of manufactured goods and raw materials. Its main export products include rice, teak and hardwood, beans and pulses, metals and minerals, including precious stones, and marine products. On the other hand, its major imports are capital goods, industrial raw materials, spare parts consumer goods, and chemicals. Foreign trade is conducted mainly with Asian countries, including China, Singapore, Japan, Thailand, India, and Malaysia. As an exporter of primary products and importer of manufactured goods, Myanmar naturally used to face unfavorable terms of trade.

Following the adoption of a market-oriented economy in late 1988, the government had permitted the private sector to engage in external trade for the first time since 1964. From 1989–1990 to 1991–1992 the share of the private sector in overall exports increased dramatically, from 36.5 percent in

1989–1990 to 50.7 percent in 1992–1993 while the share of the state in total exports declined from 63.3 percent to 47.3 percent during the same period.

Trade Agreement

Myanmar has maintained bilateral trade agreements with the Republic of Korea, People's Republic of China, Thailand, Bangladesh, India, Pakistan, and seven countries of Eastern Europe. These arrangements are of general character with the aim of further development and strengthening in every possible way the trade relations between the two countries on the principle of equality of rights and mutual benefits.

Trade System and Practices

Within the framework of market mechanism several types of trading systems have been adopted in addition to normal trade practices. These include a counter-trade system, trade on a consignment basis, import first and export later basis, border trade, and transit trade.

Trade Promotion

In order to achieve the exposure of overseas markets and to gain access to international outlets for Myanmar's exportable products, market study missions visited various parts of the world, particularly Asian countries and Europe. As a result, the private sector's participation has substantially increased in both domestic and external trade.

Training of Private Sector Personnel

In order to tide over problems encountered in the transition to a market economy and to gain proficiency in trading functions the government has initiated and organized workshops, seminars, and training courses since 1989–1990, and to date over a thousand private entrepreneurs have been trained and participated in various programs. Some of the workshops and seminars were conducted with the assistance of UNDP and UNCTAD.

Prospects

Ever-increasing methods of performing business granted by the authorities and its supportive role have created a conducive environment for private entrepreneurs in taking active part in the national development process. As the value of exports and imports are expected to increase further, the role of the private sector in external trade will also become enhanced.

Cooperative Sector

The 1970 Cooperative Law was repealed in 1992 and a new Cooperative Law was enacted eliminating socialistic aspirations of the old law that were not consistent with the market economy. According to the new law a minimum of only five members is necessary to form a cooperative society (enterprise) on an occupational basis with priority given to the formation of new farming and marketing cooperatives for oil, seed crops, beans and pulses, rubber, and marine products. This law enables the cooperative societies not only to perform more effectively and freely but also to compete efficiently with state and private enterprises in various business undertakings.

Types of cooperatives include agricultural cooperatives, which adapt modern farming methods; livestock breeding and fisheries cooperatives, which produce meat; industrial cooperatives, which now operate a large amount of mills and factories; and trade cooperatives, which by far are the largest of all cooperatives engaged in domestic and external trade.

Prospects

In order to promote cooperative exports, Myanmar Cooperative Trade Fair and Myanmar Cooperative Industrial Fair were successfully held in 1993. As the formation of more cooperatives is envisaged, particularly agricultural, livestock and breeding, and construction, more job opportunities will be created. As a cooperative bank has already been established, more financial resources can be mobilized for cooperative development, although the state banks are also providing financial assistance to the cooperatives.

TOURISM

In September 1992, the Ministry of Hotels and Tourism was established as a new ministry for the first time to set guidelines for the systematic development of the tourism industry in Myanmar. Since 1989 tourist visas have been extended from seven to 14 days and arrangements have already been made for the issuance of visas without delay. Moreover, previous limitations on tourist arrivals also have been removed and foreigners, whether on package tour groups or individuals, are welcome. At the same time, hotel accommodations have been increased considerably with the private sector's participation.

The Current Tourism Situation

Myanmar, well-known as a land of pagodas, is blessed with abundant tourist attractions, such as scenic rivers, a long coastline of unspoiled beaches and archipelagos, beautiful hilly regions, picturesque natural lakes, snow-capped mountains, and the ancient city of Bagan, which is the largest archaeological site in Asia. Traditionally, Myanmar is a cultural destination with a rich historical and cultural heritage. For ethnic interest, Myanmar has 135 national races with their own dialect, customs, and traditions.

Visitor arrivals in Myanmar are relatively low but with the recent relaxation of visa procedures and formalities they are growing steadily. A significant increase in arrivals are visitors on business trips. For the convenience of tourists and other visitors the Central Bank of Myanmar has recently issued Foreign Exchange Certificates (FECs), which are exchangeable with the U.S. dollar or the pound sterling. Payment by FECs is as good as foreign exchange and FECs are accepted by any person in Myanmar.

Although six airlines are operating scheduled flights in and out of Yangon, Myanmar also accepts non-scheduled charter flights not only to Yangon but also to other cities like Mandalay and Bagan. Besides arrival by air and sea, tourists are also now allowed and welcome across land routes from China and Thailand to border areas of Myanmar.

Hotel Industry

The hotel industry in Myanmar, although relatively small, is growing rapidly since the liberalization of tourist arrivals. The state-owned hotels, totalling 19 with 800 rooms in 1988, have increased to 43 hotels with 1,151 rooms at present. The private sector, inspired and encouraged by the government's policy, has already opened 69 hotels with 1,011 rooms. More hotels are being constructed by both the government and the private sector and so far seven hotel projects to be constructed with foreign investors have been approved.

Prospects

Although the tourism industry in some countries has already reached saturation level, countries like Myanmar, Vietnam, Cambodia, and Laos are newly emerging countries with enormous potentials for tourism development.

ENERGY SECTOR

In spite of an abundance of both renewable and nonrenewable types of energy resources in Myanmar, the actual energy consumption per capita is still low compared to other developing countries. Accordingly, the government's strategy is to develop all available energy resources in the country to increase the level of energy production and to update the energy demand surveys continuously.

Petroleum and Natural Gas

At present Myanmar produces about 15,000 BOPD of crude oil and about 120 MMCFD of natural gas. During 1989–1990 Myanmar signed a production sharing contract with foreign oil companies for exploration of both onshore and offshore areas. In 1992 similar contracts were signed with four more foreign oil companies. In 1992–1993, Total oil company discovered natural gas from two of its four appraisal (offshore) wells with an average production rate of 25 MMCFD of natural gas from each well. Similarly, Texaco oil company discovered natural gas from two of its four test (offshore) wells with a total production of 110 MMCFD of natural gas and 2,600 barrels of condensate per day. Plans are now under way to export the discovered natural gas to Thailand.

On the other hand, Myanmar's state-owned oil enterprise has also discovered new oil pools and natural gas in the shell relinquished exploration area, both onshore and offshore. Due to the shortage of domestic crude oil production, Myanmar imports crude oil quarterly and refines at one of its three refineries, which are now utilizing only 30 percent of their capacities.

Electric Power

The total installed capacities of electric power generation of Myanmar increased from 982 MW in 1988–1989 to 1,151 MW in 1992–1993. During the five-year period since 1988, 12 mini hydel projects had been constructed resulting in increased installed capacities of 59 MW. At present 315 towns and 927 villages have been electrified throughout the country. The supply of electricity is mainly derived in the form of hydro and gas turbine power.

Projects

In oil and gas, 18 blocks in Myanmar offshore and onshore areas are now available for exploration and production. In the power area, the government is seeking financing to implement the Thanlwin River Hydro Project (3,000 to 10,000 MW), the Bilin Hydro Project (240 MW), the Kun Hydro Project (84 MW), and the Pyu Hydro Project (65 MW), amongst others. Moreover, Myanmar is also planning to construct 100 MW gas turbine stations in the vicinity of Yangon. If these projects come in onstream, Myanmar will not only be self sufficient in energy utilizations but will be in a surplus position for possible exports.

CONCLUSION

During the transition period since 1988 Myanmar's economy has been managed by formulating and implementing annual plans starting from 1989–

1990 based on policy changes and reform measures undertaken with the main objectives of achieving economic recovery with stability in the short run and to lay down firm foundations for sustained growth in the long run. Accordingly, the short-term economic plan from 1992–1993 to 1995–1996 was drawn and implemented. The first year of the short-term economic plan had been designated as the Year of the Economy and was successfully implemented gaining a favorable economic foundation. The 1993–1994 annual plan was coordinated at the regional level and then with the respective organizations of the ministries at the central level, based on the implementation of the 1992–1993 annual plan, external and internal financial resources, and also on market signals. It is expected that the economic performance for the remainder of the plan period will be further enhanced.

5 THE ECONOMIC DEVELOPMENT OF VIETNAM, LAOS, AND CAMBODIA

Frederick Z. Brown

After half a century of war, civil strife, and foreign intervention, the three states of Indochina are at peace and currently engaged in the most radical economic transformation of any of the nations in Southeast Asia. Although their individual situations vary greatly, the systemic reforms of all three emphasize decentralization and privatization, and permit market forces to determine economic activity. These countries remain, however, at least two decades behind most of their counterparts in the rest of Southeast Asia with respect to the standards of living of their populations and the overall development of their economies. With the end of the cold war, they have had to recast the direction of their external political relationships and have been obliged to contemplate—with some trepidation—internal political reforms occasioned by influences accompanying a new economic orientation. In Vietnam and Laos, the communist party is still in command of the society's fundamental decisions; it is determined to retain political control. In Cambodia, pluralism and a form of democracy are mandated by the United Nations and by the new Cambodian constitution.

Beyond a history of war since 1945, and now economic reform, Vietnam, Laos, and Cambodia have little in common except their geographic proximity. The Mekong River, which runs along the southern border of Laos and winds through the heart of Cambodia and Vietnam, could become a common developmental factor, but this eventuality is decades in the future. Over the near term, their inclusion in the Association of Southeast Asian Nations (ASEAN) will be important once their economies become compatible with those of ASEAN's member states. Vietnam, and to a lesser extent Laos and Cambodia, will be the locus for ASEAN investments, particularly manufacturing for export to third countries; Vietnam is already an expanding target for products from the ASEANs, Japan, and China, not to mention high-tech communications and infrastructure equipment from the West.

Of the three countries, the Socialist Republic of Vietnam, with a population of 70 million, is by all odds the most important to the market economies of Asia and the West. Although Laos is attempting to diversify its commerce, with a population of only 4 million it seems destined indefinitely to point its primitive economy toward Thailand. Cambodia, with a population of 9 million, was devastated by the Khmer Rouge regime and the subsequent civil war and insurgency. Cambodia is just beginning the process of reconstruction, literally from the ground up. It has benefitted from massive support of the United Nations, 1991 through 1993, and hopes to have that support continued several years more.

VIETNAM

After North Vietnam's victory in 1975, Hanoi attempted to impose on the conquered South a highly centralized command economic regime along Soviet lines.[1] The socialist system that had engineered victory in war failed miserably to improve the lives of the Vietnamese people. The country continued in economic decline through and beyond the 1970s. With the invasion of Cambodia in 1978 and its 10-year military occupation, Vietnam became a political and economic leper, forbidden extensive contact with its Southeast Asian capitalist neighbors, Japan, and the West. In retaliation for unseating the Khmer Rouge government, China invaded and laid waste the northern provinces of Vietnam in early 1979. The U.S. economic embargo, honored until the late 1980s by the international community as penalty for the Cambodia adventure, added to Vietnam's woes.

Vietnam was then, and remains today, one of the world's poorest countries, with an annual per capita income of under $200. Recognizing the broad political and economic ramifications of its isolation, Vietnam began to seek a negotiated exit from Cambodia. After an internal debate lasting several years, the Sixth Congress of the Vietnamese Communist party, in 1986, approved wide-reaching domestic reforms (*doi moi*, Vietnamese for "renovation"). The aim was to move the country away from a Marxist command economy and closer to the world's free market economies. In 1989, *doi moi* was strengthened by further party edicts and government action.

Today, Vietnam is in the midst of economic revolution. The Vietnamese government has sanctioned a broad degree of private entrepreneurship in small- and medium-size enterprises, and embraced the principles of decentralization and privatization of state enterprises. Collectivism in agriculture has been all but abandoned. The communist party has agreed to reduce its suffocating presence in the day-to-day administration of the economy, and this is reflected in the new 1992 constitution. Vietnam passed a foreign investment law in 1987, refined and made more attractive in 1992. This law is judged by Western experts to be the most liberal of any communist country attempting the conversion from Marxism to a free market. Having inherited International Monetary Fund membership from the previous Saigon regime, Hanoi began to carry out structural reforms prescribed by the IMF in order to qualify for loans once the United States removed its objections.

In 1989 the Soviet Union began to curtail deliveries of fuel, fertilizer, steel, chemicals, and cotton. The shortages forced Vietnam to convert to the free market far faster than planned. Vietnamese export industries had to find alternative markets for their clothing, footwear, and handicrafts. Tens of thousands of guest workers in the Soviet Union and Eastern Europe were forced to return to Vietnam, thereby removing an important source of expatriate income and adding a source of domestic unrest. The drop in foreign aid and a weak tax collection system caused a budget deficit and spurred inflation. Prices rose 64 percent in 1990 and another 67 percent in 1991. Vietnam was also left with a large ruble debt to the republics of the former Soviet Union.[2] In retrospect, however, the sea change in the Soviet-Vietnam economic relationship, including an end to assistance from Moscow, may have been an immense blessing.[3]

With the collapse of the Soviet Union and the communist regimes of Eastern Europe, the economic aid programs that had sustained Vietnam since 1975 vanished. Although the evident bankruptcy of socialist economics around the world seems to have settled earlier arguments between Vietnamese conservatives and reformers over the country's economic path, the pace and depth (and political implications) of reforms remain open to debate. Vietnam's economic reforms are far from perfect and certainly not complete. But the accomplishments since abandoning the Soviet model have been remarkable, and the growing influx of foreign business interests indicate that potential investors do not view the economic progress to date as ephemeral. In the opinion of the IMF and the World Bank, Vietnam's reforms have been among the most successful of countries attempting similar conversions from socialism to the free market. Subsidies to government workers, communist party cadres, and inefficient state enterprises have been reduced or eliminated. The private sector now accounts for a large percentage of the nation's goods and services. The government has attempted to introduce bonds and other capitalist financial instruments; a banking system compatible with the outside world is slowly being put in place. The economy is for the most part decentralized. Prices for commodities are determined by market forces, with the exception of gasoline, electricity, and transportation. To achieve a realistic exchange rate and combat the black market, the Vietnamese *dong* was severely devalued in 1988 and then floated at a free market rate. From an artificial rate of 3,000 to the dollar, the *dong* sank to 7,000 by January 1991 and to 14,400 by December. This was an extremely dark period for Vietnam. But by November 1993 the *dong* had stabilized at 10,800 to the dollar and was fluctuating in a narrow range on the open market. It is expected that the inflation rate for 1993 will be no more than 10 percent.[4]

According to the 1992 constitution, the Vietnamese state remains *in principle* the sole owner of land. Yet, paradoxically, under a law passed by the National Assembly in 1993, individuals may use the land, transfer and divide it, and inherit those rights. Individual rights to a plot of agricultural land extend for a 50-year period, with 70 years for rubber plantations and certain other producers. Although it seems unlikely that a future government could reimpose collectivization or reverse the privatization trend in land usage without extraordinary political consequences, the question of ultimate ownership of land remains a controversial issue, which is more than theoretical.

Development Potentials and Constraints

Vietnam possesses a large labor force with craft skills, traditions of hard work and discipline, which makes it readily adaptable to economic development tasks. It enjoys a varied natural resource base that can support some expansion in agriculture, forestry, fishing, and mining industries. Its mineral deposits include coal, iron ore, bauxite, copper, chrome, and gold; their full potential has yet to be surveyed and exploited. Oil and natural gas represent an extraordinary economic boon to Vietnam, especially in the context of Southeast Asia where oil and natural gas production has been leveling off and will likely decline in the next decade, yet where consumption steadily increases. Water resources are plentiful in some areas (the Mekong and Red River deltas) but must be managed carefully to obtain further increases in agricultural development and hydroelectric power generation. The government and ruling party appear to be committed to a pragmatic policy of administrative and economic reform. Finally, Vietnam has a prime location from which to do business and trade with the world's fastest growing economic regions.[5]

One obvious constraint is the sheer scale of Vietnam's development needs in physical infrastructure. In the North, even the two main highway arteries (Haiphong-Hanoi and national route 1 extending from the Chinese border through Hanoi, then south to Ho Chi Minh City) are in poor condition. Railways are of pre-World War II vintage, were all but destroyed by bombing, and now operate in slow motion. In the South, the transportation infrastructure is in somewhat better condition but must be radically upgraded to keep pace with demands of Vietnam's industrial growth, now beginning to take off. Sea ports countrywide, including the key centers of Haiphong and Ho Chi Minh City, must also be drastically improved. The economic development zone of Quang Ninh, near Ha Long Bay, will also have to be brought to fruition.

Reform institutions are embryonic and still unproven. The implementation of regulations and administrative procedures is often absent or poorly defined. Legal codes in many areas are still being drafted. Banking officials face the task of harnessing the flow of money through overseas Chinese from Hong Kong, Taipei, and elsewhere into Vietnam via the traditional Saigon-Cholon connection. Large quantities of money are being injected into the economy from overseas Vietnamese seeking business opportunities in cooperation with relatives still in Vietnam. How to capitalize on this inflow is a major problem that remains unsolved.

Vietnam is in desperate need of training for the government and private sector personnel who will be responsible for managing economic development. Particularly in the North, there is far from adequate understanding of the mechanics of market economics or of modern technology and international practices. Corruption flourishes countrywide at all levels despite the party's rantings, endless public campaigns, and official media exposures. Smuggling from Cambodia and Mekong Delta entrepots is endemic; in the North, the illegal flood of Chinese goods threatens to destroy that region's fledgling small industries.[6] Not a few communist party cadres and government officials are profiting from the conversion from Marxism to private enterprise. The Ministry of National Defense has gone into business for itself in a variety of enterprises such as garment manufacturing, TV assembly, exports of coal, rubber, and coffee, and most prominently the hotel industry. It has formed partnerships with foreign firms from Japan, France, Hong Kong, and South Korea. One Army hospital has even signed a memorandum of understanding with a California group to build a modern hospital once the U.S. trade embargo is lifted.[7]

As in Russia and the former communist nations of Eastern Europe, privatization of Vietnamese state enterprises is mired in complications. Initially, the government sought to privatize the least efficient state enterprises. Few survived and most had to be abandoned or returned to the state. Unofficially, enterprises are now categorized as "losers" (about 40 percent), which will be liquidated eventually; "needing some help but viable" (about 30 percent); and "most efficient and able to operate under market conditions" (about 20 percent). The last category will apparently be given priority, with the state rescuing or disposing of the rest. The government hopes to sell shares to the public in successful enterprises. But the Vietnamese private sector has little investment capital and extremely limited managerial experience. As a result, most privatization has taken place in the smaller enterprises or, in the case of larger firms, in joint ventures with foreign investors.

Good results have occurred in the agricultural sector. Most state farms have been dismantled, thereby permitting farmers to farm their own land and to market the yields, with consequent increase in productivity. Vietnam exported more than one million tons of rice in 1992, and it has become the world's third largest rice exporter after Thailand and the United States. Even here there is a downside. With the marketplace determining prices and production rising faster than demand, rice farmers are no longer receiving the money income they had come to expect. Thus, the government may face the familiar dilemma of Western capitalist societies: price supports for the agricultural sector or discontent and business failures in the part of Vietnam where 75 percent of Vietnamese still live, in the villages.

If not reversed early on, environmental degradation will lead to further impoverishment of many rural areas and the relatively undeveloped Central Highlands. In a few years, Hanoi and Ho Chi Minh City could have traffic jams rivalling Bangkok. Pollution of all sorts is already a major problem. In adopting macroeconomic reforms, the government has been forced to slash drastically the national budgets for education and health services; this will have severe consequences for Vietnam's future development. Similarly, HIV/AIDS, which is beginning to become evident, could well devastate Vietnam just as it has Thailand.

The United States Embargo[8]

After 1975 Vietnam was subject to a comprehensive schedule of U.S. sanctions, including a prohibition on commercial and financial transactions and private investment in Vietnam.[9] Vietnamese assets in the United States, about $250 million with accrued interest, were frozen. The single most damaging aspect of U.S. policy was the prevention of loans to Vietnam from the World Bank, the International Monetary Fund, the Asian Development Bank, and other international financial institutions (IFI). Although Vietnam has been able since 1989 to develop lively trade relations with the outside world because of the blockage of IFI loans, major foreign investment has lagged and the country's infrastructure development has been stymied.

During 1992 the United States relaxed the trade embargo in several important ways. In April 1992, it agreed to the restoration of direct telecommunications links between the United States and Vietnam. In November the requirement that revenues accruing to Vietnam be held in escrow in the U.S. Treasury was removed. AT&T had for years lobbied for such a move, pointing out the revenues lost to Canadian and European telecommunications companies as members of the ever-resourceful Vietnamese-American community patched expensive calls to their families in Vietnam through indirect hookups. In December 1992, in response to Vietnam's increased cooperation on the issue of American servicemen missing in action or possibly held prisoner in Southeast Asia (the neuralgic POW/MIA issue), the Bush administration permitted U.S. firms to sign contracts with Vietnamese entities that could be executed once the embargo was lifted. A liberal licensing policy allowing commercial transactions relating to contracts, including opening of offices, hiring staff, writing and designing plans, and carrying out preliminary feasibility studies and technical surveys, was also put into effect.

A growing number of foreign companies, including the larger multinationals, are actively exploring business ventures with Vietnamese entrepreneurs or laying the groundwork for future deals. To mention but a few, Airbus, Canadian, Australian, and European telecommunications firms, and construction conglomerates from Japan, Taiwan, Hong Kong, and South Korea have already secured major deals. U.S. companies remain shut out and must be content with positioning themselves for future deals. What is left of the embargo acts mainly against U.S. businessmen rather than against Vietnam.

Vietnam has rich natural resources and a talented people who, had they the means, are ready to do business. As reforms in dogma and practice take hold, attractive trade opportunities for foreigners have opened up, but the market is left to Japan, ASEAN, and the "young tigers" of Asia. At the same time, Vietnam needs to have the embargo completely removed in order to become firmly integrated into international trading patterns. Psychologically, American diplomatic recognition will put a definitive end to Vietnam's isolation. In terms of security the United States is far away, China is next door—clearly, Vietnam needs an American connection.

The Petroleum Sector

In terms of national development, it would be difficult to exaggerate the importance of the petroleum sector to Vietnam.[10] It is Vietnam's biggest hard currency earner and is regarded as the prime mover of development overall. The state agency PetroVietnam estimates the hydrocarbon potential of Vietnam's portion of the South China Sea continental shelf at 30 to 37 billion barrels. PetroVietnam believes its target of 20 million barrels of crude oil production in the year 2000 is within reach. This figure is viewed skeptically by many experts in the field, but there appears to be little doubt that Vietnam's potential is significant.[11]

The effort to exploit extensive maritime petroleum resources is a top priority of the government—and an attractive foreign investment opportunity, especially for U.S. companies that pioneered seismic explorations off the southeastern coast of the Republic of Vietnam before 1975. Because of the nature of oil exploration technology in which the United States excels, this is one area where U.S. involvement is badly needed. The Mobil Corporation has become the first U.S. oil company to win drilling rights offshore; it is part of a consortium with three Japanese companies to explore the Blue Dragon field 250 miles southeast of Ho Chi Minh City, where Mobil first drilled 20 years ago. Exploitation of the field would have to await the end of the U.S. embargo, of course, but exploration could take many months or even years.[12] Vietnam at present imports 100 percent of its refined oil products. Within five years, a number of foreign-financed pipeline and refining projects will come on stream. Plans are already well underway to build a natural gas pipeline and processing facility at Vung Tau; it will cost an estimated US$550 million over two phases of construction.

Directly associated with maritime oil resources is the political question of China's possibly expansionist stance regarding territorial claims in the Spratly Island area of the South China Sea.[13] Vietnam wants American involvement in the area's energy exploration and production activities as a hedge against possible Chinese "hegemony." In this, Vietnam shares a common goal of several ASEAN countries who have big stakes in the South

China Sea and feel only slightly less threatened by China's inflated Exclusive Economic Zone, which takes in virtually all of that maritime area.

External Assistance

Vietnam's major source of external assistance during the 1980s was from the former Council for Mutual Economic Assistance (CMEA), especially the former Soviet Union, which remained Vietnam's major donor until 1991. External assistance from other donors was limited by the embargo and, perhaps because many governments had doubts about Vietnam's commitment to reform, was mainly in humanitarian areas.

Until 1992, for bilateral political reasons vis-à-vis the United States (and secondarily because of Vietnam's 1978 invasion of Cambodia), Japan kept faith with the U.S. embargo by refusing to grant Official Development Assistance (ODA). In November 1992, Japan terminated this policy and granted Vietnam a loan from its Overseas Economic Cooperation Fund of US$369 million, repayable over 30 years at one percent interest rate including a 10-year grace period. About US$200 million of this sum was allocated to pay off Vietnam's outstanding debt of US$180 million from pre-1978 loans and consequently did not represent an increase in new ODA expenditures. In 1992 Japan became Vietnam's largest donor and remains so today.

The most important modification of U.S. embargo policy took place in July 1993 when the United States, facing stiff criticism (if not refusal of the IFIs to cooperate further) from Japan, France, and other major IFI donors, withdrew its automatic veto over IFI infrastructure loans to Vietnam. In September 1993, the remainder of the embargo was kept in place pending "further results in accounting for missing Americans" and with no additional steps or timing specified. But the IFIs were free to swing into action, and Vietnam will soon become one of their largest recipients of multilateral development assistance. At the November 9–10, 1993, donor conference in Paris, Vietnam received pledges from governments and development agencies of US$1.86 billion. About 60 percent of this money will be provided by individual governments, mostly in the form of soft loans, with the remainder from the IFIs. Japan led bilateral donors with US$540 million. Other governments providing substantial amounts were Australia, South Korea, France, and the Scandinavian countries. World Bank loans totaling US$228 million were announced for education projects and highway improvements, while a third loan for an additional US$121 million for agricultural development is pending.

Following is a breakdown of Japan's 1993 aid pledges:

- US$263 million: To design and build two thermal and one hydroelectric power stations;
- US$186 million: To finance road, rail and port projects;

- US$22.5 million: To restore regional water supply systems;
- US$54 million: Grant for medical equipment;
- US$27 million: For IMF/World Bank-prescribed structural transformation program.[14]

CONCLUSIONS

Vietnam has serious weaknesses and problem areas that will adversely affect the rate at which the country is able to absorb resources from bilateral aid programs and from the international financial institutions. Perhaps most important, they will also affect Vietnam's ability to host profitable private foreign investment in the industrial and service sectors as well as in the major infrastructure projects.[15] For the next five years or so, the disparity in economic development between North and South Vietnam is likely to continue, if not increase. Many foreign investors appear to be opting for the Ho Chi Minh City-Bien Hoa-Vung Tau development triangle, in part because of natural gas coming on stream from the South China Sea and in part because the South is an easier, more efficient place to do business. Although unlikely to cause a civil war, the North-South disparity will exacerbate existing tensions within Vietnamese society. It is impossible to predict at what point the economic development and commercial adeptness of the North will draw abreast of the South.

The success of "renovation" over the long haul will, of course, determine the rate of the country's economic development. Right now, Vietnam is the darling of the international financial institutions because of its adherence to World Bank/IMF guidelines and reform stipulations even before it was eligible for assistance. Obviously, there are some savvy macro-economists influencing policy in Hanoi. They should probably share credit with former communist party Secretary General Nguyen Van Linh who in 1982 from his observations in South Vietnam understood the bankruptcy of Marxism just at the moment Vietnam's economy was about to founder.[16]

Vietnam's economic reforms, impressive as they may be when compared with the former Soviet Union and other East European nations, are still in their early stages and must be continued beyond the promulgation stage into generalized practice. As for money to carry out its ambitious development plans, Vietnam hopes to obtain funding through official government and IFI assistance, plus foreign private investment, on the order of US$20 billion by the year 2000. It also hopes to maintain annual GDP growth of 8 percent and to double annual national income to US$26.8 billion (US$400 per capita) by the year 2000. None of these goals will be easy to attain.

Finally, there remains the larger, and perhaps more important, issue of the ultimate shape of Vietnamese society. "Socialism" was one of the original goals of the communist regime's founding father, Ho Chi Minh. However one defines socialism, the word is still honored in Vietnam today. The government and the party have made clear that economic renovation and a free market orientation are the *means* of perfecting socialism and *not* ends in themselves.

LAOS

Since 1954, the national development of Laos (since 1976 the Lao People's Democratic Republic) has been heavily influenced by relationships that are based upon the hard facts of geography. The special relationship with Vietnam, the presence of China in the background, and the country's land-locked dependence on Thailand are factors that continue to play the major role in Laos's development.[17]

The cold war was cruel to Laos. Never a country that seemed intrinsically valuable, it became a buffer between Vietnam and Thailand and a battle-ground for the armies of other nations during the Indochina Wars of the 1960s and 1970s. The central government in Vientiane, which did not control the vast majority of the countryside, was at times pro-United States but grew increasingly neutralist as the war wound down. A sparsely populated land, Laos's rugged mountains and dense jungles were occupied during the war by the North Vietnamese Army, communist Pathet Lao guerrillas, and various anti-communist armed groups financed by the United States and Thailand. The Ho Chi Minh Trail, the strategic supply link from North to South Viet-nam, ran down the country's spine.

Assistance from the Soviet Bloc dried up soon after 1989. Increasingly, Laos's foreign earnings have depended on the export of electricity to Thai-land and the sale of overflight rights to foreign airlines. This situation will soon change. The new Mitraphap bridge over the Mekong River between Nong Khai in Thailand and a village near Vientiane is the first modern road link between the two countries. Due to open in April 1994, the bridge will increase the pace of commercial activity radically. The bridge will open Laos up physically—and perhaps also politically and psychologically.[18]

Like Vietnam, Laos was compelled by poverty and the loss of its tradi-tional financial backers in Moscow (and Hanoi) to introduce a market-based economy. As aid, investment, and trade increase, the government has found greater latitude in pursuing policies that are sharply at variance from those set down by its former Vietnamese and Russian ideological and economic men-tors. Again like Vietnam, the reform movement originated in 1986, when the government freed the market price of rice and other food staples. Farmers planted more and, for the first time in recent history, helped Laos establish food self-sufficiency. Encouraged by this initial success, the government floated the national currency, the kip, eased interest rates, freed trade, opened up to foreign investment, and privatized many state enterprises.

The country's first constitution was only promulgated in 1991. Since then, the government has put in place a legal infrastructure, including commercial, property, and tax laws and such institutions as a central bank. More recent reforms have involved greater access to information. In 1992, international direct dialing was allowed for telephone owners and private facsimile machines permitted. So far in 1993, individuals have been allowed to erect satellite television dishes, and foreign newspapers have been distributed openly in Vientiane after years of being banned. The government now releases economic and social statistics that are considered to be increasingly reliable. In June 1993, the government began printing a gazette of government rulings, edicts and laws, whereas previously laws and official orders were never known until invoked by the authorities.[19]

Laos's economic reforms have been guided by the IMF and the UN Development Programme. The decision to free interest rates has reduced 1989's 85 percent inflation rate to around six percent in 1993. The establishment of a foreign investment code has brought in foreign money and jobs. Total exports in 1992 rose from the previous year by 37 percent to an estimated US$85 million. Of that, foreign investment in the local textile industry helped make garments the country's top export last year, earning roughly US$35 million against US$12 million in 1991 and surpassing traditional timber and electric power exports. New foreign investments continue to flow into timber plantations and wood processing, mining, and tourism. A total of 102 inward investment permits was awarded in 1992 (as opposed to 69 in 1991), and another 79 were issued in the first half of 1993.[20] The kip, previously shunned by those with access to other currencies, is now nearly as widely used as the dollar and Thai baht; the kip's exchange rate of 720 to US$1 has held steady for the past four years.

Granted its modest successes in moving away from Marxist economics, Laos is still one of the poorest countries in the world with an estimated per capita GNP of $180. With the exception of the Vientiane area and a few small urban centers along the Mekong River, its population engages mainly in subsistence level agriculture. During the war, immense amounts of ordnance were dropped throughout the country and, today, are still dangerous to the rehabilitation of agriculture.

Laos depends heavily on the IMF, the World Bank, the Asian Development Bank (ADB), and the French, Swedish, Australian, and Japanese governments for much of its capital expenditures. Japanese ODA is especially critical. It seems unlikely that Laos can escape this dependent status in the coming decade. Foreign investment remains small, even relative to the country's small population and to its primarily agrarian character. A major factor restraining faster growth and overall national development is communications. There are at present no railroads, and the country's geography is not well suited to any sort of rail network. The road system is primitive, and most provincial towns, not to mention district towns, are unreachable by truck during the rainy season. The Mekong River is not navigable during some months of the dry season. Any countrywide transportation system would require massive amounts of investment, and then further investment to establish industry and other pillars of development. In short, Laos, for the coming decades, may have to settle for a limited development horizon emphasizing the export of electricity and wood, plus tourism and small-scale cottage industries.[21]

CAMBODIA

Cambodia is recovering from a period of national devastation—economic, political, cultural, environmental—that has few historical parallels anywhere in the world. Cambodia's troubles are rooted in a French colonial background but began in earnest in the late 1960s when the country was drawn into the Vietnam War. Cambodia suffered through extensive U.S. bombings, the U.S.-South Vietnam "incursion" of 1970, and a grinding war that ended in the defeat of the Lon Nol government in 1975. The Khmer Rouge rule inflicted grievous harm and reduced Cambodian civilization to "l'annee zero." The Vietnamese invasion of 1978 and a 12-year occupation followed, together with a bitter civil war backed by external forces.[22]

During this period, the People's Republic of Kampuchea (PRK), with aid from the Soviet Bloc and international voluntary agencies, managed to generate a modicum of economic development. Following Vietnam's lead, the PRK had in 1988 begun to move away from Marxist economics to a peculiarly Cambodian form of market economics. But by the time the United Nations-sponsored peacekeeping operation began in October 1991, Cambodia was a "failed state" in every sense of the word. Today, Cambodia is having to reconstruct its society from the ashes.

With the October 1991 "Agreements on a Comprehensive Political Settlement in Cambodia," signed by 19 nations including the five permanent members of the UN Security Council plus the four warring Khmer parties, the United Nations Transitional Authority in Cambodia (UNTAC) assumed responsibility temporarily for the future of the country.[23] National elections were held in May 1993 under UNTAC supervision. In September 1993, a new constitution was promulgated and Norodom Sihanouk was named king. A coalition government now rules.

The October 1991 Agreements provided for the rehabilitation and reconstruction of Cambodia as part of the peace process. There have been two meetings of the International Committee for the Reconstruction of Cambodia (ICORC), which was formed in 1992 to coordinate bilateral and international agency economic-assistance programs. In June 1992 at Tokyo, US$880 million was pledged by international donors; only a portion of that money was disbursed during the following year. ICORC, comprising 31 donor countries and 11 international agencies, met again in September 1993 and pledged US$119 million in new aid. An additional US$135 million is expected to be committed by early 1994.[24]

The Cambodian physical and economic infrastructure is in the worst shape of any of the Indochina countries. Its per capita GNP is well under US$200 per year. Roads (with the exception of the Phnom Penh-Sihanoukville highway), bridges, the one railway from Phnom Penh to Battambang, irrigation systems, municipal water supplies, schools—everything must be virtually rebuilt. Its human resources have been decimated. On the plus side, the international community has made a firm commitment to assist in the rebuilding effort; the new government appears to be dedicated to political compromise and to rational economic planning and development; the country has a potentially sound agricultural base; and there seems to be a remarkable desire among the Cambodian people to regenerate their country. The big question for the future is whether or not economic and social change can take place rapidly enough to forestall the return of the Khmer Rouge, (which still lurks in the background) to capitalize on the poverty and inequities of Cambodian society.

Politically, Cambodia is different. It is no longer Marxist or Leninist. It is a bittersweet irony that the land of Pol Pot's genocide and draconian rule should now be the only pluralist country among the three. A country where "democracy" (however one chooses to define that term) is getting a chance and where human rights are a concern of many people, including those in government. This tentative experiment in representative government—and it can only be described as tentative at this point—was achieved at great cost. As previously noted, its eventual success will depend in large measure on how quickly economic development and social justice can be brought to the Cambodian people.

THE PERILS OF ECONOMIC DEVELOPMENT

When the window is open, flies come in—so goes the saying. There are obvious downsides to economic development in Indochina. For example, the Lao government is of two minds about the Mitraphap Bridge's effect on the country. It desires the economic benefits yet is wary that the bridge will accelerate an "unhealthy" invasion by foreign culture and mores. Laos has always been slightly paranoid about its powerful kin on the other side of the Mekong, and it is already saturated with Thai television. The bridge could serve as a conduit for the worst excesses of development: deforestation, water pollution, prostitution, and AIDS. All are plainly evident in Thailand.

For its part, the Vietnamese government is leery of the deleterious affect of modern (read Western) culture. Vietnamese youth seem all too eager to swill Coca Cola, dance to Western rock, and covet blue jeans as a mark of sophistication. Entrepreneurship and making money have replaced "liberation" and "unification" as the goals of Vietnamese society. Prostitution, HIV/AIDS, and drug abuse are growing rapidly in Ho Chi Minh City. Underemployment and the increasing gap between rich and poor as Vietnam becomes more prosperous are also problems, particularly in the South. These and other symptoms of the erosion of Vietnam's traditional values—values that long predate Marxism-Leninism—are troubling to thoughtful Vietnamese both within and without the government, and to many Vietnamese living in exile as well.

But in Indochina it is the relationship between economic development and political liberalization that is the hotly disputed subject in both donor and recipient countries of foreign economic assistance. It is by no means a new issue. In a speech before the Philippine Chamber of Commerce in November 1992, former Singapore Prime Minister Lee Kuan Yew put the case this way:

> Contrary to what American political commentators say, I do not believe that democracy necessarily leads to development. I believe that what a country needs to develop is discipline more than democracy. The exuberance of democracy leads to undisciplined and disorderly conditions which are inimical to development. The ultimate test of the value of a political system is whether it helps that society to establish conditions which improve the standard of living for the majority of its people plus enabling the maximum of personal freedom compatible with the freedom of others in the society.[25]

A different perspective is found in a report by the Pacific Basin Research Institute written by a consortium of overseas Vietnamese scholars and professionals working with other economists from Asia and the West:

> Political stability is important, but stability must be based on representational democracy and the rule of law for sustainable economic development. Despite limited reform, the Communist Party of Vietnam keeps a tight hold of power, rejecting multi-party democracy and free elections. Without a normal democratic framework, Vietnam will not be able to achieve popular consensus or a fully integrated society. Political liberalization is necessary to achieve such a consensus, to enlist popular support for painful economic reforms and to mobilize the untapped potential of all Vietnamese outside as well as inside the country. . . . Ultimately, economic progress cannot and will not be sustained without a free and open society.[26]

The issue, obviously, is whether or not it is really possible to separate political change from economic change. The answer depends in part on how much and what kind of political change it is reasonable to expect. This in turn depends on the tangible results of economic development, on whether economic development fills the rice bowls of the population and offers them the chance to buy motorscooters and to enhance their standard of living in other ways.

The Hanoi regime faces a dilemma familiar to other communist regimes in transition: how to conduct economic reform while keeping a grip on political power. The regime has placed prime emphasis on maintaining social "stability." It has sought to avoid both the chaos of the former Soviet Union and the brutality of Tiananmen Square. In an era when ideological purity has been overshadowed by a pragmatic search for higher standards of living, this political preoccupation creates a dilemma for Vietnam's leadership. It can be argued that success in the economic realm tends to strengthen the hold of an authoritarian regime. As long as economic reforms bring tangible benefits, the Vietnamese people may indeed be prepared to accept political limitations. Similarly, while the Vietnamese Communist party may have lost the "Mantle of Heaven" and, as some observers claim, may in fact be a hollow shell, no political alternative to the party structure exists today in Vietnam. Only the most radical overseas critics of the current regime are demanding a precipitate dismantling of the party, since this would in all likelihood create a chaos that would destroy whatever economic gains have been made since 1986 and probably lead to civil war.

The problem, however, is that the Hanoi regime adamantly refuses to allow the creation of the fundamental social conditions for *any* political alternative to develop. This refusal is breeding precisely the social unrest that stability (Lee Kuan Yew's "discipline") is supposed to prevent. Since the party forbids political pluralism, any organized expression of political views different from the party's is immediately snuffed out. Even "peaceful evolution," however one defines that term, is impermissible. Thus, inevitably, the party must bear responsibility for failure to improve the lot of the Vietnamese people quickly enough and profoundly enough, and for the corruption and inefficiencies that have attended renovation.

The regime may be searching for an authoritarian model (perhaps that of Indonesia), which would offer broadened participatory governance yet maintain the pace of economic development. The party seems to be aware of its problem and is trying to improve its image with the younger generation. It has made some moves toward a "law-governed society" by making its role in government less direct and by enhancing the responsibilities of the national assembly. But this somewhat begrudging effort is moving slower than many Vietnamese in the younger and more educated class would like. As Vietnamese society modernizes, receives information, and joins the outside world, popular attitudes are changing. The facsimile, the photocopier, the computer, and the explosion of ideology by science, education, cultural exchanges, and the market place are making "peaceful evolution"—and probably some form of political pluralism—inevitable. It is difficult to imagine how the full force of Vietnam's human resources can be liberated without more running room politically and in terms of individual creativity.

Finally, it is worth noting that some international donors to Vietnam will find the regime's treatment of political dissenters and religious groups so distasteful that economic assistance will be either refused or conditioned. Certainly, when the United States and Vietnam establish diplomatic relations and the question of Most Favored Nation status arises, Vietnam's human rights record will come under hard scrutiny.

NOTES

1. See Vo Nhan Tri, *Vietnam's Economic Policy Since 1975* (Singapore: Institute of Southeast Asian Studies, 1990), and Gareth Porter, *Vietnam: The Politics of Bureaucratic Socialism* (Ithaca: Cornell University Press, 1993).

2. Vietnam still has a sizeable commercial relationship with the Commonwealth of Independent States. Two-way trade is expected to reach US$130 million in 1993. This year Russia has provided Vietnam with US$40 million in loans to complete various major construction projects.

3. See Mya Than and Joseph L. H. Tan, eds., *Vietnam's Dilemmas and Options: The Challenge of Economic Transition in the 1990s* (Singapore: Institute of Southeast Asian Studies, 1993); and William S. Turley and Mark Selden, eds., *Reinventing Socialism: Doi Moi in Comparative Perspective* (Boulder: Westview Press, 1993).

4. See The World Bank, Country Operations Division, Country Department 1, East Asia and Pacific Region, *Vietnam: Transition to the Market* (Washington, 1993); and the United Nations Development Programme, *Development Cooperation: Vietnam (1992 Report)*. (Hanoi, September 1993).

5. Ibid.

6. Smuggling goes both ways. China has good reason to seek better regulation of the border; bilateral negotiations have been in progress for some time in an attempt to limit illegal trade and maximize legitimate commerce.

7. Murray Hiebert, "Corps Business," *Far Eastern Economic Review*, December 23, 1993, p. 40.

8. On February 3, 1994, President Clinton, flanked by several cabinet members and the chairman of the Joint Chiefs of Staff, announced the lifting of trade embargo on Vietnam. The president spoke of progress made on POW/MIAs and how he was "absolutely convinced [that lifting the embargo] was the best way to resolve the fate of those who remain missing" and that the decision "will help secure the fullest possible accounting of those who remain missing." Thus the United States closed one chapter in the long, and still prickly, saga of U.S.-Vietnam relations. Relations are to be established at the "liaison office" level. Full diplomatic relations could take years to negotiate as could the granting of Most Favored Nations status and other trade benefits.

9. For extended treatment, see Frederick Z. Brown, *U.S. Policy Toward Vietnam: The Economic Dimension* (Washington: Overseas Development Council, 1992).

10. For a detailed examination, see Dario Scuka, "Oil in Vietnam: A Review of Foreign and Domestic Activities," Congressional Research Service Report 92-241 F, February 27, 1992.

11. *Indochina Digest*, October 22, 1993. Others cited in Congressional Research Services Report 92-241 F (previous endnote) put proven oil reserves at 2.2 billion barrels with natural gas reserves at 106 billion cubic meters. Adding probable and possible reserves lifts the totals to 20 billion barrels of liquids and about 500 billion cubic meters of gas.

12. *New York Times*, December 21, 1993, p. D5.

13. Scuka, *Oil in Vietnam*, op. cit.

14. From *Indochina Digest*, issues 43, 44, and 45, Vol. VI, October 29, November 5 and 12, 1993 (Washington: Vietnam Veterans of America Foundation).

15. For a candid and fundamentally pessimistic view of the problems facing Vietnam's future development, see *The Challenges of Vietnam's Reconstruction*, edited by Neil L. Jamieson, Nguyen Manh Hung and A. Terry Rambo, published jointly in 1992 by the George Mason University Indochina Institute of Fairfax, Virginia and the East-West Center, Honolulu, Hawaii.

16. For excellent analyses of Linh's efforts, see writings of Lewis M. Stern in *Asian Profile*,

Asian Affairs, and especially "Nguyen Van Linh's Leadership: A New Operational Code," *Indochina Report*, no. 18, January–March 1989.

17. For an analysis of the subtleties of Indochina relationships, see Joseph J. Zasloff, ed., *Postwar Indochina: Old Enemies and New Allies* (Washington: Foreign Service Institute, 1988).

18. Paul Handley, "Making Connections," *Far Eastern Economic Review*, November 4, 1993.

19. Ibid.

20. Ibid.

21. Stephen T. Johnson, "Laos in 1992: Succession and Consolidation," *Asian Survey*, January 1993.

22. There is a vast literature on Cambodia's plight since 1970. See especially Nayan Chanda, *Brother Enemy: The War After the War* (New York: Harcourt Brace Jovanovich, 1986); William Shawcross, *Sideshow: Nixon, Kissinger and the Destruction of Cambodia*, (New York: Simon and Schuster, 1979); and David Chandler, *Brother Number One: A Political Biography of Pol Pot* (Boulder: Westview Press, 1992), among Chandler's other books.

23. Ratified by the UN Security Council in Resolution 718, October 31, 1991.

24. *Indochina Digest*, September 10, 1993.

25. Quoted in William McGurn, "Asian Dilemmas," *National Review*, November 29, 1993, p. 32.

26. "Toward a Market Economy in Vietnam: Economic Reforms and Development Strategies for the Sate Century," p. 4. Pacific Basin Research Institute (1993), One Farsta Court, Rockville, MD 20850.

VIETNAM—BASIC DATA

Land Area: 331,033 km2

Population (1992): .... 69.3 million

Population density: 209 persons/km2

Population growth rate: 2.1%

Population distribution:

    Urban: 20%

    Rural: 80%

Proportion of females in population (1989): 51.3%

GNP per Capita (1992): .... US$220 (est.)

Land Use (thousand hectares—1990)

    Agricultural land: 6,993

    Forest and woodland: 9,395

Health

Infant mortality rate (1991): 43/1,000

Life expectancy (1990):

    Total: .... 62.7 years

    Female: .... 64.8 years

Access to safe water (1990):

    Urban: 48%

    Rural: 45%

    Total: 46%

Access to health services (1987–89): 80%

Access to sanitation (1988–90): 53%

Education

Mean years of schooling (25+ years old, 1990): 4.6

    Total: 4.6

    Female: 3.4

    Male: 5.8

Adult literacy rate (1990):

    Total: 88%

    Female: 84%

    Male: 92%

Economy

Real growth of GDP (1992 est.): 8.3%

Annual average growth rate (1986–1990): 3.9%

GDP by main activity (1992 est.):

    Agriculture: 35%

    Industry: 22%

    Service: 43%

Exchange rate (June 1993): .... US$1 = Dong 10,500

Inflation (CPI, 1992): 17.5%

Government budget (% of GDP, 1991 est.):

    Revenue: 13.6

    Recurrent expenditure: 13.3

    Public savings: 0.3

    Public investment: 2.1

Balance of payments in convertible currency (1992 est.):

Exports: .... US$2.47 billion
Imports: .... US$2.51 billion
Balance of trade: .... US$0.04 billion
Current account balance (inc. grants): ...... US$0.30 billion
External debt (1991 est.): .... Rbls 10.4 billion
                                                   plus US$3.97 billion

Scheduled debt service ratio
(1992, as percent of exports): 25.%
Principal exports: ....Crude oil, rice, marine products, coffee, coal,
                                         rubber, handicrafts, wood products, other
                                         agricultural products.

Source: General Statistics Office, SRV State Planning Committee, and UNDP Human
         Development Report.

6

THE PROSPECTS FOR DEMOCRATIZATION IN SOUTHEAST ASIA: LOCAL PERSPECTIVES AND INTERNATIONAL ROLES

Bruce M. Koppel

This chapter discusses issues concerning the prospects for democracy and processes of democratization in Southeast Asia and the roles of foreign aid in supporting or undermining these prospects and processes. The chapter is based on a series of commissioned research papers, which explored processes of political evolution in Southeast Asia.[1] The papers were commissioned through a project jointly organized by the East-West Center in Honolulu and the Foundation for Advanced Studies in International Development in Tokyo. The project was funded by the Abe Fund and included support for both the research and a series of policy dialogues involving the researchers and policymakers from South and Southeast Asia[2] and several of the major bilateral donors.[3] A specific focus of the papers was on processes of political liberalization and democratization in selected countries and the domestic and regional factors that appear most significant in shaping these processes and their outcomes.

The studies were designed in July of 1992 at a seminar that reviewed perspectives on democratization in Asia and considered the roles of bilateral aid donors in domestic and regional processes of democratization.[4] A key objective of the research focus that followed was to examine processes and problems of democratization as issues within individual contexts of political evolution as well as manifestations of the international diffusion and adoption of specific political ideologies, institutions, and practices.

Placing definition of democratization issues in the context of individual domestic processes of political change represents an important and distinguishing difference from many recent studies—which have concentrated heavily on determining degrees of conformance with particular institutional arrangements, practices, and standards—and was in fact a key reason why new studies were deemed necessary. This is not to say that the realities of international diffusion and adoption of democratic values and practices were to be ignored, but rather that they were not to be assigned preeminence *a priori.*

Consequently, this chapter directly engages crucial questions about how to define and interpret domestic democratization processes in Southeast Asia as well as how to identify and assess the influences of external forces on these processes. The thrust of these questions can be stated this way: Is it meaningful to speak of processes of political democratization as if there is a single universal model operating or unfolding—albeit with some variation—or is it more substantive to speak of processes of political evolution that may share certain "universal" issues and properties in terms of democratic content, but that fuller evaluation of the content requires serious reference to both internal as well as external criteria? This question in turn leads to a second question: if external criteria are of only limited value in assessing the democratic content in specific patterns of political evolution, then which "local" norms should be used and how can we determine and defend the authenticity of the processes that are shaping and maintaining these norms?

These questions are not simply grist for intellectual debate. They are potentially pivotal elements of both domestic and international political discourse on democracy and democratization. They speak, for example, to questions of legitimacy in domestic political organization and activity as well as to the concepts of conditionality and intervention in international political relations. Recent discussions of human rights and democracy in Asia (e.g., at the World Conference on Human Rights) have brought forward arguments that Western standards are culturally bound (i.e., not directly transferable) and that Western prescriptions for democratic choices are political anachronisms (i.e., imperialistic) in a post-cold war world. These arguments stand in sharp contrast to views that there are already (as implied in the 1948 United Nations Declaration) or should be, universal standards of human rights—including political rights—and that there is an undeniable international movement in support of political democratization—democratization, it should be added, with a limited set of conforming meanings.

But in Southeast Asia, is this a debate about different principles or competing nuances? For example, is this a discourse that *overestimates* the requirements democracy in Southeast Asia has for appeals to universal norms by *underestimating* the authenticity of indigenously formed democratic norms (what could be called the "orientalist" fallacy)? Is this a debate about the dictates of international interdependence and assumed rates and degrees of political convergence or is the debate principally about the possibilities of a more open international system and the opportunities it would create for political diversity? Do the arguments represent opposing interpretations of contemporary history and what the consequent imperatives are for political evolution or is the matter much simpler and are these arguments essentially between those who support and those who resist the extension of democracy and democratization?

THEMES IN THE DEMOCRATIZATION DEBATE

This chapter will not offer a detailed review of the resurgent interest in democracy and democratization issues among academic analysts. That would be a large task indeed inasmuch as that interest is quite vigorous and prolific.

What is useful, however, is to convey a sense of the themes that occupy much of the discussion and then later to locate the discussion in Southeast Asia in relation to this wider intellectual debate.

To begin with, it is important to note that discussions in the United States and Europe on issues of democracy and democratization have been strongly invigorated by developments in Eastern Europe in particular, but also by recent events within Asia—especially in the Philippines, Myanmar, Thailand, and China. In contrast to an earlier period, when experiences throughout Asia, Africa, and Latin America generated serious pessimism about the prospects for democratization in what was then called the "developing world," events in the 1980s led to a resurgence of academic interest in the causes, character, and consequences of democratization.

One important theme in these discussions is an optimism that democratic political evolution can be encouraged and supported—a position that is tantamount to saying that democratic institutions and practices are possible virtually anywhere provided they are appropriately designed and there is sufficient political commitment to sustain them. This is in contrast to a deep pessimism that pertained for several decades, namely that various prerequisites for democratization were not widely distributed. A focus on prerequisites implied that where prerequisites were insufficient, democratic institutions and practices could not reasonably be expected to survive. Indeed, qualitative studies of democracy have shifted away from a focus on identifying the necessary conditions for democracy as an end state and have moved towards more attention on *processes* of democratization.

There are three facets to this new optimism. The first, as already discussed, is that *democracies can be created*. This implies that the growth of democracy is not a peculiar or idiosyncratic cultural product. This leads to considerable attention to what can be called constitutional issues: how to design a democracy. The second is that *political variables are important*. This point may seem obvious, but a pessimism rooted in ideas about cultural prerequisites and economic determinism relegated political variables to marginal roles in analyses of democratization. This point says that while culture, economics, and history certainly matter, democracy is also a product of political variables. This leads to considerable attention to issues of legitimacy and renewed interests in comparative politics as a perspective on democratization.[5] The third is that *strengthening civil society is both essential and feasible*. The new assumption is that a civil society can be strengthened through deliberate acts of institutional innovation and that the possibilities for these acts and for positive outcomes from them are not wholly constrained by existing social and cultural habits. This is a crucial point because while it acknowledges the importance of how a society is functioning for processes of political democratization, it does not concede that the social basis of democracy is immutable or even predictable. This leads to considerable attention to such matters as the roles of a free press, the importance of an equitable and efficient legal system, the need to overcome gender discrimination, and the significance of patterns of free association.

However, this leaves open numerous complex issues associated with the conceptualization of democracy and democratization. For example, as implied in the previous paragraph, there are understandings of democracy as a political system and there are interpretations of democracy as a way of life, implying a specific set of cultural and moral preferences. In recent years, buoyed perhaps by the fall of authoritarian regimes across a range of cultural settings in Europe and Asia, minimalist definitions (focused on democracy as a political system only) have gained wider acceptance. However, within the terms of this apparent agreement, new issues have arisen.

One issue is a frequently confused distinction between political liberalization and democratization. There are often cases of political liberalization (e.g., civil service reforms, electoral reforms, deregulation of political parties and the press) which by themselves do not necessarily alter the fundamental responsiveness or accountability of a political system or of a specific government. Democratization, as a process, will undoubtedly include processes of political liberalization, but it will also include deepening the democratic content of existing political institutions. This can have implications ranging from conceptions of citizenship to the full range of relationships between a political system and civil society. The confusion between political liberalization and democratization stems, at least in part, from a continuing strong preference for international classifications and comparisons based on the common properties of political systems and quantitative indicators of democratic status. Such methods, based as they usually are on lists of attributes, inevitably focus on particulars at the expense of the whole. As analysts are discovering, specific policy changes and institutional innovations (e.g., electoral reform) from different political systems cannot always be treated as discrete or equivalent events for purposes of comparative assessments, at least not without extensive loss of confidence in the conclusions so generated. These changes need to be evaluated in the context of the political arrangements of which they are part and arguably from which the majority of their content. For example, the significance of electoral reforms must be assessed in the context of patterns of participation and financing.

Closely related is the important issue of democratic consolidation. Democratic consolidation does not amount to simply measuring stability, persistence, or duration of specific democratic political arrangements—although these are certainly important. These are not irrelevant indicators, but their focus tends to be quantitative and as such they court the risk of confusing the persistence of specific democratic political arrangements for the democratic significance of those arrangements. The former may be important as benchmarks in transitions to democracy. The latter, in contrast, is the issue of democratic consolidation. Democratic consolidation refers to the longer-term quality of a political system's performance where quality refers to responsiveness, accountability, and orientation. Indeed, in some opinions, the challenge of democratic consolidation will prove to be a more difficult and time-consuming one than the transition issue. What is unclear is whether this caveat should be accepted at face value or whether it is a Trojan horse for the old cultural prerequisite argument.

The point is not simply one of academic musing. Understanding the causes of democratization (as compared to determinants or prerequisites of democracy) is a compelling issue: what is propelling democratic political change? The analysis is not so simple. To start with, a focus on processes of change (rather than on conditions or states of a system) raises several measurement issues. For example, many traditional measures of political democratization (e.g., rights of assembly and speech, functioning representative institutions, "rule of law") are static properties and are not readily amenable as indicators of a democratization process—except in the limited and sometimes erroneous sense of being presumed outcomes of that process. In other words, the presence of these attributes does not tell us categorically about the processes that yielded them, or more importantly, whether they are the products of processes of democratization or, for example, the consequences of various forms of authoritarian accommodation.[6] Concerns about this point are leading to the concession that for any specific case, there will most likely be both internal and external (or domestic and international) causative and influencing factors. What is less clear—both conceptually and empirically—is what these are, how they function, and how they relate to each other.

PERSPECTIVES FROM SOUTHEAST ASIA

The individual country studies (covering Indonesia, Malaysia, the Philippines, and Thailand) on which this chapter is based cover a wide range of issues, many of them idiosyncratic to the specific countries. As noted in the introduction, the discussion that follows will be thematic rather than encyclopedic. These themes are central to the countries covered in the studies and, we believe, are central issues for considering democratization issues in Asia generally. The issues are democratization and economic development, NGOs, democratic consolidation, and external factors (security questions and democracy as an international cultural commodity).

DEMOCRATIZATION AND ECONOMIC DEVELOPMENT

An assumption is often made that economic development is not simply a prerequisite for democracy, but that economic development inexorably leads to democratization. This is associated in particular with strong confidence in market-oriented economic processes as the best path to both economic development and political democratization. Asian experience, however, suggests that while there is an association between the adoption of market-oriented economic processes and the pace of economic development, the association between economic development and political democratization is much less certain. One reason is that market-oriented economic development in Asia has not meant the absence of a significant state role in the economy—in contrast to the ideology on this point in American political debate. A second major reason, and one given special attention in the studies being reviewed here, is that there are two strong intervening variables in the relationship between economic growth and political change: the structure of economic development (e.g., sectoral composition of productivity growth) and the political economy that governs the distribution of the benefits of economic development.

What is clear throughout Southeast Asia, for example, is that there is a significant association between economic inequalities and inequalities in the distribution of and access to political power. Put differently, political power is frequently mobilized and exercised to ensure that the advantages which accrue to concentrations of economic power are maintained. These political inequalities, in turn, are not simply associated with hierarchy in the political systems in which some systematically have more power than others. Hierarchy would only imply unequal distribution, but would not necessarily imply rigidity in that distribution—for example, through substantial constraints on mobility up (and down) the hierarchy.

However, in the Southeast Asian context, the distribution of political power is frequently characterized by high degrees of segmentation. Segmentation means that hierarchies are defined by distinct levels that fix discontinuities in the distribution of power. Movement from one level to another is difficult at best. One important implication is that, effectively speaking, the hierarchy of political power is mirrored by a hierarchy of policy arenas. There are multiple political arenas with constraints on what kinds of issues can be mediated in which arenas, who is eligible to participate in which arenas, and what rules govern decision-making within each arena. This means that issues of democratization can be defined both within specific arenas as well as up and down the entire hierarchy.[7]

Two additional important points follow. First, as many analyses of electoral politics in Southeast Asia have shown, an overlay of democratic institutions and practices does not imply that these have equivalent or presumed political significance across the entire political system. This is crucial because it means that democracy cannot be viewed as a uniformly distributed political attribute associated with an assumed homogenous economic system, but rather that the progress of democratization must be measured with explicit reference to the heterogeneity of an economy. Second, economic inequalities (and associated political inequalities) are often neither temporary nor self-correcting. This is crucial because while many of the central requirements of economic development in Southeast Asia are frequently depoliticized (often at the urging of donors)—to protect the imperatives of concerns such as macroeconomic stability, economic policy reforms, and market-oriented adjustment processes—issues in the structure of economic development nevertheless are fundamentally political because they build on and have consequences for the distribution of political power. Depoliticization in these circumstances has the direct effect of suppressing open discussion of the direct political consequences of economic adjustment. More than that, though, in a context of concentrated political power associated with concentrated economic power, depoliticization tends to perpetuate a myth that economic and political inequalities will adjust "of their own accord."

In the Thai case, for example, economic development has been substantial and rapid but it has not led to fundamental changes in the character of the state. Thai society remains seriously bifurcated, with a large proportion of the labor force still in agriculture, extensive landholding problems which have contributed to the growth of a substantial level of rural unemployment and rural and urban underemployment, and an overwhelming primary city in which is concentrated much of the country's wealth and the vast majority of Thailand's middle class. Discussions about prospects for the growth of a civil society and what kind of civil society can grow cannot ignore this bifurcation.

The characteristics of a civil society growing in the medium of a bifurcated state include the rise of what can be called *authoritarian pluralism*. Patterns of industrialization that depend strongly on natural resource exploitation but that occur in social contexts characterized by severe inequalities in control over those resources can seriously inhibit the emergence of a more participative democracy. This pattern has been seen throughout the region and will often lead to close alliances between business, military, and political power in order to ensure continued control of access to natural resource supplies at favorable prices. One result is that industrialization becomes a source of intersectoral conflict—but not simply, as much development literature would have it, between the supporters of modernity and the followers of tradition, or between urban interests and rural interests. Intersectoral conflict in the context of authoritarian pluralism is between a corporate sector (military, bureaucrats, and business) and what is best called a people sector (agriculture, labor). For this reason, one of the challenges of effective democratization in Southeast Asia resides precisely in this intersectoral conflict and, more precisely, in the need for restructuring the terms of this conflict.

A second result is that in an activist bureaucratic state, democratization is often viewed as a direct challenge to the continued hegemony of the bureaucracy and its allies. Here it is important to note that strengthening the political role of the private sector (i.e., the private corporate sector)—the thrust of much political and economic liberalization under the rubric of privatization—does not equal democratization, but rather, in the political economies of Southeast Asia, often yields instead what can be called *technocratization*—where politics is viewed as problematic and not related to the judicious use of political power. One part of society is empowered (although it is debatable whether this is more a case of reallocation between corporate interests and bureaucratic interests more than any redistribution between the state and society), but the empowerment is associated with a depoliticizing of economic development. There is little evidence of democratic political trickle down from technocratization, but there is more evidence of further consolidation of political power by bureaucratic and corporate interests and often, further segmentation of the political system to ensure the security of that consolidation. For example, the levels of political power concentration in Indonesia appear to be higher than what would be required by the imperatives of macroeconomic stability or even economic growth more generally.

The success of the depoliticization project as a surrogate for democratization does frequently depend on economic performance. As long as the economic performance is there, the surrogate strategy of depoliticization appears defensible. If economic development falters, however, elites are not inclined to blame the surrogate strategy of depoliticization but rather are often eager to blame democratization. The issue can be seen in the relationship between economic growth and the legitimacy of existing political arrangements in Malaysia. As long as the size of the overall economic pie continues to expand, it is possible for the political arrangements now in place to remain fundamentally acceptable to most parties. In effect, gains of one are not always seen as exclusively the loss of another. However, if the pie does not grow fast enough or worse, if growth reverses, the legitimacy of the various arrangements that characterize Malaysian governance could be seriously shaken. Similarly, in the Philippines, a debate continues on the relative merits of democracy and "discipline," with the latter appearing more attractive to many elites whenever economic performance falters.

In this context, the concept of good governance assumes several specific meanings. In the Malaysian case, for example, it means an attempt to achieve some leveling between the principal ethnic groups. It also means a fundamental paradox. The Chinese in Malaysia apparently accept Malay domination, but the principal ruling Malay party, UMNO, cannot rule by itself. The recognized need to become one nation has been viewed with the government's economic aspirations in the form of the vision 2020 plan, which essentially says that Malaysia will be a fully developed economy by that time. The political challenges that lie ahead therefore are to establish one nation (and Malay identity), fostering and developing a mature democratic society, and promoting values that are consistent with Malay culture. These and a number of other challenges together reflect the government's concept of comprehensive security, a security that refers to the requirement that Malays overcome their insecurity. This, in turn, permits a single nation to emerge. For example, in earlier years, the threat to internal security was connected with a communist insurgency. That was defeated and today the threats to security come from federal-state relations and from a growing constituency for Islamic fundamentalism.

An important implication that follows is that structuring democratic institutions and perfecting definitions of democracy are not enough. As the Philippine case illustrates, it is equally important to focus on the *outcomes* of democratization. What are the economic consequences of democratization and for whom? While as noted, patterns of economic development structure the possibilities for democratization (a position that would see a positive relationship between breaking up excessive concentrations of economic power and opening up the possibilities for effective democratization), patterns of democratization also must be assessed in terms of their consequences for economic processes and the welfare of specific social groups. In the Malaysian case, there is an "official" concern about ownership of economic assets and in the Indonesian and Philippine cases there have been highly public challenges by the governments to the most egregious forms of economic concentration. On the other hand, democratization in terms of labor organization has been viewed as dangerous for both economic and political stability, especially in Indonesia and Malaysia. Throughout Southeast Asia, the first issue—the political consequences of high concentrations of economic power—has received much more attention than the second issue—the economic consequences of democratization.

NGOs

Given the strong concerns throughout the region about trajectories of democratization that tend strongly in elitist directions, it is understandable that increasing interest has emerged in the political significance and roles of NGOs.[8] This interest comes from within the countries as well as from a variety of external sources ranging from foreign aid donors (many of whom are very enthusiastic about working with and through NGOs) to private and charitable foundations and NGOs in the United States and Europe. Both the assumption and the hope are that NGOs help to build a foundation for participative rather than elite democracy. The bases of the assumption and the hope are that NGOs are the leading edge of an emerging civil society, i.e., of voluntary and private forms of politically significant association in the public interest.

An interesting theoretical and practical issue that arises in Southeast Asia is deciding when and if NGOs are distinct from political parties. The usual consideration is that political parties are organized in order to contest and acquire political power and control the government. NGOs, in the distinction frequently offered, are seen as interested in how power is exercised and by whom, but as not being interested in the direct acquisition of power, especially at the national level. This leads to such distinctions as between service-oriented NGOs (which tend to focus on welfare) and advocacy-oriented NGOs, which might focus on political reform. However, all of this appears less compelling the closer the examination. Clearly, NGOs in Southeast Asia can have political roles highly analogous to the roles associated with political parties. In the same way, some political parties can clearly have goals and objectives highly comparable to those associated with NGOs.

For example, in the Philippines during the Marcos years, the NGO community was often the base of the noncommunist political opposition to Marcos. In some interpretations, the NGO movement in the Philippines was a key element in ending the Marcos period and bringing Mrs. Aquino to power. In fact, the NGO community expected much from the Aquino government and was prepared to work closely with her government. When, in the NGO view, the Aquino government failed to deliver on several fundamental items (e. g., agrarian reform), the community increasingly went off on its own. The Aquino government, in its final year, sought to re-energize the alliance between government and NGOs through initiation of the *Kabisig* (literally "holding hands") movement, and there was some success in terms both of voter mobilization and ultimately electoral success in the 1992 presidential elections. In effect, the NGOs—while not political parties in terms of fielding their own candidates and directly contesting for power—nevertheless played important roles in the infrastructure of political competition.

While the Philippine NGO community today is not in a confrontational relationship with the government, neither is it tightly wedded to the government. However, increased attention to the political potential of NGOs (in terms of voter mobilization) along with increased attention from the donor community led to the emergence of many NGOs whose authenticity as peoples' organizations was suspect. For example, local elites began forming their own NGOs, not least in order to gain a share of various outside and domestic funding pools allocated for NGO support. Indeed, this led to a distinction in Philippine parlance between NGOs and POs (people's organizations). The split was symptomatic of a broader problem in the political significance of the NGO movement throughout many parts of Southeast Asia: the relationships between the growth of NGOs on one hand, and on the other hand the emergence of both new elites and the re-sanctification of old elites. These processes of emergence and re-sanctification were frequently legitimized by their NGO affiliations but not necessarily responsive to or supportive of democratic forces.

NGOs operate in sociopolitical contexts that help to explain their form and function and play important roles in defining their possibilities. Several issues emerge. One, already noted, is assessing the political significance of NGOs and, beyond that, assessing their significance in terms of democratization. Here it is instructive to consider continuities within specific countries in terms of the political roles of nongovernmental organizations. One place to look for continuities is in the traditional roles of religious-based organizations. The role of the church in the Philippines traditionally extended into the political arena. Traditionally, the church did this essentially by defending and even rationalizing the political order. It is important to recognize that the Philippine revolution in the early years of the twentieth century was channeled through religious-based organizations. Similarly, some of the most powerful criticism of Marcos came from the Church, a critique that played an important role in undermining the regime's legitimacy.

Both Indonesia and Malaysia face the issue of how to manage Islamic organizations whose political agendas are potentially quite explicit in terms of desecularizing the state. In the Indonesian case, the national ideology of *Pancasila* is a basis for precluding explicit political roles by Islamic organizations. In the Malaysian case, the issue is more contentious and, indeed, is a major theme in contemporary politics. By comparison, the role of the temple in Thai society has been much more focused on social welfare issues. The temple has not been associated with either defense or criticism of state power. The types of roles NGOs have assumed in the four countries have been strongly influenced by this background. For example, NGOs have assumed explicit political roles in Malaysia, the Philippines, and Thailand, but in these cases there are important differences in the continuities and discontinuities represented by this form of group action.

A related and more general point is that throughout Southeast Asia, while NGOs often display the technical and participatory attributes claimed for them by their international advocates, the NGOs also often reflect fundamental characteristics of the societies in which they function. This point has to be carefully assessed in considering the significance of NGO umbrella organizations.[9] These organizations have several origins, ranging from experience with foreign donors on one side to government-sponsored affiliations and sponsorship on the other. In many cases, these organizations exhibit the same hierarchical preferences that can be seen in the broader political and bureaucratic systems.

Other issues relate to the localism of NGOs. Grassroots organizations may be NGOs, but not all NGOs are grassroots organizations. There are questions about the role of NGOs as expressions of domestic political forces as compared to NGOs as extensions of external political and economic forces. There is the question of linkages with first world and third world NGOs. These linkages often take the form of significant financial subsidization, but also can take the form of ideological orientation as well. Similarly, there is the issue of interrelationships among large NGOs and small NGOs within a country as well as between countries.

For example, Malaysia has an estimated 100 issue-oriented NGOs. In the government's view, many of the NGOs are foreign supported and represent attempts to inject foreign-supported positions into the Malaysian situation. Examples include Iranian-supported Islamic fundamentalist NGOs and NGOs with Western support who press for various positions within the Malaysian political arena. As a result, for some time the government's attitude towards NGOs was highly restrictive. Lately, the government is relaxing this position somewhat and NGOs are being invited to participate in various government-NGO consortia. Nevertheless, the government maintains a substantial suspicion of the NGOs.[10]

DEMOCRATIC CONSOLIDATION

The transition to more democratic politics and political organization is an important theme in political evolution throughout Southeast Asia. However, the political transition is not the only major transition underway. There are three principal transitions that can be seen operating throughout Southeast Asia: economic liberalization, political democratization, and redefinition of citizenship. The first two are widely recognized and their interrelationships are the subject of the now classic *glasnost-perestroika* formulation. However, as experience in Eastern Europe has also demonstrated, the formulation is profoundly incomplete without reference to ongoing transitions in the redefinition of citizenship.[11] The redefinition of citizenship refers to processes that establish the boundaries of nationhood—not simply in spatial terms—but in ethnic, racial, religious, gender, class, and other social and cultural terms. The boundaries of nationhood are crucial because they establish the basic social and political space for political evolution. Expanding the boundaries of citizenship can be associated with a broadening of civil society and more inclusive democratic politics. Restricting the boundaries of citizenship can be associated with patterns of exclusion and discrimination that narrow the articulation between democratic politics and the broader society and arguably, in more extreme cases, subordinate the political order to the dictates of citizenship.

The challenge of democratic consolidation is to negotiate the terms of a balance among these multiple transitions—a balance that needs to embody the clear priority of democratic content across all three transitions. The studies point out that questions of democratic consolidation need to be placed firmly in the context of state-society relations. This says that while minimalist definitions of democracy may be acceptable as characterizations of the democratic content in processes of political evolution, processes of democratic consolidation cannot be assessed in narrow or mechanistic terms.

The notion of democratic consolidation implies no less than a relationship between the political system and the society of which it is part. This is the reason that consolidation also stands to be a more complex challenge than what can be called the transitional challenge.

Consolidation means developing linkages between a political system and a society that ensure that the democratic content in the political system will be nurtured, protected, and respected. This implies economic practices that do not systematically subvert principles of open competition and it implies concepts of nationhood and citizenship that do not systematically assign differential rights based on social or cultural attributes. Two types of consolidation strategies follow from the notion of democratic consolidation as a balance and both can be seen in Southeast Asian political debates.

Democratic consolidation as a balance can be viewed partly as a social compact that establishes basic relationships among the multiple transitions. This can be seen as a constitutional strategy. Constitutional strategies seek to combine an acknowledgment of contemporary differences in forms and levels of power with the values of stability and predictability in future relationships among the transitions. It is a fundamentally conservative strategy, which treats deviation from a defined balance as problematic.

Democratic consolidation as a balance also has to be viewed as an agreement that democratic principles and qualities will characterize both the processes that adjust relationships across the transitions as well as the objectives of those processes. This can be seen as an ideological strategy. Ideological strategies view existing relationships among transitions as passing and are focused more on establishing agreement about where change is going and how the change will occur.

It is in the context of these strategies—both constitutional and ideological—that one can ask questions about whether democratic processes can be introduced, and whether they can be sustained. At this level, the issue of democratic consolidation basically asks: what factors and indicators are most crucial in supporting a judgment that democratic innovations can be sustained—whether they were endogenously formed, borrowed from elsewhere, or both? Consolidation clearly refers to institutionalization and maintenance, at the least within the political system and ultimately between the political system and a committed civil society. There is also a crucial additional criterion: democratic consolidation implies a very low likelihood of reversibility.

However, in Southeast Asia, these guidelines need to be tested in political crucibles where civil-military relationships have not all been settled in a manner or to a degree that ensures the security of democratically determined political choices; where concentrations of significant economic power along with the persistence of significant levels of poverty and social exclusion raise serious concerns about the implications of an incomplete civil society for the durability of democratic processes; and where questions about the relationships between the growth of middle classes and their demonstrated commitment to the values of stability raise concerns about premature closure on democratic consolidation.

EXTERNAL FACTORS

Three external factors appear to be especially important as influences affecting prospects for democratization. One is the question of security issues and how these relate to statism, the role of the military, and the values placed on unity. A second area is cultural and focuses on the question of democracy as an international cultural commodity. And the third is foreign aid and the roles of donor countries in particular as explicit agents of change.

Security and Democratization

Concerns about internal security have been a well-established feature of both support for and resistance to democratization in many parts of Southeast Asia. Concerns about internal security have led to the adoption of political liberalization and democratic reforms in several cases. These steps have been taken as part of efforts to strengthen regime legitimacy (in both domestic and foreign circles) and to weaken support for insurgent elements in particular—for example by holding out the possibility of orderly government change. The problem frequently encountered in these cases—both in Southeast Asia and elsewhere—is that the commitment to these steps has tended to erode as the challenges presented by insurgents have receded.

Concerns about internal security also have been associated with persistent resistance to political liberalization and democratic reforms. This is because problems of internal security are seen as making open political competition potentially destabilizing and divisive, especially in multiethnic societies. In other cases, concerns about insurgent ideologies have placed a high value on indications of loyalty and support and have significantly depreciated the legitimacy of opposition politics. Finally, the requirements of political stability for economic growth and confidence have generated cautious reactions to political evolution that would introduce external perceptions of domestic political instability and thus threaten the continuity of economic growth policies.

Concerns about regional security have been an important element as well in political debates about democratization in Southeast Asia. Before the end of the cold war, discussions of regional security and of prospects for democratization within specific countries were distinct discussions. This distinction reflected the low institutionalization (compared to Eastern Europe) of the security discussion, and the hostility throughout the Asia-Pacific region to political conditionalities in international relations. The latter theme still functions (e.g., the Thai-Myanmar relationship). However, rudimentary relationships appear to be developing in Southeast Asia among three issues: economic interdependence, regional security, and political development.

There are important changes underway in the structure of international political, economic, and security relations in the region and in the prospects for domestic political evolution in specific countries. These changes include the increasing power within the Asia-Pacific region of China and Japan. There are also the increasingly important indicators of growing regional interdependence, but a regionalism for which the United States by itself cannot be a prime supporter—as was the case in the emergence, for example, of ASEAN. This is due to the growing economic power of the region, the strains on the American economy, and the growth of middle-rank powers (Korea, Taiwan, Thailand, Indonesia) whose rise weakens American hegemony. This also reflects an important underlying change in the structure of international relations within and affecting the region: there is the absence of a permanent political and security polarization overlay. Against this background, overall political change is likely to be incremental. Changes in the structure of interaction between states, however, will lead to changes in the structure of international relations in the region. This will make the question of regional norm-setting in matters related to security, human rights, and democratization increasingly important. This point has been recognized through recent regional initiatives on security and human rights.

Democracy as an International Cultural Commodity

There is a substantial body of opinion in Southeast Asia that argues against the direct transfer of democratic standards and strategies from external sources. This argument actually takes two forms. One form says that each country needs to discover and apply its own unique democratic definitions and solutions. This does not exclude the possibility of borrowing parts of these from the experience and practice of others, but the validation would lie not in the practices themselves or where they came from, but rather in the determination of their appropriateness in the cultural and historical circumstances of a particular country. The notion of a universal democratic norm is accepted only in the broadest sense—that it legitimates local determinations of what the norm means. There is a second view that agrees that there cannot be a successful literal transfer of democratic strategies from one cultural and political context to another. However, from this perspective, there are reservations that a relativist position about the meaning of democracy implies that there are no widely accepted standards or norms as to what constitutes democratic institutions and behavior. For example, there is the idea of an ethical universalism in support of democratization that cannot be falsified because a particular government or party finds it inconvenient.

The debates on this point appear most vigorous where there are difficulties in the transitions affecting concepts of citizenship. Implicit in Western concepts of democracy are standards regarding human rights. These rights are only narrowly political. They have broader reference to social and cultural expression and are therefore foundations of citizenship as well as political democracy. In Southeast Asia, the individualism associated with these standards is often attacked as incompatible with cultural emphases on the group. In other cases, explicit concerns are raised, especially in multiethnic situations, that acceptance of a conflictual political process, based on the legitimacy of opposing individual views along with rights of free association, would be formulas for communal conflict and severe internal instability.

For example, in evaluating how much democracy Malaysia has achieved, the argument is often made that progress needs to be measured in terms consistent with Malaysia's situation and not against criteria that may be acceptable in other more advanced settings. For example, there are difficult issues of culture and education and the issue of the role of vernacular education. To what degree does vernacular education perpetuate ethnic differences that are problematic? Arguments such as this have led to discussions about a communitarian rather than a Western liberal perspective on democratization. The communitarian perspective defines rights in terms of social groups and the importance of stable relations (i.e., nonconflictual relationships) among groups. The significance of participation in political democratization rests on definitions of citizenship. Those definitions are made in terms of membership in social groups. To use the distinction made earlier, democratic consolidation in this mode is principally constitutional—it seeks to fix intergroup relations as a framework within which democratic content can be defined and institutionalized.

Proposals for communitarian democracy should be distinguished from concerns about "over-democracy." In some cases, these are expressions referring to dangers of instability and can be associated with a minimalist perspective. They are often associated with underdeveloped party systems, difficulties of managing political conflict, policy gridlock, indecisive governance, etc. There is also a maximalist perspective on problems of over-democracy that is closely tied to a fundamental critique of the liberal model of democracy. This critique focuses on the association between liberal democracy and what are frequently viewed as social and cultural excesses. Rather than a democracy characterized by the clash of individual interests and the consequent dissolution of social and moral standards, a democratic process is needed—characterized by stability, peace and order, the upholding of shared moral and cultural values, and the priority of communitarian interests.

The question of communalism versus individualism also needs to be addressed in the context of economic scarcity. Cultural diversity often appears to be more tolerable when the perceived senses of economic scarcity are limited. When perceptions of scarcity run strong, then attention can turn in various directions for criteria to govern the allocation of scarce resources and services. In these circumstances, criteria associated with the hegemony claims or aspirations of a particular group can effectively convert the reality of cultural diversity to a reality of cultural stratification.

Finally, another important issue in the debate between communalism and individualism hinges on the often subtle dividing lines between consensus, conformity, and compliance. In principle, the idea of democracy is associated with ideas about access and participation. In specific social and political contexts, however, "democratic" behaviors that yield high consensus (e.g., voting) may not necessarily represent expressions of agreement, but rather may reflect more conservative patterns of conformity with pre-democratic forms of leadership and decision-making. The latter could happen, for example, where patterns of economic relationships (e.g., high incidence of tenancy in a rural area) have created expectations for conformity with local leadership or, more generally, where community leadership remains wedded to older autocratic modes even though the broader system may have formal democratic characteristics. Where conformity is essentially imposed (e.g., through single candidate elections or compromises in ballot secrecy), then the consensus becomes compliance and processes of participation reflect the exercise of state power rather than the articulation of popular voice.

FOREIGN AID AND DEMOCRATIZATION

Bilateral foreign aid has some history of supporting processes of democratization in Asia. As elsewhere, this support has taken two major forms. Support that *indirectly* and implicitly supports democratization has focused on economic development, infrastructure provision, health and education, and domestic security. In different ways, each of these was rationalized—at least in part—by the impacts they could or did have on prospects for democratization. Support that *directly* and explicitly supports democratization has been much less frequent. In these cases, the focus historically has been on assistance for managing elections, educational opportunities for legislators and senior policymakers, and assistance for members of the press. In recent years, donor relationships with NGOs have expanded and in so doing, have bridged both the direct and indirect paths between foreign aid and democratization. Until recently (specifically the end of the cold war) the links between aid and progress towards democratization in Asia were never made a condition for aid,[12] although in a few instances movement away from democratization and concerns about human rights abuses were made a basis for suspension of aid by some donors.

With the recent surge of interest in democratization, however, donors are looking more explicitly at how their aid can be used to support processes of democratization. In Southeast Asia, this shift in strategy is juxtaposed with several other issues related to foreign aid and Asia generally. These include the role of foreign aid to middle-income countries (a growing issue for Southeast Asia), issues of persistent poverty (especially in south Asia), and interactions of trade, aid, and international political relations (especially with China). All these matters together—along with constraints on aid budgets faced by many donors—place significant challenges on existing donor capacities and preferred modalities for functioning.

The democratization issue requires donors to have considerably broader and deeper understanding of domestic political processes in recipient countries. The democratization issue also requires donors to proceed very carefully in their relationships with domestic groups in recipient countries to avoid compromising indigenous democratization processes. Four themes in particular are important in assessing the roles of foreign aid and democratization in Southeast Asia: strengthening good governance, working with Asian NGOs, promoting democratization, and understanding the limits of bilateral influence.

Foreign Aid and Good Governance

A key issue in foreign aid strategies to support democratization in Southeast Asia is the matter of good governance. However, can foreign aid contribute to strengthening good governance? Good governance can be viewed as a compromise between the imperatives laid out by the ethical universalism of democracy and the possibilities permitted by the dictates of political prudence. However, in the Southeast Asian context, the issue of good governance should be examined carefully. Is good governance an instrument of power or is good governance power itself? If good governance is interpreted strictly as the latter, the results may simply be efforts to make a nondemocratic government more efficient or less corrupt. There are numerous examples of this outcome throughout Southeast Asia.

The real question, and the deeper challenge of good governance, is that accepting the principle of good governance makes the exercise of power instrumental. This, in turn, forces the question: for whom and for what purposes is power being used? In a democratizing society the presumption will be that in some nontrivial sense the answer to the question will be: for the people and for purposes they deem important through meaningful representative expressions.

In one sense, this means that foreign aid in support of good governance must focus on reforms *within* government. This focus becomes necessary because the bureaucracy frequently will not be sympathetic to political liberalization and democratic initiatives that appear to require reductions in their prerogatives. However, this focus does not mean that foreign aid should be *state-centric.* The larger challenge of good governance in Southeast Asia is to strengthen the capacities of the civil society to both support and if necessary demand its role in determining how power is both used and limited. What this means for the question of how foreign aid can relate to good governance is that external pressures in favor of good governance must be strongly *social-centric.*

Foreign aid to support good governance and democratization must be directed at specific social groups rather than the state as such. In cases such as the Philippines and Thailand, but also in many other developing country circumstances, aid which has the effect of strengthening the existing state (e.g., by making the bureaucracy more efficient) will not by itself guarantee the growth of authentic democratization processes. For foreign aid to support good governance, aid that improves the efficiency of governing must be accompanied by aid that strengthens the role of the governed. This means that new forms of policy dialogue are needed between donors and recipient countries, dialogues that go beyond the existing state-to-state format. To support such dialogues, donors will need to develop much more subtle understandings of democratization processes in recipient countries.[13]

Foreign Aid and Asian NGOs

For most bilateral donors, the principal recent entry point to the issue of democratization in Southeast Asia has been work with Asian (and donor country) NGOs. Three issues concerning the relationships among donors, Asian NGOs, and democratization were identified in the studies: selection, funding, and "ownership."

The selection issue relates to what types of NGOs are identified, what criteria are used to make these choices, and what processes are employed to apply the criteria. Concerns have arisen about selection for several reasons. First, there are concerns about the range of issues that donors appear to want to associate with NGOs. The general conclusion now is that donors should use NGOs especially for people-oriented issues such as community forestry, election monitoring, skills training, etc. However, as the election-monitoring example sometimes illustrates, both governments and nationalist forces (who may otherwise be opposed to their government) are suspicious that the NGOs are not being supported in their own right but rather as instruments for a donor's political agenda. From this perspective, there are serious concerns that when donors rely heavily on NGOs, what they are attempting to do is to blunt the sharper edge of their political intervention.

Second, there are concerns about in-country hierarchies among NGOs. Some argue that donors should function through "umbrella" organizations for NGOs rather than with NGOs directly. Others argue that umbrella organizations can represent NGOs whose principal asset is their familiarity with donor procedures and accessibility to donor overtures. The implication is that such NGOs would not necessarily be in touch with or sympathetic to the range of NGO interests in-country. Related to this is a concern coming from more grassroot NGOs that umbrella NGOs simply reflect hierarchies of power in the society at large. Indeed, in several countries, umbrella organizations that are basically federations of large NGOs have emerged. However, these are being alienated from more grassroots organizations. This is because a very high proportion of the umbrella NGO funds come from outside (usually international) sources. Finally, umbrella NGOs have not escaped the problems of bureaucratization. From this perspective, working through umbrella NGOs may not offer significant advantages over working with state institutions directly.

The issue of funding is developing into a sensitive issue on several fronts. One reason is that NGOs in general are vulnerable to high dependence on individual donors. This is problematic, as will be noted, where ambiguity arises as to who "owns" the NGO. Where NGOs have or are believed to have political roles, the dependence on donor funding can compromise the integrity of the NGOs and of the evolving democratic processes of which they are presumably a part. The availability of funding—often actively promoted—has encouraged the formation of NGOs in several countries, but the organizations so formed and their explicit dependence on donor funding raise serious questions. In the Philippines, for example, a distinction is made between NGOs and POs. POs are people's organizations and are viewed as more authentic. NGOs may be people's organizations, but their authenticity is considered more tentative.

The issue of ownership follows from the issues of selection and funding. Donor selection represents more than a form of endorsement. In the political and funding environment throughout Southeast Asia, donor selection of an NGO often represents empowerment. Donor funding endows an NGO with the resources to function. In these circumstances, subtle problems can arrive on the part of the NGOs and those they deal with. Are the NGOs free associations acting independently or are they the agents of those who fund them? This question is often brought into sharp relief by donors themselves who take several steps that more closely bind the identity of the NGO to the donor. These steps range from high visibility and frequent visits to the NGO organized by the donor to incorporation of the NGO into the donor's budgeting practices. By insisting, for example, on exemption of the NGO from conventional in-country budgeting practices, the effect is to highlight that the NGO is in the donor's orbit.

As the democratization process unfolds, and as countries move into phases where relationships between political change, economic reform, and redefinition of citizenship and social rights become more open and politicized, the scope of voluntary group action may increase beyond technical matters to explicitly political issues. It will be important in these instances for donors to be cautious about what constitutes an NGO as compared, for example, to a political faction. This characterization cannot be based on some abstract classifications, but instead must be clearly based on an understanding of the political significance of these organizations in their own political and cultural contexts. This understanding will also have to make a distinction between a government's assignment of political significance to NGOs (a step that can come very fast) and an independent assessment that considers the validity of an assignment in terms of broader state-society relationships. At the same time, donors will need to give very careful attention to how relationships with NGOs can be best defined and managed from the perspective of contributing to the construction of a strong and independent civil sector. This raises issues not only for donors, but for recipient country governments as well, since they too may have interests in NGOs as "development partners."

Several implications follow. The clearest of these is that working with NGOs will require new forms of policy dialogue involving donors, governments, and NGOs. This issue has to be seen at several levels. Country-specific forums are needed, but these need to be trilateral—involving governments, donors, and NGOs. However, this will not always be feasible, especially where NGOs are viewed with suspicion by government and most especially where governments may see explicit alliances between donors and NGOs as political intervention. From another side, however, it is important to recognize that NGOs are often at the forefront of independent political activity and group action and are a foundation for the building of open political dialogue. From yet another side there is the complex issue of cooptation. NGOs have become very wary of their relationships with both their own governments and foreign donors and foundations. This is the reverse side of the ownership issue discussed earlier: the issue of NGOs having to sacrifice their independence as a price for funding and worse, as a cost of legitimation. The failure to handle this issue sensitively—especially by donors—can seriously complicate efforts to build independent group action.

Consequently, issues in the regulation and suppression of NGOs have become a key playing field for the formation of a civil society and not coincidentally also for the exercise of state resistance to expanding social and political rights. This establishes an important line, a line that holds significant promise from a democratization perspective, but which also holds considerable danger if the reality of the line is miscalculated or underestimated. For example, NGOs can be labeled by the state as political groups (rather than technical or charitable organizations only) early on. This kind of labeling in many parts of Southeast Asia can disqualify NGOs from receiving donor support (this would be political intervention) and from protected status in domestic political arenas as well (by virtue of being nonpolitical).

There is an important additional point. Where this line between strengthening the civil society and inviting repression actually lies across the region and is the core of a debate about the meaning of human rights in the Southeast Asian context. Donors must be careful about their involvement in this debate. However, one role donors can play is to support the process of regional norm-setting. Donors can recognize a need for regional forums across several countries that permit cross-national dialogue among NGOs as well as among governments and donors. Dialogues are needed in several forums beyond the traditional government-to-government mode: within donor governments, between officials and NGOs within donor countries, among international NGOs, among NGOs in one country, between government and NGOs in one country, expanding bilateral donor-recipient dialogues to include other parties (NGOs), and initiating regional multilateral dialogues involving donors, NGOs, and recipient country officials (on policies, not projects). Multilateral forums are important not as much for what they can contribute to consensus building (although this is important, especially in terms of norm-setting), but for the roles such forums can play in clarifying expectations that donors, recipients, NGOs, and others will have of each other.

Donor involvement with NGOs did not originally emerge as part of commitments to support democratization. In most cases, NGOs were seen as offering a more efficient alternative to state agencies for implementing projects addressing a range of rural development and rural resource management issues. This is still true, even given the link of NGOs to participatory development. This is because principles of participatory development have been applied by donors to projects, but not to the basic relationships between state and society. Nevertheless, NGOs are certainly a visible step into a democratization strategy. However, beyond the specifics of NGOs, what roles can donors play in the democratization process?

Promoting Democratization

As noted earlier, the studies that underlie this chapter emphasized the importance of avoiding the imposition of essentially imported strategies. Solutions and paths need to be found that will function within specific historical, political, and cultural circumstances. A second conclusion is that bilateral conditionalities to pressure democratization choices have been neither effective nor ethical. However, multilateral conditionalities, i.e., agreement and coordination among the donor community to support certain democratization paths, could be considerably more effective and can avoid the ethical problems of one country, in effect, dictating matters of domestic political choices to another country. The assumption in some quarters would be that the donor community as a whole is a more credible representative of wider norms than any individual bilateral donor. This interpretation can be applied, for example, to the role of the UNTAC in Cambodia.

However, it is unlikely that the donor community—even in the form of a multilateral approach—will always be able to substantiate a role in this area. Throughout the region, for example, the number of highly educated business people is growing. More generally, the size of the middle class in countries across the region is growing. These developments can be associated with greater demands for further government efficiency, less corruption, and possibly the adoption of democratic values. However, these developments can also be associated with greater confidence in the articulation of indigenous norms and the rejection of external imposed norms. Earlier waves of NGOs that focused on religious-philosophical and intellectual issues are being supplanted by a new wave of NGOs with stronger political orientations. These too can also be associated with possible commitments to democratic values, commitments as well to indigenously identified strategies for realizing these values, and suspicions about the roles of foreign capital and interests in domestic political processes. In this context, what is the role of foreign aid? Foreign capital, as such, is seen as supplementary, i.e., it is not necessarily seen as posing a problem for nationalism. The problem arises around perceived conditionalities. While most countries in the region have been willing to accept economic advice from donors, they have been much less willing to consider noneconomic conditionalities. This is not to say that nothing can be done. Several things can be done with existing foreign aid programming that have strong potential to support democratic processes.

First, one can ask who gets the foreign aid. Democratization can receive added support if more foreign aid goes to sectors such as health, education, and rural infrastructure—sectors that are more likely to reach the economically and politically less well off. Second, regional (within ASEAN for example) dialogues on good governance supported by foreign aid can help create a more conducive environment for democratization. The dialogue could consider perspectives on human rights. This would be especially valuable since there are presently no regional arrangements or forums for this purpose. Inadequate and obsolete norms and standards for good governance, democratization, and international arrangements within the region are creating a strong need to develop and operationalize norms and standards for good governance, democratization, and international cooperation in support of these. The absence of regional norms and of processes to develop such norms constitutes a significant impediment to sustainable international cooperation in support of democratization.

These points illustrate that the influence donors can have on democratization need not be confined to explicit patterns of influence on political reform in the political system. Another example resides in the relationships between the demands of economic growth and the requirements for political stability. Donors have often accepted the argument that economic growth requires soft authoritarianism. However, it is becoming increasingly apparent to many that this relationship is considerably more complex. For example, the early phases of macroeconomic reform appear to benefit from a political environment that does not subject the reforms to challenges from affected elites. However, as macroeconomic reforms proceed and sectoral reforms unfold, experience in Southeast Asia suggests that sustaining these reforms (rather than simply adopting or initiating them), requires forms of constituency development and mobilization that can benefit from processes of political liberalization and democratization. This point parallels the argument about the relationships between political stability and investor confidence. In the early stages, stability is undoubtedly a prerequisite for investor confidence. But past a certain point, authority is associated with bureaucratization, conservatism, and corruption—points that hardly strengthen investor confidence.

Consequently, while some argue for an Asian model of democracy based on soft authoritarianism, others notice it is governments and elements of the military and business sectors who are making these arguments. And indeed, the levels of political power concentration in several countries appear to be higher than what could be required by the imperatives of economic growth. These levels also exceed what could be required by the demands of internal security. The threat of communism and domestic insurgency, a significant issue in several countries in the 1950s and 1960s and one that justified strengthening state police powers, is no longer a significant force in the internal security prospects of most countries in Southeast Asia. The level of education has increased—a point that should imply an increasing level of tolerance for diverse political views. And the rise of middle classes has reduced tolerance for inefficiency and corruption.

Again, the challenge for donors in this context is not to impose their views, but on the other hand, not to restrict their understanding of the debate to what governments and their most obvious allies have to say. Donors have a legitimate responsibility to be aware of broader democratic processes operating in a society and to conduct their own affairs with sensibility to the consequences of their actions for those processes.

The Limits of Bilateral Influence

The role just described represents a significant challenge to contemporary donors in terms of their existing capabilities, usual strategies, and preferred modes of operation. Faced with this challenge, can the donor community effectively play what is a highly complex role? The donor community has, by and large, not been inclined to collectively and formally raise issues related to domestic political evolution within most countries of Southeast Asia (with the possible exception of China). When views are raised, they are usually raised informally and out of public view, or are contained in soft public statements of concern. Miscalculation here can lead to problems. For example, Japan's implied characterization of the May 1992 crackdown in Bangkok as normal politics by Thai standards widened the gap between Japan and many of the democratic forces in Thailand. Indonesia's break with Dutch aid after the Dutch government publicly critiqued the Indonesian government's behavior in Timor can be seen as an example of two points. First, recipient countries will not necessarily lightly tolerate public criticism of their political arrangements by aid donors—especially if there are hints of aid conditionality in the critique and if there are no other major mitigating economic factors at risk in the relationship between the donor and the recipient country. Second, aid donors who wish to maintain an active aid portfolio in a country should be cautious about how and where they offer views on internal political issues in a recipient country.

Given these sensitivities, and given until recently the preference of most donors to avoid direct programming in Southeast Asia on democratization, it is not surprising that both bilateral and multilateral discussions between donors and recipient countries have predominantly focused on matters of economics—economic policy reform, trade matters, foreign investment policies, external debt management, etc. Donor consultative group forums (for specific countries) offer an annual opportunity for donors and a recipient country government to review past performance and future plans and commitments but these meetings have exhibited serious limits as mechanisms for either conveying donor views on democratization progress or for domestic interests in a recipient country to somehow aggregate or voice their own perspectives to the donor community.[14]

An important distinction that should be made here is that between conditionality and facilitation. Throughout Southeast Asia, governments are not pleased with the specter of what they see as political conditionalities. On the other hand, there is considerable debate about facilitative roles donors can play. Some donors and international NGOs appear to prefer to become involved in direct support of the construction of political parties. They do this through various forms of technical and financial assistance and through encouraging affiliations in some cases with political parties in Europe. This is often both welcomed and opposed—in both cases for the resources and linkages it brings. Other donors and international NGOs get involved frequently in "turf" battles over which parts of the democratization process are "theirs." This competitive pattern is not restricted to democratization issues, of course, but on such issues it forces out problems of ownership discussed earlier and raises questions about the autonomy and even the integrity of local political groups so aided.

These patterns of donor involvement in local efforts at political change suggest that donors are not always clear about where the line is between intervention and facilitation. The studies suggest that donors should stick to facilitative issues (e.g., steps that help the public to become better informed about issues and choices in democratization processes), but donors should not become directly involved in support of political institution building. For example, donors can focus on the democratic fulcrum effects of their aid, i.e., the political consequences that might flow from specific areas of support (e.g., health, agriculture). This may resemble the historic focus on indirect strategies, but it should be noted that what is implied here is not simply restating an old rationale for investment in health, education, and infrastructure, but rather is calling for serious analysis of the impacts of project assistance on matters such as political participation. Facilitation is also advised on the grounds that in the end, it is crucial for domestic political interests to be able to say that they developed a strategy for democratization themselves. This would not exclude technical assistance on strategies and methods employed elsewhere, but from this perspective direct support of institution building is seen as inappropriate.

These are complex issues. Donors do not exhibit consistent practice within Southeast Asia on these issues. Many donors are strongly inclined (and politically propelled from domestic sources) to approach democratization issues through a norm-imposing approach. However, for other donors, dialogue strategies that take the shape of norm-imposing forums would not be acceptable. In these cases, donors are inclined to adopt a "soft" approach. This means that a donor would play a cautious role in the process of finding the core factors constituting democratization (and which it would promote), and in identifying those bottlenecks and constraints for which foreign aid can be a constructive part of a problem-solving strategy.

What Southeast Asia sees, however, is that some donors are troubled by the concept of a soft approach—however defined. These donors argue that a soft approach is too vulnerable to abuse, in effect rationalizing business as usual among those not especially interested in progress on democratization. Others argue that the concept of the soft approach is too vague. It implies applying the concept of democratization with multiple standards. The issue here is disagreements among donors and governments in Southeast Asia about how to understand what are the core factors constituting democracy.

It is also important to recognize that existing modes of foreign aid management by several donors present numerous limits on the capacity and relevance of foreign aid as a strategy for supporting democratization. Factors ranging from patterns of organization (such as characteristics of centralization and decentralization), staffing skills and distribution, relationships to nongovernmental groups in donor countries as well as in recipient countries, and the imperatives of budget cycles and contracting rules all have significant bearings on what a foreign aid system can actually do in terms of programming on democratization. At the least, for many donors, there is an increasingly pressing need to bring ends and means on democratization into closer correspondence. This point is apparent to many sectors in Southeast Asia.

However, this does not mean that bilateral influence is insignificant. For example, an important area where donors can influence the prospects for democratization comes from the relationships between the prospects for democratization and the deconcentration of domestic economic power. Donors have achieved considerable influence in areas of economic policy reform and these reforms, if extended to attacking distortions that reside in the structure of the economy as well as in the choice of inappropriate economic policies, would carry significant potential for positive impacts on prospects for democratization.

Where donors have been weak, however, is in recognizing that economic policy reform is only one side of the coin in reorienting an economy to more market-oriented principles. The other side of the coin is the structure of the economy, represented by the concentration of economic power and the rules for entry, competition, collusion, and exit that characterize the private sector. While economic policy reforms can certainly alter the incentives and signals that government sends to the economy, the relationships between government and the economy are hardly this simple or unilinear. The political economies in Southeast Asia are considerably more complex and if economic change is to have an impact on the distribution of political power, then there is no sidestepping the importance of the need to reform the organization of economic power. The issue here, of course, is whether donors have either the capacity or the will to embrace this challenge—especially in the growing and increasingly powerful economies of Southeast Asia.

CONCLUSION

There is an increasingly vocal discussion in Southeast Asia about the quality of society as an indicator of developmental success. However, a fundamental and contentious difference remains to be settled: Whose concept of quality will pertain? Specifically, there is wide discussion both in and about Southeast Asia that questions the applicability and appropriateness for Southeast Asia of Western understandings of democracy, democratization, and human rights. Broadly speaking, two sides to the discussion can be identified.

On one side is the belief that there is a unique Asian perspective on democratization, democracy, and human rights. This perspective represents a set of historical and cultural experiences which, while significantly influenced by the West through colonialism and more recently communications and trade, is nevertheless distinct. This distinctiveness along with the premise that the political system of any society—if it is to be authentic—has to reflect and be consistent with the deeper cultural themes of that society, leads to the conclusion that Western liberal democracy in both its minimalist and maximalist forms, is inappropriate. Asian experience, according to this perspective, plays down the importance of individual rights and especially the role of the individual as the legitimate arbiter of a political order and gives preeminence to the imperatives of economic growth, social unity, and political stability. This is the so-called "consensual" model. The "worth" of democracy is not denied, but rather is defined in terms of the responsiveness of a government to the imperatives of economic growth, social unity, and political stability—imperatives because these goals bring the greatest benefits to the largest number.

On the other side is the argument that the impetus for democratization, democracy, and human rights reflects an ethical universalism, a global endorsement of democracy as a normative good accessible to all. This ethical universalism—as a moral principle—is not seen as "foreign" to Southeast Asia but rather as convergent with emerging political and social forces within Southeast Asia. This ethical universalism, however, does not mandate precise reproduction of specific institutional strategies employed elsewhere nor, in fact, does it mandate foreign intervention in the name of external standards. What it does say, however, is that the imperatives of democratization cannot be satisfied by the substitution of what amount to antidemocratic philosophies. From this perspective, the ethical universalism in favor of democracy and democratization can be defined as referring to certain core values. How these values are institutionalized can reflect the diversity of particular historical and cultural contexts without violating the meaning of the values, but the core values—by definition—cannot be said to vary.

The studies summarized here do not categorically resolve this argument, but they do make two important points with direct relevance to the argument. First, the desire for wider democratization in Southeast Asia along lines that are recognizable globally is stronger than many elites apparently are prepared to accept. The major evidence against the claimed desire for wider democratization—the claimed support for the principle of diversity and the preservation of unity and stability—is certainly compelling, but the studies suggest this evidence is problematic as a counterweight to democratization.

Undoubtedly there is diversity between the West and Southeast Asia, but the deeper issue is the significance of diversity within individual societies. Ethnic, religious, and cultural diversity are recognized as potential problems for social stability and the integrity of the nation itself, but the studies suggest that what matters is the political significance assigned to diversity and, more specifically, the political processes that assign and maintain this significance. The core of the political implications of diversity resides in definitions of the nation. The studies suggest that it is certainly possible to embrace strategies to manage ethnic, religious, and cultural diversity through restricted definitions of nationhood. There are two dangers, however, with this strategy. One is that maintaining class differences and elite defense of their political and economic prerogatives are often masked as strategies to preserve the nation. In effect, rather than "preserving" diversity, politics in these cases creates diversity for purposes of defining who are excluded. The second is that there is not clear evidence that strategies to manage diversity by definitions of nationhood that concentrate on ethnic, cultural, or religious status rather than civil status have been correlated with or principally responsible for either social unity or political stability.

At the same time, identifying a point that is shared by the opposing sides in the argument, the studies conclude it is crucial for Southeast Asia's societies to find their own ways to realize and institutionalize emerging democratic values. For donor countries, this requires recognition that there is indigenous support for and, indeed, conceptualization of democratic values and processes in Southeast Asia. The challenge this establishes is for donors to spend less time encouraging the transfer of their own experience or measuring the conformance of Asian political processes by the criteria of their own experience. Instead, donors need to spend more time on understanding indigenous democratic processes within Asian countries and the impacts of the donor country's overall relationship with a country on the prospects for democratic elements in that country.

For all this to happen, however, there needs to be greater agreement on norms for the core values of democracy, democratization, and human rights than there is now. There also needs to be a greater effort to construct a dialogue for norm-setting that reaches beyond established elites. These steps will not come easily, even among Asian countries themselves. Without efforts to establish norms based on a broad dialogue, however, donor efforts to support democratization in Southeast Asia are likely to be reactive, of very limited value, and arguably only marginally effective at best. The studies confirm that forces are operating within Southeast Asia's societies that can be associated with an emerging process of democratization. Donors will need to learn how to understand these forces without compromising them.

Finally, donors will also need to give serious attention to the implications of international relations within the region on prospects for democratization. In the same way that norm-setting is required with regard to the core values of democracy, democratization, and human rights, norm-setting will also be needed to establish the core values of security. This point is crucial for two reasons.

First, processes of norm-setting involving dialogue—especially between donors and countries in Southeast Asia—will need to face very clearly the realities of differences in understandings about both the importance of culture as well as the significance of cultural differences. Cultures in Southeast Asia generally assign less importance to confrontation, competition, and change than cultures in the West. Concepts of security may vary accordingly, with greater concerns about the preservation of certain core cultural values than the impregnability of physical borders (although the latter would never be unimportant). As discussed earlier, one problem for donors will be to assess whether the core values associated with security are for a culture as a whole or for the maintenance of specific power arrangements within a culture.[15]

Second, there are serious democratic forces within Southeast Asia. However, the most subtle danger to their health is the growing possibility that redefinition of security within Southeast Asia will incorporate notions of democracy based on the principles of unity, stability, and consensual politics. The results will be to strengthen the legitimacy of "soft authoritarianism" as the "Asian way," preserve the notion of diversity as problematic, deepen the role of the state as interpreter of the imperatives of economic growth and political stability, and weaken the possibilities for an emergent civil society.

NOTES

1. The papers are: Bruce Koppel and Chai-Anan Samudavanija, *Democracy and Democratization in Southeast Asia: Imposition or Evolution?*; Mohamed Jawhar, *Problems and Prospects for Transitions in Governance and Democratization: Malaysia*; Mikoto Usui, Yasunori Sone, Shinsuke Hirai, Ken Fujimura, Naonobu Minato, and Yumi Horikane, *Challenges and Opportunities for Innovations in Policy Dialogue and ODA Management*; Djisman Simandjuntak and Amir Santoso, *Problems and Prospects for Transition and Democratization in Indonesia*; Muthiah Alagappa, *The Political-Security System in the Pacific: Towards a New Equilibrium*; Chai-Anan Samudavanija, *Problems and Prospects for Transitions in Governance and Democratization in Thailand*; Carolina G. Hernandez, *Problems and Prospects for Transition in Governance and Democratization: A Case Study on the Philippines*; Doh C. Shin, *On the Global Wave of Democratization: A Synthesis of Recent Research Findings*.

2. Indonesia, Nepal, the Philippines, and Vietnam.

3. Australia, Canada, Germany, Japan, Sweden, and the United States.

4. Foundation for Advanced Studies in International Development, *International Workshop on Democratization and Economic Development in Asia* (Tokyo: July 2–3, 1992).

5. For a recent example, see the very provocative article by Margaret Somers: "Citizenship and the Place of the Public Sphere: Law, Community, and Political Culture in the Transition to Democracy," *American Sociological Review*, vol. 58 (October 1993), pp. 587–620.

6. For example, the establishment of the *Batasan Pambansa* by Marcos did create a representative institution, but the process that did this had far more to do with the consolidation of authoritarian power in the Philippines than it did with democratization.

7. For further discussion on this point, see: Bruce Koppel, "The Politics of Economic Reform: Insights from Indonesia, the Philippines and Thailand," in David Timberman, ed., *The Politics of Economic Reform in Southeast Asia* (Manila: Asian Institute of Management, 1992), pp. 117–147.

8. The term NGOs refers to "nongovernment organizations."

9. NGO umbrella organizations are usually based in capital cities and are especially interested in either administering or brokering development project contracts from international aid agencies and foundations. They have become a favored agent for these purposes.

10. Along with China and Bangladesh, Malaysia took the lead in pushing for the exclusion of NGOs from the Vienna conference on human rights.

11. A good recent discussion is: Joseph Held, ed., *Democracy and Right-Wing Politics in Eastern Europe in the 1990s* (New York: Columbia University Press, 1992).

12. The term "never" is used because although considerable aid (especially to Indochina in the 1950s and 1960s) was rationalized as supporting democracy and in some instances was

increased because of political reforms in those states, overall these steps are more properly characterized as support for anti-communism rather than support for democratization per se. Similarly, considerable support to Pakistan and the Philippines in the 1970s and 1980s was occasionally advertised as support for democratization, but its primary purposes were related to international and regional security issues. Finally, the efforts of several donors during the 1980s to encourage economic policy reforms supportive of more market-oriented economic processes were sometimes described in terms of their consequences for democratization, but these consequences were not the pivoting point for the determination of how much aid would be provided or when it would be released.

13. One strategy recognized (although not necessarily equally feasible) in most countries is grassroots research, which generates greater understanding of how the social sector is configured and performing. The term "grassroots" is used to convey the importance of getting a perspective that is from the foundations of an emerging civil society. A second strategy proceeds from the need to recognize that prospects for democratic outcomes in specific countries reflect the peculiarities of different histories. This argues for qualitatively oriented case studies developed along lines that are very sensitive to indigenous concepts and concerns.

14. Actually, in most cases the donor groups have not been especially effective even for coordinating donor policies on economic issues. In principle, what made the Philippine multilateral aid initiative different was that there were explicit commitments to coordination and monitoring.

15. The same point can be made, of course, about similar debates within donor countries (e.g., McCarthyism and the "Moral Majority" in the United States, xenophobic neo-Nazism in Germany, etc.).

7 GOVERNMENT AND BUSINESS IN THAILAND

Daniel Unger

Institutions linking state and society help to affect both political and economic processes. Particularly critical are those institutions tying business and government. The effectiveness of these institutions helps to determine the relative success national economies achieve in exploiting the challenges posed by the international economy. The particular form of the institutions is a critical factor influencing the development of a country's political system. In this chapter I describe the broad forces shaping business-government relations in Thailand. I begin, however, by discussing in general terms the differences between business-government ties in Southeast Asia (Indonesia, Malaysia, the Philippines, and Thailand) and Northeast Asia (South Korean, Taiwan), as well as the differences among the former group. I then go on to analyze in greater detail the patterns of cooperation and conflict between business and government in Thailand. In the conclusion, I suggest how those patterns will influence Thai economic and political development.

James Steuart, the eighteenth century Scottish political economist, observed that:

Trade and industry . . . owed their establishment to the ambition of princes . . . principally with a view to enrich themselves, and thereby to become formidable to their neighbors. But they did not discover, until experience taught them, that the wealth they drew from such fountains was but the overflowing of the spring; and that an opulent, bold, and spirited people, having the fund of the prince's wealth in their own hands, have it also in their own power, when it becomes their inclination, to shake off his authority. The consequence of this change has been the introduction of a more mild, and a more regular plan of administration.

When once a state begins to subsist by the consequences of industry, there is less danger to be apprehended from the power of the sovereign. The mechanism of his administration becomes more complex, and . . . he finds himself so bound up by the laws of his political economy, that every transgression of them runs him into new difficulties.[1]

Steuart's description of an entrepreneurial class throwing off the shackles of state absolutism is a classic statement of the rise of capitalist classes in the early industrializing nations: traditional landed authority, in its greed, became dependent on the golden goose of industry and was compelled to refrain from suffocating it. In time, the rising forces associated with the new urban economies were able to shake off monarchical authority and establish their own rule.[2] Inherent in this interpretation of political changes accompanying the rise of capitalism is a conflict of interest between the state and at least some sectors of society over the extent and nature of state intervention in the economy as well as over the right to rule.[3]

This stylized sequence of historical events and the relationship between the state and private capital contrasts sharply with that in many late industrializing nations. And state-society relations in the late industrializers of Northeast Asia (Japan, South Korea, Taiwan) contrast even more sharply with Steuart's model.[4] As in the other late industrializers, the entrepreneurs of Northeast Asia were not prepared for the tasks of catch-up industrialization. Therefore, state officials in Japan, and later in South Korea and Taiwan, set about strengthening domestic capital to enhance national autonomy, as well as regime legitimacy. State elites sought the most effective wealth-creating instruments available to them, including markets, concentration of market power (this was less true in Taiwan)[5] and, to greater and lesser degrees,[6] the regulated participation of foreign capital.

Whereas capitalists in the early industrializing nations won jurisdictional victories limiting state power, in the late industrializers the states used capital and capitalists in pursuit of substantive development goals. The resulting differences in the states' economic roles are characterized by Johnson as the regulatory and the developmental state.[7] As Johnson notes, "The very idea of the developmental state originated in the situational nationalism of the late industrializers, and the goals of the developmental state were invariably derived from comparisons with external reference economies."[8] In the late industrializer, the state is not a regulator gradually taking on additional functions neglected by the normal operations of the market. Rather, it acts as a vanguard forced "to drag a complaining, half-awakened nation of merchants and peasants after them."[9]

This distinction between developmental and regulatory state is broadly consistent with that made by Lindblom who notes that polyarchies seek to constrain rather than mobilize authority.[10] Lindblom argues that in capitalist societies critical (investment) decisions are privatized. Hence, entrepreneurs can be viewed as public functionaries.[11] In the Northeast Asian late industrializers, the perception that private investments yielded collective goods helped to establish a normative basis for close cooperation between entrepreneurs and state officials.

Business-government links in Southeast Asia, however, appear to differ significantly from those in Northeast Asia. Yoshihara, for example, argues that in the former, rent seeking is the principal concern of entrepreneurs.[12] As a result, economic expansion fails to generate a self-sustaining dynamic driven by indigenous technological capabilities. Instead of authentic capitalists, Yoshihara sees rent-seekers, crony and bureaucratic capitalists.[13] This assessment echoes the earlier judgment of Norman Jacobs who, looking at Thai economic growth in the 1960s, saw "growth without development."[14] Why, in these scholars' views, should Southeast Asia fail to produce authentic capitalism? The explanation generally centers on the survival of traditional patrimonial norms that persist because of the ethnic cleavages in Southeast Asian countries between indigenous political and Chinese economic elites. In fact, however, with the partial exception of the Philippines, these countries have undergone dramatic shifts in the nature of dominant political norms, the role of ethnicity in national politics, the extent to which politically favored actors are able to reap profits free from significant competition, in the broad regulatory framework within which economic activity takes place, and in the nature of business-government ties. As economic growth becomes an increasingly prominent policy goal, these states less frequently "resort to approaches that can be regarded as 'making policy by default.'"[15]

The Southeast Asian cases considered here also, of course, vary in their respective institutions and the nature of links between business and government. These differences help to account for divergent economic performances (see table 1).

Indonesia and Malaysia both rely on elements of corporatist strategies through which political elites can channel communications with business and other social groups. In the Indonesian case, this corporatism rests on "functional" groups (e.g., farmers, labor, women) and is more statist (top-down) in nature. In Malaysia, by contrast, corporatist groups are ethnically based, somewhat more autonomous, and their organization to some degree predates the efforts of state elites to coopt them. Relative to the Philippines and Thailand, however, Indonesia and Malaysia both have relatively insulated, technocratic policymaking processes dominated, in Indonesia, by the Cabinet, the Economic Stabilization Council, and the Monetary Board, and, in Malaysia, by the Economic Planning Unit. These agencies are closely tied to the executive's authority in both countries. They do not, however, reflect the cohesion and concentration of economic policymaking authority seen, for example, in South Korea and Taiwan.

The degree of insulation of economic policymaking in the Philippines and Thailand has varied over time, depending on the government in power. Some Thai governments have been able to insulate technocratic decision making to a great extent, while others have been either unable or disinterested in providing such distance between particular pressures and the policy process. In the Philippines, even when executive authority has provided such insulation (under Marcos), the effects have been more malign than otherwise as Marcos's policy preferences were far from consistent with those of economic development in the Philippines.

In all four Southeast Asian cases, state officials concerned to have access to foreign exchange and government revenue had an easier time of it than did their counterparts in South Korea and Taiwan. Looking within the four, the "easiest" case has been Indonesia while the Philippines has been the "hard-

TABLE 1
Economic Performance of Southeast Asian States

	Average Annual % Growth in GDP 1960–1990	Recent Expansion in Exports ($billions) 1986	1991
Indonesia	3.2	14.8	29.1
Malaysia	3.95	14	34.4
Philippines	1.4	4.8	8.8
Thailand	4.81	8.9	27.6

Source: Vinod Thomas and Yan Wang, *The Lessons of East Asia, Government Policy and Productivity Growth, Is East Asia an Exception?* (Washington, DC: World Bank, 1993), p. 14; ASEAN Centre, *ASEAN-Japan Statistical Pocketbook* (Tokyo: ASEAN Centre, 1993), p. 19.

est." Reaping revenue has been relatively easy (compared to the Northeast Asian cases) for all four because each has been able at various times to rely heavily on exports of agricultural and mineral commodities. In Indonesia, the combination of a small and politically docile Chinese business class, military-backed rule, and enormous gas and oil reserves have made the tasks of realizing revenue relatively easy (ignoring the arguably far more difficult development and governance tasks Indonesian elites have faced). Malaysian state officials have enjoyed neither the same military backing, nor have the Chinese been as quiescent, nor has the energy sector been as dominant. Rather, Malaysian officials have had to rely on the export of commodities produced under concentrated, private ownership (e.g., rubber plantations). In Thailand, the business class has become increasingly assertive politically and the energy sector provides little revenue and no foreign exchange. Commodity exports, however, particularly in the past (rice), were privately owned but ownership was fragmented so that producers faced enormous collective action problems in mobilizing for political action. The Philippines has posed the greatest difficulty given a strong business class and government dependence on privately owned, but relatively concentrated ownership of, commodity exports.

In contrast to the imagery of the capitalist developmental state in which the state elite acts as a modernizing vanguard, the evolution of state-society relations in Thailand is tracing a path more reminiscent of the early industrializers. The Thai case, however, is distinctive in that state restraint is less a result of the rise of the political power of capital than of the state's eventual choice of restraint as a means of limiting intra-elite competition as well as a means of development. That choice resulted from a mixture of ideological appeal among Thai technocrats and influential foreign advisers and institutions, the evident failure by the 1960s of a more activist state strategy,[16] and the particular context of political struggle when Field Marshal

Sarit Thanarat came to power and laid the political and institutional bases for rapid growth in Thailand in the early 1960s.

Politics in Thailand are perhaps most accurately represented by a pluralist model of the state in which policy outcomes result from a process of bargaining among elites pursuing divergent goals:

The so-called liberal policy of Thailand thus appears more like classical liberalism, where business is guided by the hidden hand of competition mainly because checks and balances make the government relatively weak, than like a modern liberal policy of using the price system as a regulating and decentralizing instrument.[17]

In the words of former Prime Minister Anand Panyarachul, Thailand features "laissez-faire by accident."[18] The confusion of policies in Thailand amid a tangle of bureaucratic agencies allowed Thailand's energetic Sino-Thai entrepreneurs, in concert with foreign capital, to exploit a large domestic market behind protectionist tariffs. Particularly beginning in the 1980s, Thailand's approach has attracted foreign capital on a far larger scale, propelling Thailand's industrial expansion.

Scholars have made a great deal of the absence in Asia, with the critical exception of Japan, of feudal societies. Indeed, Jacobs' work on Thailand, *Modernization Without Development*, opens with the question:

Why have the societies of Asia, with the notable exception of Japan, in spite of tremendous changes and despite the considerable advisory and material aid which they have received, especially in recent decades, not developed?[19]

Muscat and Jacobs emphasized the patrimonial nature of the Thai elite in explaining the lack of Thai economic development from the mid-nineteenth century to the mid-twentieth century.[20] Muscat also noted that for 80 years Thailand ran trade surpluses to balance its exports of capital, primarily remittances to China by resident Chinese.[21] During those years capital goods imports were limited while there were considerable imports of gold bullion. State development investment was modest[22] and, in general, "the government played an unusually passive role in the country's economic development."[23] Most important, however, was the absence of a legal and normative framework conducive to capitalist development, particularly guarantees that the state would not compete with or in other ways harass private sector producers.[24]

In order to examine the issues introduced, I now turn to a more detailed analysis of the Thai case. In the following section I discuss the (minimal) role of the Thai state in guiding the economy, the impact of Chinese-Thai political accommodation, the organization of Thai business interests, and the partial exclusion of both the military and much of rural Thailand from a new business-government compact.

STATE ROLE IN THE ECONOMY

With the exception of relatively brief and unsuccessful periods of extensive state ownership of the economy, private owners have dominated economic activity in Thailand. In 1955, state officials reprivatized the rice trade, the heart of the Thai economy at that time. Previously, the government Rice Bureau had controlled that trade. As the international market became more competitive, however, the government turned the rice trade over to the private sector, thereby cutting sharply the potential for rent-seeking by bureaucrats and politicians.

Privately owned commercial banks have dominated Thailand's financial sector. Neither has the state played an important indirect role in mandating credit allocation. State officials have contained growth of the Thai public sector, including slower rises in public employment during the 1980s. Under Prime Minister Prem Tinsulanonda in the 1980s, the government instituted zero-growth budgets. With revenue growth and state surpluses in the late 1980s, fiscal austerity has been abandoned. Nonetheless, state spending as a share of GDP remains modest (see table 2).

In the 1980s and into the 1990s, Thai officials have worked to reduce further the extent of state ownership of the economy, and to sell off state-owned enterprises. The latter effort has met numerous obstacles. Nonetheless, officials have sold some state firms and have made progress even with successful, profitable ventures such as Thai Airways International and the Electrical Generating Authority of Thailand.[25] The 63 remaining state-owned firms, as a group, run profits and employ just over a quarter of a million workers. As Thai officials attempted in the late 1980s to rapidly expand the country's badly overstrained infrastructure, the impetus to privatize grew stronger. Planned expansion of port facilities as well as urban mass transportation schemes involve privately run concessions.[26] Unfortunately, as a result of political conflicts and overlapping jurisdictions, for the most part these have been no more successful than public sector efforts.

An overall sense of the limited direct state role in the economy is evident in table 2.

Thailand's economy is dominated by market forces. The country is basically open to foreign trade, although tariff levels until very recently remained fairly high (see table 3). This was largely due to the Thai state's dependence on trade taxes for revenue. Tariff policies have aimed at bringing the country's current account into balance, industrial promotion, and revenue collection. Recent state budget surpluses provided the government with opportunities to move decisively in cutting tariffs: those that previously ranged from 5 percent to 60 percent ad valorem are scheduled for sharp cuts. In September 1990, the Chatichai government reduced machinery duties from 30–35 percent to 5 percent. The Anand government reduced duties on raw

TABLE 2

Relative Shares of Private and Public Ownership (%)

	FY 1982	FY 1984	FY 1986	FY 1988
Consolidated public spending and net lending*	24.9	24.0	24.5	21.7
Private spending and net lending	75.1	76.0	75.5	78.3

*Includes central and local governments and state firms.
Source: From Kraiyudht Dhiratayakinant.[27]

materials as well as automobiles.[28] And Thailand's commitment to the ASEAN Free Trade Area will require further major tariff cuts into the next century.

To what extent are businesses in Thailand dominated by rent-seeking entrepreneurs intent on using state protection and subsidization? Kunio Yoshihara argues that this posture characterizes businesses throughout Southeast Asia.[29] In Thailand, however, many sectors of the economy are dominated by private interests who enjoy only modest support from government officials. In many cases, that support does not extend to assuring against the entrance of new firms posing competitive challenges.

State officials long have protected the Thai financial sector from competition. Nonetheless, in recent years that competition has become more significant, particularly as larger firms gain access to foreign sources of loans or local direct finance through the booming equities market. The privileges that banks enjoyed in the 1950s and 1960s are largely a thing of the past. At that time, banks provided revenue sources for competing political cliques.[30] Bankers would include top government officials on the boards of directors of banks and related firms. The banks also helped to finance the 100 state enterprises that constituted another base of wealth for the politicians. The most important case of this pattern concerned the Bank of Ayudhya's association with the National Economic Development Corporation (NEDCOL), a holding company for five manufacturing firms run by the dominant (Phin-Phao) clique that Marshal Sarit ousted in coming to power in the late 1950s.[31]

The links with politicians also were helpful to the banks. Government officials rented out protection against ethnic nationalist threats that the officials themselves had created. Through this process, the Chinese were at times able to use discriminatory policies in their favor, obtaining state resources in exchange for the provision of benefits to government officials.[32] A case in point was the Bangkok Bank's success in convincing the Ministry of Finance to increase the government's share in the bank's registered capital to 60 percent in 1953.[33]

There are few formal restrictions on freedom of entry into business activities. The Ministry of Industry is responsible for issuing factory licenses, but

TABLE 3

Effective Tariff Rates of Protection for Selected Industrial Groups

agriculture	15.88	plastic products	213.36
food	97.65	glass and glass goods	115.39
textiles	307.35	iron and steel	62.93
leather	119.33	machinery	111.29
chemical products	94.39	electrical machinery and appliances	80.27

Source: Mehdi Krongkaew, "Recent Economic Management and Structural Adjustments in Thailand," Foundation for Advanced Information Research Conference in Fukuoka, August 1989.

in most sectors this represents only a nuisance factor. More important has been the practice of awarding Board of Investment (BoI) privileges. In many cases, business executives have viewed privileges as necessary to overcome various disincentives in Thai tariff and tax structures. In situations where some firms have access to privileges, those without comparable access can be working at an insuperable disadvantage. Moreover, during most periods the BoI has discriminated systematically against smaller firms.

Thai academics long have criticized various BoI policies. When in office, Prime Minister Chatichai also attacked the BoI, talking of dismantling it altogether. The Anand government took steps to reduce the Board's influence. Most important, by reducing tariff and tax rates, the Anand government sharply cut the number of disincentives that needed to be overcome and which made Board privileges important.

The weaknesses of BoI policies, as well as Ministry of Industry licensing of factories, have been evident in the development of the Thai textile industry. Since the adoption of import-substituting policies in the late 1950s, the state has shown no commitment to liberalizing textile policies, on the one hand, and little ability to rationalize promotional policies, on the other. While the state employs capacity controls, rarely does it do so according to a long-term plan for development of the industry. Even with a plan, state officials generally lack the requisite data for successful implementation. In any case, firms often bypass controls. Firms' ability to evade controls does not mean, however, that regulations are essentially neutral. Their limited effectiveness is sufficient to stifle the industry's capacity to respond to changes in demand. And the ability to overcome state controls is not distributed evenly among all producers. With large producers better able to avoid restrictions, those firms' dominance grows. Controls also result in imbalances in industrial structure.

Control of entry in the financial sector represents a special case given concerns about the stability of the economy and issues of moral hazard. For these reasons, as well as the considerable political clout of the country's commercial banks, financial officials have been reluctant until recently to issue any new banking licenses. State officials have overcome the resulting financial rigidities, in part, by allowing the expansion of the unregulated finance and securities companies beginning in the 1970s. These grew rapidly and precipitated the crash of the local stock market and, eventually, led to a massive bailout by state officials of financial institutions in the 1980s.

A tradition of conservative fiscal and monetary policies long has dominated in Thailand. This stemmed partly from the effects of neocolonialism on the Thai economy in the nineteenth century. Thai technocrats, for their part, often used their links to foreign sources of funds to limit raids on the Thai treasury by local politicians. In some instances, technocrats opted for foreign loans bearing higher rates of interest because auditing requirements for those loans helped the technocrats guard against politicians' abuse of state funds. While the state also enjoys considerable control over the budgetary process, its autonomy is more pronounced in the area of monetary policy, largely due to the role of the Bank of Thailand. Thai political leaders have most consistently delegated to technocrats financial and monetary policymaking.

The Bank of Thailand (BoT) enjoyed high status from its origins as a result of its having deterred Japanese economic domination during the war and maintained its own professional integrity during a period in which inflation and smuggling encouraged corruption among civil servants. To encourage its independence, the government placed the BoT outside normal bureaucratic control and granted its personnel salaries significantly higher than those in the civil service. The BoT's position was also strengthened by the quality of its leaders. Central bank influence also drew on its linkages with the IMF and World Bank (which it joined in 1949). The BoT was able to use consultations with and loans from these institutions to limit corruption and inflationary spending.

The leading Thai technocrats in the 1960s were not so much concerned with economic growth as with maintaining stability. In his study of money and banking in Thailand based on research from that time, Silcock noted that:

> throughout most of its existence the Bank of Thailand has been preoccupied with maintaining the external and internal value of the baht, and only recently has its leadership become concerned with economic growth.[34]

Economic technocrats dominate the Thai budgetary process. The role of the legislature in shaping fiscal policies is very limited. Thai budgeting does not appear to be subject to any electoral cycles.[35] (One result of this is that politicians are forced to use sectoral policies[36] to gain the pork they need to sustain their bases of support and to buy access to high-level political positions.) The National Education and Social Development Board (NESDB), the Bureau of Budget and the Fiscal Policy Office within the Ministry of Finance draft the budget and submit it to the prime minister who then submits it to the

Cabinet. The Cabinet acts as a rubber stamp. Of the other actors in the process, all are technocrats with the occasional exception of the finance minister. The budget then is sent to the various ministries, but their influence also tends to be very limited. When the government then presents the budget to the legislature, it must act quickly and based on little information. In any case, the legislature's powers are limited to making cuts in allocations: it cannot dictate additional spending.

Technocrats under Prem tried to implement various tax reforms, including establishing overall tax neutrality. The Anand government enjoyed considerable success in implementing the unfinished agenda from the Prem years, including greater tax neutrality. Most crucially, the government finally adopted the long discussed value-added tax. The government of Chuan Leekpai, however, suggests the persistence of a pattern in which technocrats enjoy considerable autonomy in making macroeconomic policies, but politicians have free rein to dole out privileges in other policy areas.

Overall, Thailand has enjoyed considerable stability in economic policy. The government generally has implemented policy shifts in an incremental fashion. The stability of prices has helped policymakers avoid the necessity of sharp swings in policy and has helped businesses concerned to predict the impact on their investments. An exception to the general rule of policy incrementalism was the sharp (by Thai standards) devaluation of the baht in 1984. While recognition of the necessity of a devaluation was widespread, most did not expect it to occur until the following year. The resulting hue and cry was impressive. By now it is widely agreed that this step had a beneficial impact, along with the further devaluation resulting from the weight of the dollar in the basket of currencies against which the baht moves, on the Thai export boom of the late 1980s.

As we have seen, Thai politicians, to greater and lesser degrees, have protected Thai technocrats from excessive political or social pressures, leaving the technocrats free to pursue stable macroeconomic policies. A variety of factors has made this possible,[37] including what Callaghy refers to as "internal cohesion," such as "informal recruitment and performance networks," that is, "the fusion of connection and competence." Thailand has only more recently, however, moved toward forging links between bureaucratic and social groups, including business.[38]

Stable macroeconomic policies have provided the fundamental conditions for rapid capital accumulation and enhanced economic efficiency in Thailand. To build on these conditions, however, Thai business and government elites also had to achieve a stable political accommodation among their interests. Further, economic growth transformed Thai society and required ongoing adjustments in the business-government relationship. Thai elites achieved the first of these steps in the early 1960s. The second step involves a longer process, one that began in the mid-1970s and continues today. While Bangkok-based business leaders and government officials have been developing increasingly cooperative relations, other social (labor, farmers) and regional (beyond Bangkok) groups largely have been excluded from this new accommodation.[39]

STATE-SOCIETY RELATIONS IN THAILAND

It is natural to couple a discussion of the Chinese in Thailand with a history of the country's economic development. As Suehiro notes,

The growth of capitalism and wage labour in Southeast Asia is essentially related to the history of overseas Chinese.[40]

Chinese have been coming to Thailand for centuries in a variety of capacities.[41] The major immigrations, however, occurred late in the nineteenth century and early this century, peaking in the 1920s, and effectively halting in 1949. Eager to earn money, the Chinese initially were free agents operating outside the system of Thai values and the largely commodity-producing economy.

A critical step in realizing a modus vivendi between Thai and Chinese elites, and hence between business and government elites, was the practice of having leading Thai politicians and bureaucratic elites serve on the boards of directors of Chinese firms.[42] This provided Thai leaders with incomes sufficient to support their political followers and thereby reduced incentives to create state enterprises to serve that function. For the Chinese, having Thai elites serve on the boards of their firms offered guarantees against arbitrary state action against their interests. It also offered the hope of reaping inside contracts and privileged information. While this arrangement was not satisfactory in the long term (a business could be hurt, and some were, by associating with members of a losing political faction), it was of critical importance in establishing the new bases for economic growth in Thailand.

The institutionalization of this protection racket limited competition between Chinese in procuring patronage while establishing cooperation between the two sets of elites.[43] Both sets of elites shared common interests, most importantly the desire to promote the interests of their firms. A less positive legacy was the tradition of using political connections to assure state protection, monopoly status, or other privileges. While this tradition threatened long-term Thai economic growth, its collapse in the late 1950s cleared the way for rapid expansion.

Under Sarit, relations between the Thai and Chinese improved dramatically. Local Chinese responded to the new investment incentives and increased their involvement in manufacturing, often in joint-ventures with

Japanese firms. Sarit curried close relations with the Chinese Chamber of Commerce.[44] He declared the state would neither create new enterprises nor compete with private investors who were granted investment promotional privileges. As Muscat observes,

Probably the single most important development policy by any Thai government in the past forty years was the decision of the Sarit regime around 1958–1959 to repudiate the Thai ethnocentric state dirigisme—economic intervention and the creation of state commercial and industrial enterprises to preempt economic development from non-Thai control—that had marked socioeconomic policy since the coup that ended the absolute monarchy in 1932.[45]

Since the 1950s, the Chinese business community has moved from being a pariah to establishing itself as the backbone of Thailand's industrial and commercial community. Sino-Thais not only control almost all of the largest firms and financial institutions in Thailand, but also dominate the major trade associations, including peak organizations such as the JPPCC.[46] Sino-Thais with roots in business are increasingly well represented in Thai politics, dominating the main political parties and increasing business representation in parliament and in the Cabinet.[47] In addition, trade associations have become more assertive in expressing business policy preferences.[48] The easing of communal tensions has made possible a dependence on private enterprise without which Thailand's economy could not have performed well given the considerable limitations on its administrative capabilities.

Successful Thai-Chinese accommodation has been of fundamental importance for Thai economic growth. Chinese entrepreneurial energy has been critical in bringing the peasantry into the market economy, in establishing and supporting manufacturing industries, in attracting foreign capital to Thailand, and in finding overseas markets for Thai exports. Van Roy argues that during the nineteenth-century rice export boom,

the Chinese played the crucial role of culture broker, serving as the link and buffer between the international market and the indigenous entourage arrangement.[49]

In many respects this same kind of argument holds true even today. In the broadest terms, the Chinese were clearly outward-oriented long before most indigenous Thais and used their external links to develop economic ties between the Thai and international economies.

The easing of communal tensions has made possible a dependence on private enterprise that has produced Thailand's rapid economic growth. Coexistence among Chinese and Thai elites, as well as the communist victory in China in 1949, which foreclosed continued access by Sino-Thai to their original communities, stemmed capital outflows from Thailand and made available for local investment the profits earned in merchandizing goods in Thailand.[50] Indeed, Ayal suggests that the unleashing of Chinese energy with the establishment of limits on the bureaucracy's patrimonial privileges may have been more important in ushering in high economic growth rates in the early 1960s than investment promotion, stable political rule, or "rudimentary" national planning.[51] Muscat also notes the importance of reducing the Chinese sense of vulnerability if they were to move from highly liquid investments, primarily in services, to longer term investments stimulating Thailand's industrial development.[52]

The new ethnic compact brokered by Sarit, together with a new economic policymaking regime, cleared the way for rapid economic growth in Thailand. Over time, this produced a politically significant middle class in Bangkok, more powerful business figures in Thai politics, and a fundamental alteration in Thai politics. Thailand's bureaucratic polity has disappeared.

Political participation in Thailand, previously limited to small circles of top-level bureaucrats, increased rapidly during the 1970s and 1980s. By the 1980s, political parties in some cases were able to protect the powers of Parliament against military encroachments. This was dramatically evident in 1992, when students and members of Bangkok's middle class played key roles in stymying military efforts to reestablish their dominance of Thai politics. The increasing participation of businessmen in parties and cabinets attests to their hopes of being able to serve their interests through the institution of Parliament.[53] The bureaucracy's dependence on technocrats and businessmen for their technical and managerial expertise has enlarged the scope for those groups' input into the political process. Peak business organizations play increasingly active consultative roles in economic decision making.[54]

In general, however, the growing presence of businessmen in Parliament and cabinets has not been translated into a commensurate rise in policy influence, although this varies considerably by government and issue area. Prime Minister Anand, like Prem and Field Marshal Sarit before him, gave technocrats considerable influence over government policy.[55] Under the more democratic civilian Chatichai administration, business influence expanded considerably, albeit not necessarily through formal institutional channels. In terms of issue areas, technocrats maintained policy dominance over macroeconomic issue areas while politicians exercised greater influence over sector issues.[56]

ORGANIZATION OF THAI BUSINESS

Thai businesses long have been organized into a host of sector and linguistic (among different groups of Chinese) associations. The old Chinese associations served social, political, and economic roles. Newer business associations are now of far greater importance. Business associations are prohibited by law from having any links with political parties. This does not preclude, of course, individuals from maintaining such links. Indeed, most political parties are bankrolled by prominent business figures.

The Third-Five-Year-Plan (1972–1976) formally recognized the legitimate role of private enterprise in Thailand.[57] Business associations played active roles in the NESDB policy subcommittees by the late 1960s. These business groups expressed interest at the time in creating a federation of business organizations akin to Japan's Keidanren.[58]

Business interest associations became more influential in the late 1970s when a former deputy prime minister and textile industrialist headed the Association of Thai Industries (now the Federation of Thai Industries), a former minister of finance headed the Thai Bankers Association, and a future minister of industry headed the Board of Trade and Chamber of Commerce.[59] The secretary general of the NESDB, Snoh Unakul, facilitated the development of these organizations and the development of links between them and the government.[60]

Under Prem, Snoh took the initiative in supporting the establishment of the Joint Public-Private Consultative Committee (JPPCC), chaired by the prime minister and with the NESDB serving as the secretariat. The JPPCC represented the continuation of a long established trend of increased business concerns, business influence remained strong, but increasingly was expressed through political parties, the ruling Chart Thai party in particular. This in fact served as an umbrella organization over the various peak business organizations.[61] Over the 1980s, with assistance coming from the United States Agency for International Development, the government established regional chambers of commerce in every province in Thailand.

Despite the rapid gains in formalizing business-government links, these were set back during the Chatichai years. Emphasizing particularistic concerns, business influence remained strong, but increasingly was expressed through political parties, the ruling Chart Thai party in particular. This in fact represented the continuation of a long established trend of increased business representation in parliament and government cabinets. (See tables 4 and 5.)

Generally speaking, business figures have viewed the state as an obstacle to achieving their goals. While cooperation between individuals in government and business has been common, this usually has been in order to serve particular interests. Bureaucratic obstacles to business practices encouraged such alliances. While government interference with private interests has not been great, this resulted only in part from any commitment to liberalism. The bureaucracy's inability to keep up with business and the exercise of informal checks and balances within the government itself helped to assure business of a reasonable degree of room for maneuver.

This situation changed considerably over the 1970s and, particularly, the 1980s. As Thailand became wealthier and more urban, as state employment growth slowed, and the differential between private sector and public sector wages ballooned, the prestige of private sector employment increased relative to that in the public sector. With slow growth in the mid-1980s and fiscal stringency, the Sixth Five-Year-Plan's (1987–1991) emphasis on the private

TABLE 4
Business Figures in Parliament

Date of Election	Business Figures	Total Representatives
November 1933	15	78
November 1937	18	91
November 1938	20	91
January 1946	20	96
August 1946	9	82
January 1948	22	99
June 1949	7	21
February 1952	25	123
February 1957	42	160
December 1957	44	160
February 1969	100	219
January 1975	93	269
April 1976	82	279
April 1979	112	301
April 1983	124	324
July 1986	186	347

Source: Suriyamongkol, p. 37; see note 57.

sector's leading role expressed a growing consensus among Thai elites in public and private sectors. The increasing importance of private investment to stimulate economic growth had its political counterpart in the strengthening of the role of political parties and the Parliament. The military posed the principal challenge to the emerging consensus in favor of markets and political democracy.

THE ROLE OF THE THAI MILITARY

Through much of the 1980s, however, divisions within the military decreased the likelihood of its acting in united fashion to overthrow the emerging order (though there were coup attempts by military factions in 1981 and 1985). It was only with the concentration of power under Class Five officers that it became possible for the military, with minimal opposition, to overthrow the Chatichai government in February 1991. When the military, however, was slow to reestablish parliamentary rule, large street demonstrations eventually forced the military to step aside, clearing the way for new elections and the establishment of the Chuan government.

Laothamatas argues that government-business ties have moved from a relationship based on clientelism to more of an equal partnership. This allows for more business input into policymaking as well as increased corruption.[62] Samudavanija's view of the relationship is less favorable: while urban business interests have achieved an accommodation with political and state elites, this has come at the expense of rural business and agricultural interests.[63]

TABLE 5
Business Figures in Cabinets

Head of Government	Business in Cabinet	Total Cabinet
Sarit	0	14
Thanom I	1	18
Thanom II	1	25
Thanom III	3	28
Sanya I	4	28
Sanya II	3	31
Seni	8	30
Kukrit	16	27
Seni II	11	31
Thanin	2	17
Kriangsak I	2	33
Kriangsak II	9	43
Kriangsak III	5	38
Prem I	17	37
Prem II	12	40
Prem III	17	41
Prem IV	21	44
Prem V	31	45
Chatichai I	33	45

Sources: Suriyamongkal, p. 39, see note 57; William S. Cole, Somboon Suksamran, Gary S. Merritt Suwannarat, unpublished manuscript.

Many in the military continue to promote themselves as guardians of the national interest. This perspective tends to make the military suspicious of businessmen and political parties. Military leaders have described parties as "trading companies" and insisted that the military has a responsibility to protect the people from unscrupulous "capitalists" and "dark influences."[64]

In recognition of the lack of voice given to the interests of the majority of the population, the military, many of whose members have rural roots, perceives itself as being closer to the people and having a legitimate role in advocating their interests. This sometimes leads the military to play a direct role in economic policy, for example in purchasing and distributing rice in an effort to raise its price, when the military believes that the civilian bureaucracy is failing to address problems.[65]

CONCLUSION

The limitations of Thai public administration led Muscat to suggest for Thailand

a development strategy that minimizes direct government intervention in the market place and permits maximum concentration on the not inconsiderable range of infrastructure, technical and other requirements of development which must be met by the public sector.[66]

Indeed, Thai-style public administration could have inspired Keynes' discussion, from *The End of Laissez-Faire:*

But above all, the ineptitude of public administrators strongly prejudiced the practical man in favour of laissez-faire—a sentiment which has by no means disappeared. Almost everything which the State did in the 18th century in excess of its minimum functions was, or seemed, injurious or unsuccessful.[67]

With the partial exception of a narrow range of monetary policies aimed at stabilizing and alleviating external imbalances, Thai leaders have had difficulty designing and implementing coherent development policies. Yet the strong record of Thailand's economic growth is undeniable. The conclusion may be that "government in Thailand has been irrelevant to the kingdom's success, except in the negative sense of having maintained an open economy, not having squandered the kingdom's credit, and having (generally) stayed out of the way of the Sino-Thai entrepreneurial class."[68]

A robust private sector in the absence of competent public administration, however, has been unable to address the needs associated with long-term economic growth in Thailand. In 1986 Thailand still suffered from uneven development and unemployment. The public sector deficit was almost one-fourth the size of the budget. Efforts to increase revenue collection during the fifth plan had largely failed, partly due to rampant tax evasion. With a quarter of the budget going to service debt, only about 16 percent of the budget went to capital outlays. Infrastructure remained underdeveloped.[69]

The dramatic turnaround in Thai economic fortunes beginning in late 1986 resulted in major part from external factors. Oil prices fell as did interest rates. In 1988 various commodity prices increased sharply. Most important was the depreciation of the baht relative to the currencies of the major East Asian exporters of manufactured goods while those countries' currencies appreciated against the U.S. dollar. Together with rising wages and the loss of preferential access to the U.S. market, these forces pushed manufacturing industries offshore from Japan, South Korea, and Taiwan. With the surge in manufacturing exports from Thailand resulting from that shift, Thai public sector deficits disappeared, at least temporarily, allowing increased spending for badly needed infrastructure. Unemployment decreased sharply as well. These externally driven forces produced a major structural adjustment of the Thai economy in the direction of an export-oriented industrialization regime.

To sustain these gains, however, Thailand must establish an effective and stable political regime. The incoherence and delays surrounding efforts in recent years to launch new transportation systems in Bangkok are doleful reminders of some of the costs of the current style of Thai political decision making.[70] Ultimately, the underpinnings of a more effective, institutionalized, political pluralism are likely to be shaped by the ways in which business-government relations evolve over the coming years.

While Thai politics have changed significantly since 1974, that change has been gradual. With the exception of the brief period of authoritarian rule under Thanin, it is not easy to talk in terms of different types of political regimes. Clearly the Chatichai government was, and the Chuan government is, more democratic than any of those that followed the Thanin government. After all, Chuan himself and the members of his Cabinet are members of Parliament. The gap between the Chuan government and the fifth Prem government, however, is probably no greater than that between the first and fifth Prem governments. Over the years, political parties played increasingly important roles under Prem.

Relatively free markets also have dominated the Thai economy since the late 1950s. By speeding up the processes of wealth creation, urbanization, and the spread of education and mass communications, markets have stimulated the development of political pluralism.[71] Clearly the expansion of a middle class and the need to afford business greater autonomy as the economy grew more complex helped to undermine the Thai bureaucratic polity.

The central political problems in Thailand remain: 1) the weaknesses of institutions that mediate between state and society and 2) the difficulty of finding means to institutionalize a political compromise between business and the military. Military intervention has stunted the development of Thai democracy, but it is hard not to conclude that in the absence of that intervention Thai democracy would, at least for some time, have produced outcomes worse than those evident under military rule. A democracy lacking strong political parties would likely produce continued vote buying and, perhaps, a pattern of social and economic development somewhat more like cronyism in the Philippines.

Clearly Thailand's emphasis on market solutions to economic problems has been most evident under relatively authoritarian regimes: the Sarit and Anand governments. Nonetheless, it would be a mistake to suggest that military rule always results in the depoliticization of economic policymaking. A coup overthrew the Kriangsak government after it was unable to implement policy changes necessitated by oil price increases in the 1970s and ensuing macroeconomic instability in Thailand. The Prem government implemented important economic reforms, but also faced political obstacles that slowed the pace of change. The recognition that political conflict continues under all kinds of regimes is particularly important in the Thai case. One result, characteristic of most Thai governments, has been an inability to provide many of the public goods (technical education, adequate physical infrastructure, environmental protection, limits on regional and class income inequalities) that help to sustain economic expansion over the long term and enhance the quality of life. Differences in regime type have had a more significant impact on macroeconomic policies than on the provision of these public goods.

Further development of democracy may also endanger Thailand's long-standing macroeconomic stability. Evidence of this emerged during the Chatichai years when, for a time, a key Chart Thai leader held the finance portfolio. The result may be a decline in the finance ministry's interest in protecting the central bank from political pressures. Such insulation may decline as a result of parties expanding their linkages with firms favoring expansionist policies; the legislature becoming more important in fiscal policy; and successful macroeconomic policies generating fiscal surpluses sufficient to fuel demands for such policies.

Thailand's long-term stability and economic expansion depend on maintaining some of the technocrats' traditional policymaking autonomy, enhancing the capacity of the policymaking machinery to make crucial (e.g., related to the provision of infrastructure) decisions, and finding means of addressing critical political and social issues, including economic inequities and public health scourges such as that associated with the spread of AIDs.

NOTES

1. James Steuart, quoted in Albert O. Hirschman, *The Passions and the Interests* (Princeton, NJ: Princeton University Press, 1977), pp. 83–84.

2. Joseph Schumpeter provided a more nuanced version of these processes. Joseph A. Schumpeter, *Capitalism, Socialism and Democracy*, 3rd edition (New York: Harper and Row, 1950.)

3. Perry Anderson, *Lineages of the Absolutist State* (London: Verso, 1979).

4. Chalmers Johnson refers to the "Meiji-Bismarckian pattern of late economic development." See "The State and Japanese Grand Strategy," in *The Domestic Bases of Grand Strategy*, ed. Richard Rosecrance and Arthur A. Stein (Ithaca: Cornell University Press, 1993), pp. 201–23.

5. This was also important, however, particularly in the case of Taiwan. See Karl Fields, doctoral dissertation, University of California, Berkeley, Department of Political Science, unpublished.

6. Particularly during the postwar years, Japan was very careful to limit foreign capital's access to its market.

7. Chalmers Johnson, *MITI and the Japanese Miracle* (Stanford, CA: Stanford University Press, 1982.) This distinction is introduced in pp. 17–26.

8. Ibid., p. 24.

9. E. H. Norman, quoted in John W. Dower, *Origins of the Modern Japanese State* (New York: Pantheon, 1975), p. 19.

10. Charles E. Lindblom, *Politics and Markets* (New York: Basic Books, 1977), p. 165.

11. Lindblom, *Politics and Markets*, pp. 172–75.

12. Philip Bowring contrasts the slow development of automobile industries by relatively independent firms in Japan and South Korea with Tommy Suharto's recent purchase of part of Lamborghini SpA. "Young Suharto's Fast-Track Approach is Hardly the Tigers' Way," *International Herald Tribune*, December 27, 1993, p. 4.

13. Kunio Yoshihara, *The Rise of Ersatz Capitalism in Southeast Asia* (Singapore: Oxford University Press, 1987).

14. Norman Jacobs, *Modernization Without Development* (New York: Praeger, 1971).

15. John Stopford and Susan Strange with John S. Henley, *Rival States, Rival Firms* (Cambridge: Cambridge University Press, 1991), p. 10.

16. By and large I avoid using the term "strategy" in referring to Thai development policies. The term is misleading for obvious reasons that were well described by a leading Thai economist:

   Like the bourgeois in Moliere's play who one day suddenly discovered that he had been speaking prose all his life, the BOI discovered in 1970 that it had been promoting import substitution all its life.

   From Ammar Siamwalla, "Stability, Growth and Distribution in the Thai Economy," in the Bank of Thailand's *Finance, Trade and Economic Development in Thailand* (Bangkok: Sompong Press) p. 38.

17. T. H. Silcock, "Summary and Assessment." In *Thailand: Social and Economic Studies in Development*, ed. T. H. Silcock (Canberra: Australian National University Press, 1967), p. 294.

18. Interview, Bangkok, 1987.

19. Jacobs, *Modernization Without Development*, p. 3.

20. Suthy Prasartset (*State Capitalism in the Development Process: Thailand 1932–59*, Institute of Developing Economies, Tokyo, 1979) makes a similar argument with the addition of constraining external linkages.

21. Robert J. Muscat, *Development Strategy in Thailand: A Study of Economic Growth* (New York: Frederick A. Praeger, 1966), p. 34.

22. Ibid., pp. 34–39.

23. Ibid., p. 37.

24. Ibid.; James C. Scott, "Corruption in Thailand," ed. Clark D. Neher, *Modern Thai Politics* (Cambridge, MA: Schenkman Publishing Co., 1979), pp. 294–316. For a different view stressing the constraints on patrimonialism in Thailand, see Jeffrey Race, "The Political Economy of New Order Indonesia in Comparative Regional Perspective," in *Indonesia: Australian Perspectives*, ed. James Fox, Mackie et al. (Canberra: Research School of Pacific Studies, Australian National University, 1980).

25. *Far Eastern Economic Review*, June 27, 1991, p. 48. The state, however, does not require these firms to pay business taxes.

26. Ibid.

27. "Role of the Private Sector in the Thai Economy: Now and in the Future," in *Thailand on the Move: Stumbling Blocks and Breakthroughs*, ed. Suchart Prasith-rathsint, (Bangkok: Thai University Research Association and Canadian International Development Agency, 1990), table 6.4, p. 105.

28. Ajanant et al., *Trade and Industry in Thailand* (Bangkok: Social Science Association of Thailand, 1989); General Agreement on Tariffs and Trade, *Trade Policy Review Mechanism, The Kingdom of Thailand*, June 1991.

29. Kunio Yoshihara, *The Rise of Ersatz Capitalism in South-East Asia*, (New York: Oxford University Press, 1988).

30. Parts of this discussion draw on Richard Doner and Danny Unger, "The Politics of Finance in Thai Economic Development," in *The Politics of Finance in Developing Countries*, ed. Stephan Haggard, Chung Lee, and Sylvia Maxfield (Ithaca, New York: Cornell University Press, 1993).

31. Silcock, op. cit., p. 184.

32. Scott R. Christensen, "The Politics of Democratization in Thailand: State and Society Since 1932," background paper (Bangkok: Thailand Development Research Institute, 1991).

33. Akira Suehiro, *Capital Accumulation and Industrial Development in Thailand* (Bangkok: Chulalongkorn Social Science Institute, 1985), table 3.

34. T. H. Silcock, "Money and Banking," in *Thailand: Social and Economic Studies in Development*, ed. T. H. Silcock (Canberra: Australian National University Press, 1967), pp. 170–205.

35. Richard Doner and Anek Laothamatas, "The Political Economy of Structural Adjustment in Thailand," in *Voting for Reform*, ed. Stephan Haggard and Steven Webb (New York: Oxford University Press), forthcoming. The following discussion of the budgeting process draws on this work.

36. Scott Christensen et al., *The Lessons of East Asia, Thailand, the Institutional and Political Underpinnings of Growth* (Washington, DC: World Bank, 1993), p. 23.

37. Richard Doner and Danny Unger, "Financial Liberalization in Thailand," in *The Politics of Financial Liberalization in Developing Countries*, ed. Stephan Haggard, Sylvia Maxfield, and Chung Lee, (Ithaca: Cornell University Press, 1994); (see #35).

38. Thomas R. Callaghy, "Visions and Politics in the Transformation of the Global Political Economy: Lessons From the Second and Third Worlds," in *Global Transformation in the Third World*, ed. Robert O. Slater, Barry M. Schutz, Steven R. Dorr (Boulder, CO: Lynne Rienner, 1993), p. 169.

39. Chai-Anan Samudavanija, "Thailand, Economic Policymaking in a Liberal Technocratic Polity," in *Economic Policymaking in the Asia-Pacific Region*, ed. John W. Langford and K. Lorne Brownsey (Halifax, Nova Scotia: Institute for Research on Public Policy, 1990), pp. 181–202.

40. Akira Suehiro, *Capital Accumulation in Thailand, 1855–1985* (Tokyo: The Centre for East Asian Cultural Studies, 1989), p. 71.

41. The literature on the Chinese in Southeast Asia is extensive. Among those works that include the Chinese in Thailand are: William G. Skinner, *Chinese Society in Thailand: An Analytic History* (Ithaca: Cornell University Press, 1957); *Leadership and Power in a Chinese Community in Thailand* (Ithaca: Cornell University Press, 1958); "Change and Persistence in Chinese Culture Overseas: A Comparison of Thailand and Java," in *Southeast Asia: The Politics of National Integration*, ed. John T. McAlister (New York: Random House, 1973); *Journal of Southeast Asian Studies*, issue on "Ethnic Chinese in Southeast Asia," Singapore University Press, Singapore, vol. 12, no. 1, March 1981; Leo Suryadinata, *'Overseas Chinese' in Southeast Asia and China's Foreign Policy* (Singapore: Institute of Southeast Asian Studies, 1978); R. J. Coughlin, *Double Identity: The Chinese in Modern Thailand* (Hong Kong: Hong Kong University Press, 1960); Linda Y. C. Lim and Peter Gosling eds., *The Chinese in Southeast Asia* (Singapore: Maruzen Asia, 1983); Kenneth P. Landon, *The Chinese in Thailand* (London: Oxford University Press, 1941); Fukuda Shozo, *Kakyo Keizai ron* (on the Overseas Chinese economy), (Tokyo: Ganshodo, 1940); Chung-hsun Yu, *Kakyo keizai no kenkyu* (Research on the Overseas Chinese economy), (Tokyo: Institute for Developing Economies, 1969); Suehiro Akira, *Capital Accumulation and Industrial Development in Thailand* (Bangkok: Chulalongkorn University Social Research Institute, 1985); Krirkiat Phipatseritham and Yoshihara Kunio, *Business Groups in Thailand* Singapore: Institute for Southeast Asian Studies, 1983).

42. Skinner (1957), see note 41; Fred Riggs, *The Modernization of a Bureaucratic Polity* (Honolulu: East-West Center Press, 1966).

43. Scott (see note 24).

44. Patcharee Thanamai, "Patterns of Industrial Policymaking in Thailand: Japanese MNCs and Domestic Actors in the Auto and Electrical Appliances Industries," Ph.D. thesis, Department of Political Science, University of Wisconsin, Madison, 1985, p. 46.

45. Robert J. Muscat, *Thailand and the United States: Development, Security, and Foreign Aid* (New York: Columbia University Press, 1990), p. 276.

46. Pisan Suriyamongkol and James F. Guyot, *Bureaucratic Polity at Bay*, National Institute of Development Administration, no. 51, Bangkok, 1986.

47. See Anek Laothamathas, "Business and Politics in Thailand: New Patterns of Influence," *Asia Survey*, 33 (April 1988), pp. 601–21.

48. Ibid.

49. Edward Van Roy, "The 'industrial organization' of a pre-industrial economy and some development implications," *Journal of Development Studies*, (April 1971), p. 24.

50. Muscat, op. cit., p. 276.

51. Eliezer B. Ayal, "Private Enterprise and Economic Progress in Thailand," *Journal of Asian Studies*, 26, 1 (November 1966).

52. Muscat, op. cit., pp. 235–242.

53. See Anek Laothamathas, "Business and Politics in Thailand: New Patterns of Influence", *op. cit.*; Pisan Suriyamongkol and James F. Guyot, *The Bureaucratic Polity at Bay*.

54. Ibid., p. 51.

55. Ibid., p. 47.

56. See Scott Christensen and Ammar Siamwalla, *Beyond Patronage: Tasks for the Thai State* (Bangkok: Thailand Development Research Institute, 1993).

57. Pisan Suriyamongkol, *Institutionalization of Democratic Political Processes in Thailand: A Three-Pronged Democratic Polity* (Bangkok: National Institute of Development Administration, 1988), p. 29.

58. Richard Doner, *Driving a Bargain* (Berkeley: University of California Press, 1991).

59. Ibid.

60. Interview, Bangkok, 1987.

61. The best and fullest treatment of this issue is in Anek Laothamathas, *Business Associations and the Political Economy of Thailand: From Bureaucratic Polity to Liberal Corporatism* (Boulder: Westview Press, 1992).

62. Ibid.

63. Chai-Anan Samudavanija, "Economic Development and Conflict or Conflict Resolution: Case of Thailand," mimeo, 1993.

64. Chain-Anan Samudavanija, "Thailand: A Stable Semi-Democracy," in *Democracy in Developing Countries*, ed. Larry Diamond, Juan Linz, Seymour Martin Lipset (Boulder, CO: Lynne Rienner, 1989).

65. Chai-Anan Samudavanija and Sukhumbhand Paribatra, "In Search of Balance: Prospects for Stability in Thailand During the Post-CPT Era," *Toward a Durable Regional Stability: Options and Alternatives* (Singapore: Regional Strategic Studies Programme, Institute of Southeast Asian Studies, 1987).

66. Muscat, op. cit., p. 280.

67. Quoted in *Asean Investor*, 4 (August 1985), p. 35.

68. The Asian Strategies Co., op. cit.

69. *Asian Wall Street Journal*, October 6, 1986.

70. These have included a confusing array of different proposals, each of which has encountered a dizzying diversity of obstacles. Most recently, many Thais are arguing against some of the proposed elevated transit systems in favor of subterannean ones. With something like 1.3 million cars on the road in Bangkok and that number expected to double over the next ten years, the city's abysmal traffic will only grow much worse (*Bangkok Post Weekly*, November 12, 1993, p. 20).

71. Here I refer to pluralism rather than democracy. It is not clear the extent to which it is appropriate to argue that the Chatichai government was more democratic than the last of the Prem governments. Given the roles of vote buying and the dominant role of finance in determining the fortunes of political parties, it is hard to argue that most Thais exercise meaningful roles in selecting those who occupy top positions in the state apparatus. The value of elections is then twofold: 1) the conviction that if enough were at stake, most Thais would use their right to vote to exercise meaningful influence; 2) the belief that over time mediating institutions develop sufficient strength so that the direct influence of finance is diminished and broader ideological or programmatic appeals become more decisive.

8

TRADE AND INVESTMENT IN SOUTHEAST ASIAN DEVELOPMENT

Stephen Parker

Southeast Asian countries have grown rapidly and consistently over the last 20 years, setting a standard for development policy throughout the developing world (see table 1).[1] It is important to remember, however, that as recently as the mid-1960s, many Southeast Asian countries, especially Indonesia, were considered basket cases with little prospect of long-term growth. Although many Southeast Asian countries have historically been important exporters of various raw materials (agricultural products, petroleum and minerals), the recent boom in economic growth is highly correlated with surges in manufactured trade and related investment. The key role of foreign investment in this expansion sets the Southeast Asian growth model apart from the more inward-looking Korean and Japanese development strategies.

The surge in foreign trade and investment over the 1980s occurred in response to a combination of forces. Most importantly, the ASEAN countries (excluding the Philippines) had set in place by the mid-1980s market-driven, private-sector-led economic policy regimes with special attention to improving the foreign trade and investment business environment. The Plaza Accord realignment of exchange rates made Southeast Asian labor-intensive manufacturing very competitive relative to Japan, Korea and Taiwan. As well, the world economy, especially world trade, grew steadily following the 1982–1983 recession, which when combined with generally open market access to most developed countries, provided strong demand for Southeast Asian exports.

Prospects for continued economic growth, and growth in foreign trade and investment, in most Southeast Asian countries are encouraging. Growth rates will likely moderate a bit from the high levels of recent years, primarily because of conservative internal macroeconomic management. Economic management in the ASEAN countries increasingly aims toward steady (5–8 percent), well-managed, broad-based economic growth. Increasingly growth in the rapidly developing Southeast Asian countries is being generated more from increases in domestic consumption and investment rather than trade, although trade does continue importantly to stimulate domestic productivity gains and to finance foreign debt service requirements (see table 2).

There are several indications, however, of reductions in foreign investment into these countries, just at the time that many of them are trying to upgrade their industries into more sophisticated and higher-value-added production. Foreign investment (and non-equity contributions by foreign busi-

TABLE 1
Real Growth Rate of GDP
(percentage)

	Average 1971–80	Average 1981–90	1987	1988	1989	1990	1991	1992	Forecast 1993	Forecast 1994	* 1993	* 1994
Singapore	7.9	6.3	9.4	11.1	9.2	8.3	6.7	5.8	5.8	6.0	6.1	6.5
Southeast Asia (less Singapore)	7.4	6.1	6.2	8.4	8.8	7.7	6.3	5.8	6.5	7.1	8.3	6.8
Indonesia	7.7	5.5	4.9	5.8	7.5	7.1	6.6	5.9	6.3	6.7	6.1	6.5
Malaysia	7.8	5.2	5.4	8.9	9.2	9.7	8.7	8.0	8.0	7.8	7.8	8.1
Philippines	6.0	1.0	4.8	6.3	6.1	2.7	-0.7	0.0	2.8	4.5	1.5	3.5
Thailand	7.9	7.8	9.5	13.2	12.0	10.0	8.2	7.5	7.8	8.5	7.7	8.1
Vietnam	–	6.1	4.0	5.2	8.0	5.1	6.0	8.3	7.5	8.2	–	–

Source: Asian Development Outlook 1993, The Asian Development Bank.
*Forecast from Pacific Economic Outlook 1993–94, PECC.

nesses) has played a key role in introducing quickly and efficiently a wide range of management, technology, and market linkages that have contributed vitally to the recent export surge and will be needed for these countries to step up the productivity ladder. If foreign investment indeed falls significantly over the next couple of years, the cost of advancing into higher value-added production will be much higher, both in terms of domestic resource requirements and time.

Given the breadth of the assignment to review the role of trade and investment in Southeast Asian development, this chapter attempts to distill the key elements of this relationship over the last two decades, with a special emphasis on the manufacturing boom since the mid-1980s. Included also is an examination of the prospects for these economies over the 1990s. It is important to note the limits of this chapter, since the generalizations that are forced by this format undoubtedly will overly simplify any number of complex relationships within and among these countries.

THE ROLE OF TRADE AND INVESTMENT IN SOUTHEAST ASIAN DEVELOPMENT

The story of economic development in Southeast Asia, and the role of foreign trade and investment, has a number of themes and diverse plots.[2] Indonesia, Thailand, Malaysia, and Singapore have meandered through various forms of economic policy regimes, starting first with shifts in political conditions, primarily in the 1960s, that established governments with strong commitments to economic growth. Early development regimes in each of these countries centered on import-substitution and inward-looking sectoral policies.

TABLE 2
Contributions to Real GDP/GNP Growth Rate, 1992–1994

		GDP Growth Rate	Personal Contr. Exp.	Gross Private Dom. Invest.	Government Purchases	Net Exports
Indonesia	1992	6.4	2.4	4.3	1.6	-1.9
	1993	6.3	3.1	1.3	1.0	1.8
	1994	6.5	3.3	1.4	1.7	1.8
Malaysia	1992	8.5	4.0	3.0	2.8	-1.3
	1993	7.6	1.5	2.0	1.4	2.3
	1994	7.5	1.4	1.7	1.0	3.4
Philippines	1992	2.5	1.8	0.5	0.1	-0.3
	1993	3.3	2.7	2.0	0.1	-0.9
	1994	6.7	4.0	3.3	0.3	1.0
Singapore	1992	6.0	2.2	6.3	0.9	-3.4
	1993	6.0	1.6	3.6	0.7	0.1
	1994	6.1	1.7	3.6	0.7	0.1
Thailand	1992	8.6	4.6	4.1	0.5	0.3
	1993	7.9	4.0	3.3	1.7	0.8
	1994	8.4	4.0	3.7	1.9	1.9

Source: Pacific Economic Outlook 1992–93, 1993–94, PECC.
Net contributions may not equal the GDP growth rate due to "statistical discrepancies" and/or "other."

Singapore shifted first to an export-oriented, free-trade strategy, followed by Malaysia.[3] Singapore has maintained an export orientation with an ever-present strong government role in managing (in some cases leading) the structural shifts accompanying higher wages and shifts toward services and high-value-added production. Malaysia has maintained a relatively open trade and investment environment, although it regressed somewhat into a more inward-looking, state-dependent policy regime in the 1970s and early 1980s under the New Economic Policy (NEP). Although not all of the social and economic interventions of the NEP have been eliminated, in general Malaysian economic policy since the mid-1980s has been solidly outward-looking and market-oriented. Thailand also committed to an export-oriented growth strategy early on, and has refrained from major expansions in the state sector. Nevertheless, Thailand has moved in and out of costly and inappropriately capital-intensive, import-substitution initiatives. By the mid-1980s, Thai economic policy firmly encouraged foreign trade and investment. The policy shift was most pronounced in Indonesia, which embarked on a major and sustained effort of economic deregulation and pro-trade policy reforms in the early to mid-1980s, following decades of heavy state investment and economic management stressing import-substitution objectives. Economic growth in all four of these countries has been strong throughout the late 1980s and into the 1990s (see table 1).

Building Momentum in the 1960s and 1970s

It is remarkable that the buoyant economic growth in Southeast Asia over the last 10 years that is now almost taken for granted is a relatively new phenomenon. As recently as the mid-1960s, outside observers of Southeast Asia remarked about the hopelessness of long-term economic development throughout the region. Gunnar Myrdal, a Nobel Prize winner and author of *The Asia Drama*, essentially called Indonesia a basket case. Even Singapore could not escape outside pessimism, illustrated by a 1967 report in the *Far Eastern Economic Review* by David Bonavia that concluded independent Singapore had no future.[4] The one country that attracted the most optimism during the 1960s, the Philippines, has been the least successful of the ASEAN branch of Southeast Asia, although the new Philippine government has raised expectations significantly about prospects for stronger growth over the next several years (see table 1). Myanmar also looked somewhat promising during its initial independence period, but has retrenched into an extremely isolated and antigrowth regime. Indochina essentially stood still, or regressed severely in the case of Cambodia, in the aftermath of the Vietnam War. Vietnam, and to a lesser extent Laos, have now made a commitment to economic growth and have initiated a number of market-oriented shifts in economic policy.

The role of foreign trade and investment has also varied significantly over time and among countries. All Southeast Asian countries (even Singapore as a processor and transshipper) have traditionally exported a range of raw materials, including oil and gas from Indonesia and Malaysia, and some combination of rubber, coffee, palm oil, coconut, spices, various food crops, and various minerals from all the countries. Southeast Asian countries also have traditionally imported consumer and capital goods.

Although foreign trade and investment played a role during this stage, predominantly in the form of investments for the export of raw materials, and investments in import-substitution sectors, trade and investment flows were not a major element of these early stages of growth.[5] Each country started a modern development process with political stability and a combination of macroeconomic stability, a group of large (often state-owned) investments commonly supported by import-substitution policies, relatively strong agriculture and rural development programs, growing investment in human and physical infrastructure, and a mass of small and often informal rural and urban businesses.[6] Substantial private sectors existed in all the ASEAN countries, but many private firms operated either at the behest of the government through preferential licensing and policy arrangements (clientelism typically among larger firms) or informally around pernicious government interference (the vast majority of smaller firms).

The windfalls of the OPEC increases in oil prices during the 1970s supported these programs in Indonesia and Malaysia. Foreign assistance also played an important role in Indonesia, Thailand, and the Philippines. An important consequence of these inward-looking policies was intermittent balance of payments problems that forced domestic retrenchments, often including the cancellation or rescheduling of large, capital-intensive projects.

The Trade and Investment Boom in the 1980s and 1990s

At the heart of the transformation from rural, agricultural-based to thriving manufactured-led economies that has been the engine of growth for Southeast Asia over the last 20 years has been shifts in foreign trade and investment policy. Non-oil foreign trade and investment first became the driving force for Southeast Asian development in the mid-1980s, although Singapore and to a lesser extent Malaysia had taken steps to attract export-oriented foreign investment well before. Indonesia most profoundly, but also Thailand, began broad economic reform programs, with policies that encouraged foreign investment and exports at its center. Malaysia enhanced its attractiveness to foreign investors by shifting away from the NEP into a more outward-looking National Development Policy. The continuation of political instability and anti-trade policies in the Philippines caused it to lose its relative competitiveness compared to the other ASEAN countries (and China). These economic reforms greatly improved the business environment for both foreign and domestic investors. The surge in foreign investment introduced not only financial capital but, probably more importantly, management and technical capacities and access to international marketing channels. This, combined with macroeconomic stability and already high domestic savings rates, set the stage for strong and broad-based economic growth.

The aggressive encouragement of foreign investment has been one of the most distinctive elements of the Southeast Asian development strategy (see table 3). Southeast Asia was one of the first regions to court successfully export-oriented foreign investors. This sets Southeast Asia apart from Korea and Japan, which have been more closed to foreign investment. Latin America and Africa, partly in response to the success of Southeast Asia, have just begun to promote foreign investment for manufacturing exports, even though they have a long and controversial history of foreign investment related to natural resources and import-substitution sectors.

Just as the Southeast Asian countries were unilaterally reforming their economic policies, the Plaza Accord agreement in 1985 initiated a major restructuring of exchange rates throughout Asia. The currencies of Japan, Korea and Taiwan all appreciated significantly relative to the U.S. dollar. At the same time, the Southeast Asian currencies not only followed the dollar down relative to the Northeast Asian currencies, but in several cases governments further devalued their currency relative to the dollar (note the major devaluation of the Rupiah in 1986). In addition, wage levels in Northeast Asia were growing independent of the exchange rate changes as economic growth pressured domestic labor markets and inward immigration was restricted.[7] The relative competitiveness of production in Southeast Asia compared to Northeast Asia shifted overwhelmingly in 1985 and 1986. As well, world economic growth was steady and reasonably strong from 1984 until the early 1990s, and foreign trade grew even faster, as developed countries and their multinationals began to develop international assembly and purchasing programs that searched out low-cost suppliers worldwide. Trade barriers remained low to moderate in the United States and the European Community, to some degree disciplined by the GATT agreements and responsibilities.

This fortuitous combination of events—economic reforms at home, the favorable realignment of exchange rates, and good market access to most developed country markets—fired the manufactured export boom in Southeast Asia that has run from the mid-1980s until now. As trade and investment boomed, so did real estate and construction, and more generally domestic consumption and domestic investment, stimulating a broad-based economic surge that kept pace with rapid growth in Northeast Asia and exceeded growth in any other region of the world over this period.

Much of the foreign investment flowing into Southeast Asia since 1985 has involved a shift in the production of labor-intensive products for export from Northeast Asia, but also from North America and Europe. Japanese investment has been important, but over the last five years the Asian NIEs—Korea, Taiwan, Hong Kong, and Singapore—together surpassed Japan as the largest foreign investor in Southeast Asia.[8] This highlights the ease of transferring labor-intensive production across borders. Investments from the United States and Europe in manufacturing exports have also risen steadily.

Growth in manufactured exports in the four ASEAN tigers has been impressive, generally growing in the range of 15 to 30 percent per year over this period (see table 4). Exports of textiles and apparel, footwear, electronics and computers, various assembly components, plywood (for Indonesia), and fabricated materials have led this surge. Many of these exports originated from intrafirm transactions within multinational businesses who invested in Southeast Asia (particularly in computers and electronics). Other exports involved foreign buyers operating through contract manufacturing agreements with local businesses (either domestic-owned or from Asian foreign investors that had shifted production from, e.g., Korea, Hong Kong and Taiwan to Indonesia, Thailand, and Malaysia). Under these contract agreements, foreign buyers often supplied technical and management support, and provided marketing channels, but did not take any equity position.[9] These contract arrangements are the most footloose type of exporting arrangements. Without the vital inputs of the foreign investors and buyers, however, it would not have been possible to develop competitive production capabilities in Southeast

TABLE 3
Foreign Direct Investment
(millions $US)

	1986	1987	1988	1989	1990	1991	1992
Indonesia	258	385	576	682	1,093	1,482	1,774
Malaysia	489	423	719	1,668	2,332	4,073	4,118
Philippines	127	307	936	563	530	544	228
Thailand	261	182	1,081	1,726	2,303	1,847	1,979
Singapore	1,529	2,630	3,538	1,891	3,911	3,235	4,288
Korea	325	418	720	453	-105	-241	-497
Japan	-14,250	-18,350	-34,730	-45,220	-46,290	-29,370	-14,520
China	1,425	1,669	2,344	2,613	2,657	3,453	7,156

Source: International Financial Statistics, IMF, September 1993.

Asia as quickly as occurred over this period. This was also shown clearly by the key role of Hong Kong and Taiwanese businesses in the Chinese experience.[10]

Singapore was well ahead of this trend. By the early 1980s, Singapore had attracted substantial amounts of foreign investment, becoming somewhat of a Southeast Asian center for U.S. and other foreign companies. The composition of investment in Singapore, though, has changed over the last 10 years, shifting from labor-intensive manufacturing to a preponderance of services and high-value-added production. This shift occurred in response to a clearly stated policy by the Singapore government to raise wages in Singapore, in conjunction with a long-standing commitment to strong education and training levels, forcing the economy to sink or swim as a high-wage economy. Foreign investment now makes up around three-quarters of all investment in Singapore, and the Singapore standard of living is now at a developed country level. Nevertheless, the Singapore government still plays a very active role in managing sectoral policies and through state ownership of many key elements of the economy.

Not only have exports and foreign investment expanded rapidly over the last 10 years in Southeast Asia, but imports have grown almost as strongly (see table 6). A key element of the trade and investment policy reforms throughout the region has been the implementation of duty drawback systems (or comparable free trade or export processing zones) that allow exporters to import duty-free intermediate and machinery inputs. When combined with pro-trade exchange rate management and generally competitive labor markets, domestic producers had access to high-quality imported inputs at world prices in combination with quite favorably priced labor inputs. Imports of consumer goods have expanded in Southeast Asia, as the rising ASEAN middle classes increase their consumption of a broad range of consumer products. As well, economic growth in the region has placed considerable

TABLE 4
Growth Rate of Merchandise Exports
(percentage)

	Exports* 1991	1987	1988	1989	1990	1991	1992	Forecast 1993	Forecast 1994
Singapore	56.8	28.7	38.3	13.8	17.2	12.1	6.0	8.6	9.0
Southeast Asia (less Singapore)	102.7	25.4	21.1	20.2	15.3	15.1	13.8	14.5	15.4
Indonesia	29.4	19.5	13.4	17.8	16.7	9.8	13.5	13.0	13.0
Malaysia	33.9	31.1	17.4	18.3	17.1	17.3	11.0	14.0	15.0
Philippines	8.8	18.1	23.7	10.6	4.7	8.0	9.8	11.5	11.2
Thailand	28.2	31.7	36.1	25.7	15.0	23.8	17.8	18.4	18.7
Vietnam	2.0	8.2	21.6	87.4	23.5	-18.0	25.6	22.2	22.0

Source: Asian Development Outlook 1993, The Asian Development Bank.
*f.o.b., billion $US.

pressure on domestic infrastructure. Large government, and increasingly private, investments in infrastructure have required large amounts of imported goods and services. Southeast Asia is increasingly an important export market for the rest of Asia, as well as for developed countries throughout the world.[11] Nevertheless, even though each country has significantly lowered many tariffs and non-tariff barriers to imports, each country also still maintains high levels of protection for a number of key sectors.

The Role of the Private Sector and Ethnic-Chinese Business. Even though the role of state-owned enterprises remains important in all Southeast Asian countries—there has been little effort to privatize state firms—it has been the growth of the private sector in Southeast Asia that has fueled the surge of economic growth, and especially foreign trade and investment in the region.[12] Except for raw material exports, state firms rarely have played an important role in the Southeast Asian export drive. Concerns regarding the ethnic composition of the private sector, however, have importantly influenced economic policy throughout Southeast Asia.

As is well known, the private sector in each of the Southeast Asian countries has been dominated by an ethnic-Chinese minority (this obviously does not hold for Singapore, where ethnic Chinese are a majority, dominating political and economic power). In Indonesia, the Chinese minority represents less than 5 percent of the total population, while Malaysia sets the other bound with an ethnic-Chinese minority of around 35 percent. The proportion is between these two extremes in Thailand, the Philippines and Vietnam.

The fear by the ethnic majority of domination by a Chinese-led private sector contributed importantly to the initial desire of Southeast Asian governments to favor state and quasi-state owned firms, where ethnic-majority leadership could be administered by government dictate.[13] This issue was a driv-

TABLE 5
Direction of Merchandise Exports
(percentage share)

	Developing Asia		Japan		USA		EEC		Other	
	1985	1991	1985	1991	1985	1991	1985	1991	1985	1991
Indonesia	17	26	46	37	22	12	6	12	9	14
Malaysia	40	44	25	16	13	17	14	14	9	10
Philippines	21	18	19	20	36	36	14	18	10	8
Singapore	38	41	9	9	21	20	10	13	21	17
Thailand	29	22	13	18	20	22	18	19	20	20
Vietnam	50	35	17	38	—		5	11	27	17

Source: Asian Development Outlook 1993, The Asian Development Bank.

ing force for Malaysia's NEP, which is the most comprehensive example in Southeast Asia of a national program to promote the ethnic-majority position. (Note that the NEP in the early 1980s also supported a major effort at state-owned, capital-intensive industrial development, which largely failed and was reversed by 1985.) Although a number of large Chinese family-owned firms developed before the 1980s in each country, primarily behind preferential trade and licensing barriers designed to stimulate domestic investment, the majority of the Chinese firms were small to medium sized involved with domestic and international trading and smaller-scale production. Economic deregulation provided the opportunity for many of these mid-sized firms to expand. Although data is not available, much of the initial manufactured export surge in Southeast Asia appears to have occurred from this platform of medium-sized, family-owned Chinese firms. The large conglomerates, benefiting from protection, in many cases were not particularly competitive in world markets and did not contribute importantly to the early stages of the export boom. In fact, many of the Southeast Asian conglomerates fought hard to maintain their protection, only gradually diversifying into export markets.

Much of Southeast Asia's economic growth, and especially growth in trade, therefore, can be traced directly to the role of ethnic-Chinese firms. The dilemma is that ethnic-Chinese firms have grown faster in response to economic reforms than the ethnic-majority firms, aggravating in many cases long-standing animosities by the majority against the more prosperous ethnic minority. In order to maintain political support for economic reform, expanding the majority business class throughout Southeast Asia, most profoundly for Indonesia, is a key task for governments over the 1990s. Unfortunately, advancing the wide participation of the majority business class in the growth of the economy is much more complex than the now widely accepted package of macroeconomic and sectoral reforms.[14]

TABLE 6
Growth Rate of Merchandise Imports
(percentage)

	Imports* 1991	1987	1988	1989	1990	1991	1992	1993 Forecast	1994 Forecast
Singapore	60.9	27.8	34.9	13.3	22.1	9.2	4.0	8.6	9.2
Southeast Asia (less Singapore)	107.7	20.6	27.5	25.7	27.5	15.4	10.3	11.9	13.9
Indonesia	24.6	5.0	10.4	17.9	31.5	14.8	10.0	10.5	11.0
Malaysia	34.0	15.7	28.4	35.6	29.9	26.3	6.0	10.0	12.0
Philippines	12.1	33.6	21.1	27.7	17.2	-1.3	14.6	13.3	13.0
Thailand	34.2	42.8	48.6	27.4	29.9	15.8	12.8	15.0	17.0
Vietnam	2.2	13.9	12.3	-6.9	7.3	-20.2	14.1	24.7	28.0

Source: Asian Development Outlook 1993, The Asian Development Bank.
*f.o.b., billion $US.

Prospects for Future Growth in Southeast Asia

Will Southeast Asia continue to sustain its impressive economic growth results over the 1990s? Short to medium-term forecasts for the Southeast Asian countries all show a continuation of steady economic growth (see table 1). For the first time in almost a generation, forecasters are optimistic about the Philippines. Vietnam is expected to grow rapidly over the next several years. The forecasters point to continued growth in manufactured exports and imports for Southeast Asia. Increasingly, however, as their economies mature, domestic factors are providing the main source of economic growth, not trade. Results reported in last year's *Pacific Economic Outlook* show that increases in domestic consumption and domestic investment are now accounting for the bulk of the economic growth in the region (see table 2). Economic growth in Southeast Asia, therefore, will increasingly depend on domestic macroeconomic management and internal competitiveness policies. Exports are still important to these countries, especially as a stimulus for productivity gains and covering debt service requirements, but growth in imports is expanding equally rapidly, offsetting the net macroeconomic impact of trade flows on the economy.

Growth rates are moderating a bit relative to the recent go-go years, as Indonesia, Thailand, Malaysia, and Singapore have taken measures to dampen domestic economic growth in the face of perceived macroeconomic overheating. This reinforces the Southeast Asian countries' traditional support for conservative macroeconomic management underlying steady, well-managed long-term growth. As a sign of economic maturing, each country is working to develop more sophisticated financial markets and (indirect) monetary control instruments that will facilitate fine tuning rather than the "sledge hammer" effect often caused by resort to direct credit and administrative controls. Southeast Asia's commitment to conservative macroeconomic policies is another hallmark of the Southeast Asian development story.

The strong growth in Eastern (Southeast and Northeast) Asian economies in general has increased demand throughout the region. As a result, Southeast Asian countries are increasingly diversifying their export markets toward non-Japan Asia as a rival to the United States and to the increasingly important European Community (see table 5). The strength of the non-Japanese economies has provided a vital cushion of foreign demand that has helped the Southeast Asian economies weather the weak economic conditions in Japan, Europe and the United States. As the Eastern Asian countries become increasingly integrated, each Asian economy benefits from a more diverse and thus stable international demand for its exports. On the other hand, this integration also injects greater competition throughout the economies of the region. To maintain competitiveness both in export markets and now increasingly in home markets, governments are forced to keep up with their neighbors in terms of improvements in their business environment and in terms of physical and human infrastructure. This is a self-propelling process of competitive, unilateral deregulation done without access to any formal negotiating or reciprocity structure.

What are the most important risks to this optimistic forecast? Assuming a continuation of sound macroeconomic management, the following risks are assessed: the impact of the emergence of China; threats to international market access from increased protectionism; and, possible indications of a sustained decline in foreign investment in Southeast Asia.

The Emergence of China. The emergence of China injects a major infusion of competition into the Southeast Asian economies. Not only is China a major alternative for foreign investment and supply to export markets, but China is increasingly exporting inexpensive, some say dumped, goods to Southeast Asia. For example, legal and smuggled Chinese exports into Vietnam are perceived as one of the most difficult constraints to a rapid deregulation of import policies and to a limitation of sectoral industrial policies in Vietnam. Foreign investment is booming in China, while there are signs of reductions in foreign investment in Southeast Asia. Clearly, businesses in Taiwan, Hong Kong, and now Korea and Japan as well, are increasingly attracted to China, both for export and for sales into the huge domestic market.[15] Although it is difficult to measure, there are reports of expanding investments by Southeast Asian ethnic-Chinese firms in China.

International Market Access. Given the diversity of export markets for most Southeast Asian countries, they have benefited greatly from the GATT umbrella of open market and nondiscriminating principles that have disciplined trade policy in most of the countries of the world. The ASEAN countries' increasing support of the Uruguay Round of the GATT reflects these fundamentals.[16] Alternatively, Southeast Asian countries are vulnerable to a breakdown in the GATT talks and to any regression into economic regionalism in Europe or North America. Even given Asia's increasing integration, any major reduction in access to the large developed countries' markets would seriously threaten the continuance of their strong export trends, and thus their overall economic growth.

Tensions within countries from the impact of increased trade and investment flows are occurring simultaneously with the greater benefits arising from trade. Strong restructuring pressures in the developed countries, including not only North American and Europe, but now also Japan, raise demands for protection and domestic subsidies to maintain uncompetitive industries. It will become increasingly important for the fast growing developing countries and the mature developed countries to understand the political and economic pressures underlying each other's trade policies. More and more pressure will be exerted on Southeast Asia to continue to open their markets to foreign competition. Much of this protection is in capital-intensive intermediary inputs, machinery and "high-tech" goods, and sophisticated service sectors. These sectors are where the developed countries are strong and where the developing countries have ambitions to grow. Developed countries, therefore, will pressure the Southeast Asian countries to keep these sectors open to their exports just as the Southeast Asian countries are pushing to expand these sectors in their development plans. Southeast Asian countries, on the other hand, will push for expanded market access in developed countries for labor-intensive exports, just as developed countries work to ameliorate domestic declines in these vulnerable sectors.

International and regional trade agreements will also be important. The successful resolution of the Uruguay Round is the most important indicator of the likelihood of open foreign market access for Southeast Asian countries. The ASEAN Free-Trade Agreement (AFTA) will most likely not have much affect on Southeast Asian economies in the near to medium term, as ASEAN struggles to negotiate and implement the complicated regional trade agreement. AFTA will become more important toward the end of the decade as the policy reforms are implemented and as trade linkages within ASEAN expand over time. The Asia Pacific Economic Cooperation (APEC) forum holds more immediate promise, especially in terms of expanding the communication and understanding of economic issues in Southeast Asia (the largest group of developing countries in APEC) and the United States. Almost every APEC economy is committed to expanding regional trade and investment flows within a context of "Open Regionalism," which emphasizes steadily declining trade and investment barriers in a nondiscriminatory context. The recent passage of the North American Free-Trade Agreement, again within the context of open regionalism, combined with advances in all other international trade forums, leads to the prospect of minimal increases in protection and the likely reduction of barriers within the region and the world. Market access limitations, therefore, should not be a serious constraint to Southeast Asian growth over the 1990s.

Possible Persistent Decline in Foreign Investment. The most serious threat to a continuation of trade and growth in Southeast Asia, barring any major political changes or ethnic conflicts, may be new trends in foreign investment throughout East Asia. Approvals of foreign investment in Indonesia, Thailand, and Malaysia have fallen significantly.[17] Domestic investment has also declined, in response to tight-money-induced high interest rates. Foreign investors' interest in the region is not disappearing, but there are indications that the ease of the recent boom in foreign investment in Southeast Asia may be over.[18]

Japan and Korea are struggling with internal slowdowns that are reducing business confidence and the supply of capital for overseas investment. The recent strong appreciation of the yen may offset this to some degree, but it will be hard for Japan to lay off domestic workers in response to a shifting of production overseas. To the degree that Japan and Korea are investing overseas, an increasingly large proportion is going to China, not Southeast Asia. Taiwan and Hong Kong, as well, have found China more attractive recently than Southeast Asia. European and North American investment, which is significant but relatively small compared to Asian investment, still shows an interest in Southeast Asia, but there are no signs of escalated interest to offset the Asian decline.

It is important to note that actual investment levels as reported by the national income accounts are showing a leveling off and in some cases a slight decline from the recent historic peak levels. Only investment approvals have shown significant declines, and the new levels are still relatively strong unless compared to the historic highs of recent years. Furthermore, investment approvals are a notoriously imprecise gauge of investment, given the ability of one or two large investments to dominate the aggregate numbers. Nevertheless, for the first time since the Southeast Asian manufactured export boom, there are signs of trouble.

The possible reduction in foreign investment in Southeast Asia comes at a particularly inappropriate time. Many Southeast Asian governments now are planning a range of economic development pushes that move beyond low-wage production into more sophisticated, higher-value-added production. Noting the key role that foreign investors have had in stimulating the export boom, the costs of developing these sectors purely from domestic resources may be quite high. The key domestic capacity for domestic-driven advance is the quantity and quality of education and training. Singapore is well along this track, and Malaysia and interestingly the Philippines may be best positioned for skill-related economic advance. Both Malaysia and the Philippines, and possibly even Vietnam, have invested heavily in developing a skilled work force. (For example, Philippine managers and crafts people have played a key and understated role in the growth of many Indonesian firms.) Indonesia and Thailand, on the other hand, have successfully increased basic literacy rates through investment in elementary schools, but overall spending for high school, technical training, and higher education has lagged far behind the impressive standards of the rest of Eastern Asia.

Summing up, the prospects for continued moderate to strong economic growth in most of the Southeast Asian countries are high. Trade and investment flows will continue to expand and contribute importantly to Southeast Asia's push toward prosperity. There are indications, however, of a decline in foreign investment interest in the region that may have important consequences as these countries struggle to upgrade the technical levels of their production of goods and services to accommodate the increases in real wages that are fundamental to raising broad-based standards of living.

REFERENCES

The Asian Development Bank (1993). *Asian Development Outlook 1993*. Manila, Philippines.

Bhattacharya, A., Pangestu, M. 1993. *Indonesia: Development Transformation and Public Policy*. The Lessons of East Asia. Washington, DC: The World Bank.

Christensen, S., Dollar, D., Sianwalla, A., Vichyanond, P. 1993. *Thailand: The Institutional and Political Underpinnings of Growth*, The Lessons of East Asia. Washington, DC: The World Bank.

Encarnation, D. (1992) *Rivals Beyond Trade*, Ithaca, NY: Cornell University Press.

Hill, H. (1993). "Southeast Asian Economic Development: An Analytical Survey." Economics Division Working Papers of the Research School of Pacific Studies at Australian National University, Canberra, Australia.

Pacific Economic Cooperation Council. (1993) *Pacific Economic Outlook 1993–1994*. Washington, DC.

Ramstetter, E. 1993. "Prospects for Foreign Firms in Developing Economies of the Asian and Pacific Region," *Asian Development Review*, 11(1): 151–185.

Salleh, I., Meyanathan, S. (1993). *Malaysia: Growth, Equity and Structural Transformation*, Lessons of East Asia. Washington, DC: The World Bank.

Soon, T. K., Tan, C. S. (1993) *Singapore: Public Policy and Economic Development*, The Lessons of East Asia. Washington, DC: The World Bank.

Yue, C. S. (1993). "Foreign Direct Investment in ASEAN Economies." *Asian Development Review*, 11(1): 60–102.

NOTES

1. Southeast Asia represents a diverse group of countries, usually including: the six ASEAN countries—Indonesia, Thailand, Philippines, Malaysia, Singapore and Brunei; the Indochina countries of Vietnam, Cambodia and Laos; and Myanmar. Due to their size, Brunei, Laos, and Cambodia will not be included in most of the analysis, while Myanmar will not be examined because of its still extreme isolation from world markets. Most of the discussion in this chapter will be generalizable among the ASEAN countries, except for the Philippines, which has lagged far behind in its economic development program. Vietnam will be included as much as possible, even though the Indochina countries (and Myanmar) are just beginning to address economic reforms seriously, setting them more or less at the same position as Indonesia in the late 1960s.

2. See Hill (1993) for an excellent overview of the Southeast Asian development experience.

Hill notes on page 8, "As one surveys economic developments over the past 25 years, and especially during the 1980s, a recurring message in the literature is the importance of pragmatic, effective and outward looking policy reform. Banking sectors have been liberalized, protection reduced, state enterprises reformed, taxation structures overhauled, and incentive systems re-evaluated."

3. See the references for the World Bank's Lessons of East Asia series for more detail on the evolution of each country's economic policy regimes.

4. See T. K. Soon and C. S. Tan, *Singapore: Public Policy and Economic Development, The Lessons of East Asia* (Washington, DC: The World Bank, 1993).

5. Japan was the leading non-oil foreign investor in Southeast Asia during the 1970s, especially in terms of investment in manufacturing largely in response to import-substitution incentives. U.S. investment during this period concentrated in natural resource extraction efforts, especially oil and gas in Indonesia.

6. Except for Singapore, all Southeast Asian countries have been, and still are, predominantly agricultural and rural. As has been the case throughout Asia, Southeast Asian countries have supported advances in their agricultural sectors, both through rice intensification programs and generally favorable programs for agricultural commodity exports. Malaysia more than any other country in the region has benefited from strong agricultural commodity exports. Good agricultural policies offer many benefits. Higher food production reduces food imports and generates a secure supply of basic grains at affordable prices. Exchange rate and export policies benefit rural agricultural commodity exports, generating foreign exchange through exports and rural income growth. Favorable policies toward agriculture in general enfranchises a significant proportion of the population to the growth and development programs of the government, as well as generating high rural savings and surplus rural workers for release to the manufacturing and service sectors. Southeast Asian policies toward agriculture have been much more successful than often debilitating policies in South Asia, Africa, and Latin America. An interesting dilemma confronting Southeast Asian governments is how their agricultural policies will evolve as the role of agriculture in their economies falls. In most developed countries, governments have implemented income support and protectionist policies toward agriculture as their industrial sectors became dominant. So far Southeast Asian governments in large part have resisted this trend. More stringent GATT rules toward agriculture will make such moves all the more difficult to justify internationally.

7. Later in the 1980s and early 1990s, political reforms in Korea and Taiwan opened the door for more aggressive union representation, further increasing wage levels, especially in Korea.

8. See H. Hill, "Southeast Asian Economic Development: An Analytical Survey," Economics Division Working Papers of the Research School of Pacific Studies at Australian National University, Canberra, Australia, 1993.

9. The important role of contract manufacturing is one explanation for the relatively low amount of U.S. foreign investment in Southeast Asia (and China) relative to the large amount of trade interaction. U.S. firms rarely invest overseas in labor-intensive production. Most competitive U.S. technologies are labor saving, or require skilled labor. Much of the incentive for production in Southeast economies, on the other hand, is to take advantage of low wages. Thus, it makes much more sense for U.S. buyers to develop non-equity contract manufacturing relationships. U.S. investment does make sense for higher-technology and intellectual property-driven production such as telecommunications and computers, for many business services such as banking and insurance, and for investment in immobile natural resource extractions. An important policy implication, therefore, is that U.S. foreign investment in Japan is a much more important lever for expanding U.S. exports to Japan than is U.S. investment in Southeast Asia (see Encarnation, 1992).

10. Ramstetter (1993, page 184) notes correctly that "rapid growth of foreign firms has almost always gone hand in hand with rapid growth of local firms and that local firms . . . not foreign multinationals, have been the backbone of rapid growth in Asia." What needs more development here is the key role of foreign investors and non-equity foreign business relationships in stimulating the growth of local firms, especially through new stages of product, technology, and marketing sophistication.

11. For example, the *China Post* on November 23, 1993, reports that "Southeast Asia has replaced the United States as Taiwan's largest export market, absorbing 32.1 percent [of Taiwan's total exports] or US$22.7 billion. . . . The U.S. was second with 27.6 percent or US$19.6 billion, and Hong Kong came in third with 21.6 percent or US$15.3 billion."

12. Given the interest in privatization in Latin America and Europe, it is surprising that there has been little effort to privatize state-owned firms in Southeast Asia, or for that matter all of East Asia. In Indonesia, for example, a privatization drive began to build in the late 1980s, but it quickly lost force. The difficulty was not so much ideological nor even fiscal, but primarily the practical problem of who to sell the state firms to. Potential private owners, even if privatized through public stock issues, appeared to be concentrated among friends of the government, ethnic-minority businesses, or foreigners, none of which met political and equity standards. In addition, the political push for privatization was dampened within governments because state-owned firms were not major drags on government spending, and these firms provided the largest grouping of ethnic majority management in the economy.

13. The political and economic role of ethnic-Chinese businesses are important in every Southeast Asian country, but often in different forms and degrees. It is impossible to detail the subtleties of these relationships in each country in an overview chapter such as this.

14. One explanation contributing to the difficulty of developing a broad, multiethnic business class involves the weak commercial law environment throughout Southeast Asia (and the rest of Asia). Chinese family groups have learned to do business effectively in conditions of chaos and weak formal legal structures by developing informal contract and enforcement systems that reduce transaction costs within the group. Transaction costs with outsiders, however, can be much more costly because of insufficient contract enforcement mechanisms. A Chinese business person, in many cases, may find it less costly to trade with a Chinese business person from another country than with a non-Chinese business in their own city. All concerned are out to maximize returns in response to clear profit incentives; non-economic preference for in-group trading is insignificant. Improving commercial law systems, however, is difficult. Writing new commercial laws is not particularly daunting, but developing an effective judicial and enforcement system is costly in both funds and time, often introducing difficult political considerations as well. Few Asian countries have a sophisticated and widely used formal commercial law system, including Japan.

15. For example, note this report in the *China Post* airmail edition on November 13, 1993. "Taiwan has invested a total of US$4.5 billion in Indonesia over the past years, with a peak of US$1 billion in 1991. Yet the figure dropped to US$500 million in 1992 and further slid to less than US$100 million as of now in this year. The downfall mainly resulted from a boost of Taiwan investments on the Chinese mainland, a practice which has alarmed Southeast Asian nations. Chiang [the Taiwanese Economic Affairs Minister] told Indonesian officials that the government of the Republic of China would very much like to see its mainland-bound investments become diversified, fearing that Taiwan will someday be economically held hostage by the mainland."

16. Indonesian President Suharto made this comment at a November 20, 1993, dinner in Seattle during the APEC leadership meeting. "Open regionalism is the key to the economic advances of Indonesia and our partners in APEC. Even more important, however, is open internationalism. The success of the Uruguay Round cannot be underestimated for the developing economies of the world. Ensuring that markets remain open, that trade will function under well-known international rules is critical not only to the major economies of the world, but to the new entrants as well. Only through dynamic interaction among the world's economies can we guarantee efforts of eradicating poverty, improving the health and well-being of the world's population, and easing international tensions."

17. Major declines in foreign investment approvals over the last two years for Indonesia, Thailand, and Malaysia were reported during a San Francisco talk on September 24, 1993, by Ian Buchanan, head of SRI's Southeast Asia Regional Office.

18. "ASEAN has been highly successful in attracting FDI in the recent past but risks losing its competitive edge as investors face rising costs in Singapore, infrastructural and skill bottlenecks in Indonesia, Malaysia and Thailand, and continuing political and economic uncertainty in the Philippines, on the one hand, and intensified global and regional competition

for FDI, on the other. . . . Within Asia, ASEAN can expect strong investment competition from Viet Nam and the People's Republic of China as these countries embark on economic liberalization, particularly for investments from Japan and Asian NIEs; investments from these sources have already slowed down in various ASEAN countries." See Yue (1993) pp. 97–98.

9

MANAGING RENEWABLE RESOURCES IN SOUTHEAST ASIA: THE PROBLEM OF DEFORESTATION

Gareth Porter

After decades of ignoring environmental decline, Southeast Asian countries have begun to recognize that such neglect carries a severe price. By the late 1980s, one Southeast Asian government after another was under pressure to take new actions aimed at stemming the degradation of renewable but fragile resources and vital natural support systems. But the momentum of environmental degradation is such that no Southeast Asian country is yet on a development path that is environmentally sustainable.

Southeast Asian countries have to cope with a wide range of environmental problems, of which some of the most serious are land degradation, declining groundwater levels and land subsidence, pesticide contamination of water and soil, depletion of marine fish stocks from overfishing, urban air pollution, and pollution of rivers and streams by industrial and residential wastes.

But this chapter will analyze the Southeast Asian environmental problem that has attracted the most attention worldwide: the loss of the region's forests. Deforestation is not only a problem for Southeast Asian countries but a global environmental issue, affecting all mankind. It is a source of emissions of carbon dioxide, thus contributing to the threat of global warming, and it is also the single most important cause of biodiversity loss worldwide, since tropical forests are believed to hold 50 to 90 percent of the earth's biological diversity.

This chapter highlights some similarities among Southeast Asian countries in the patterns of forest loss, the causes of deforestation, and the physical and economic consequences of forest loss. It will show that commercial logging overshadows shifting agriculture as the main cause of deforestation, that export markets have been a powerful pull factor in speeding up the destruction of forests and that all Southeast Asian countries have experienced remarkably similar consequences for their watersheds from the denuding of once-forested hillsides.

Finally, the study examines the main policy responses of regional governments to the problem of deforestation: various kinds of bans on logging or log exports and national forest plans. It concludes that most such plans have not yet reflected the political will to make policy changes necessary to stem the destruction of Southeast Asia's forests.

EXTENT OF DEFORESTATION

Southeast Asia's tropical forests have been one of the world's great storehouses of not only tropical timber but of biological diversity. Indonesia alone has 10 percent of the world's tropical forests and about 90 percent of the remaining undisturbed tropical hardwood forests in Asia.[1] It is also considered by biologists as the second most important "megadiversity" country in the world, because of the number of the plant and animal species to which its forests are home. Indonesian forests hold about 10 percent of all plant species, 12 percent of mammals, and 17 percent of birds worldwide.[2] The forests in Malaysia's Sarawak state have what specialists believe to be the richest forest in the world in terms of the biodiversity of the trees themselves, with several thousand tree species. Some of these species could be 10 million years old, and some of the trees are 150 feet tall.[3] Burma has 80 percent of the world's remaining teak forests, now that Thailand's teak forests have been cut down.[4] And it is home to Asia's largest remaining wild elephant herds. Thailand's Khao Yai National Park has been designated as one of eleven sites in the world known as "Vavilov Centers," meaning that it has some of the most valuable species in the world in terms of genetic materials for the development of new drugs.[5] Other Southeast Asian countries all have endemic plant and animal species that face extinction if the destruction of rain forests is not halted.[6] Even now, three-fourths of the 44 primate species known to exist in the region have suffered a serious decline in population because of they have lost at least half their range due to vanishing forests.[7] And forests provide vital environmental services in protecting watersheds from soil erosion and maintaining climate and hydrological balances.

Before the onslaught on Southeast Asian forests that began in the 1960s, most of the land area of Southeast Asia was covered by a lush forest cover. Only Vietnam and the Philippines had less than half of their land area under forest cover. Cambodia, Laos, and Indonesia all had 70 percent of their land area under forest cover in the 1950s and 1960s (see figure 1).

Estimates of forest cover and forest loss in the region are often based on inadequate data, and when the data come from government agencies, frequently they have been unreliable. Nevertheless, the estimates available indicate how rapidly the region's forest resources have been depleted and how far the process has already gone. The Philippines, Thailand, and Vietnam have dangerously little forest cover, and Laos, Burma, and Cambodia are not far behind. Malaysia and Indonesia still have more than half of their forest cover, but have lost their forest resources over the past few decades at an alarming rate (see figure 2).

Thailand, the Philippines, and Vietnam have the lowest level of forest cover remaining in the region. Thailand probably had only about 15 percent of its land area still under forest cover by 1992—significantly lower than the official government estimate.[8] Commercially valuable timber is confined to remote mountain areas. That figure suggests Thailand was losing about 719,000 hectares of forest, or 2.6 percent of its 1961 forest every year over the 1961–1988 period.[9] The rate of deforestation slowed dramatically to 235,000 hectares from 1985 to 1988 and since 1888 is estimated at 40,000 hectares annually.[10]

The Philippines had between 14 and 20 percent of total land area under forest cover in 1990.[11] These estimates stand in contrast to the minimum of 54 percent forest cover that Haribon, the leading Philippine environmental organization, considers necessary for the stability of the ecosystem.[12] Undisturbed primary forests in the Philippines have been reduced to 800,000 hectares or 1.8 million hectares, depending on which source is believed, out of an original 6.5 million hectares.[13] The official figure for annual forest loss as of 1992 was 100,000 hectares, but unofficial estimates suggest it could be two and a half times greater.[14]

Vietnam has only 16 to 19 percent of its land area (5.4 to 6.2 million hectares) remaining under forest cover, depending on whether higher or lower estimates of annual deforestation are used.[15] Although most of these are classified as primary forests, less than 2 million hectares of primary forests of commercial quality remain intact, and these are widely scattered.[16] If the higher estimate of current rates of deforestation continue, Vietnam will have lost almost all of its primary forests by around 2010.[17]

Cambodia, Laos, and Burma constitute a second group of countries having approximately 30 to 40 percent of their land area under forest cover. Cambodia had a forest cover estimated at 38 percent in 1992.[18] UNDP estimated that Cambodia was losing its forests at a rate of 250,000 hectares annually at the time of the formation of the "Supreme National Council" in 1992.[19] At that rate of destruction, Cambodia would lose all its natural forests by 2020.[20]

Laos has between 28 and 34 percent of its land area under forest cover.[21] Of its remaining forests, only about 1 million hectares (17 percent of the total) are considered to be commercially exploitable for timber because they are intact and accessible.[22] If the high end of the estimates for the annual deforestation rate in Laos, 400,000 hectares, were to continue indefinitely, it would exhaust the existing forest cover of Laos around 2010–2012.[23]

Burma is now estimated to have 30 to 33 percent of its land area under forest cover. The range of estimates of the annual rate of deforestation is from 600,000 hectares to 1 million hectares. Depending on which rate is used, the continuation of such rates of deforestation would result in the loss of all of Burma's forest cover sometime between 2011 and 2028.[24]

Malaysia claimed that 59 percent of its land was under forest cover as of 1990, and that Sarawak had 71 percent of its land area under forest cover.[25] However, given the estimates of the actual rate of logging of Sarawak's forests over nearly 30 years and the destructive impact of that logging, the

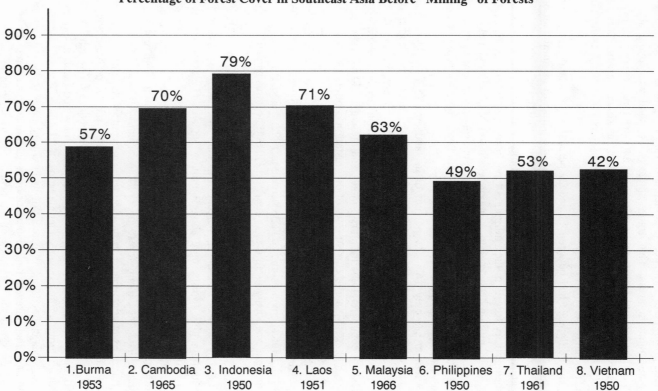

FIGURE 1
Percentage of Forest Cover in Southeast Asia Before "Mining" of Forests

actual percentage of land still under *effective* forest cover (i.e., forest cover that fulfills essential environmental functions) in Sarawak is now probably only about 56 percent.[26] Thus, Malaysia as a whole is now estimated to retain only 47 percent of land area under forest cover.[27] In 1990, the World Bank and the International Tropical Timber Organization (ITTO) warned that the Malaysian state of Sarawak would have logged over all primary forests within 11 years if the rate of deforestation continued at its 1989 rate.[28] The Malaysian state of Sabah is expected to be completely logged over as early as 1995.[29]

Indonesia, with the largest forests in the region, has an estimated 54 percent of its total land area under forest cover.[30] But Indonesia has been destroying its forests at a rate of 1.3 million hectares annually.[31] The government of Indonesia projects that from 1990 to 2030 the country will lose 750,000 hectares of forest land per year, which would leave that country with only 38 percent of its territory under forest cover by the end of the period.[32] By 2050, according to the World Bank, natural forests in Indonesia would be insufficient to assure the survival of the plant and animal species dependent on the them for habitats.[33]

Papua New Guinea has the highest percentage of land area under forest cover in the region, with 76 percent in 1992.[34] Its annual loss of forests was estimated in 1992 at 200,000 hectares, or 6 percent of the forest cover then existing (although one specialist believes the annual rate was 75 percent

References for Figure 1

1. Seema Agarwal, *The Scope of Biological Diversity in Burma*, Agency for International Development, Rangoon, December 1987, p. 9.

2. John V Dennis and Gregory Woodsworth, *Report to the United Nations Conference (UNCED); Environmental Priorities and Strategies for Strengthening Capacity for Sustainable Development in Cambodia*, submitted to UNDP Phnom Penh, April 7, 1992, p. 9.

3. Charles Barber, Nels Johnson, and Emmy Hafild, *Breaking the Logjam: Obstacles to Forest Policy Reforms in Indonesia and the United States*, Washington, DC: World Resource Institute, forthcoming, p. 10.

4. Marcha Belcher and Anegla Gennino, eds., *Southeast Asia Rainforests: A Resource Guide and Directory* (New York: Rainforest Action Network and The World Rainforest Movement, 1993), p. 20; and Larry Lohmann, "Lao People's Democratic Republic Tropical Forestry Action Plan (First Phase), Main Report, August 1990: A Critique," November 20, 1990, p. 20.

5. This figure is calculated from statistics in *Southeast Asia Rainforests*, p. 24; and *A Report on the Tropical Timber Industry in Sarawak, Malaysia, Report of a Congressional Staff Study Mission to Malaysia, March 25–April 2, 1989*, to the Committee on Foreign Affairs U.S. House of Representatives, September 1989, p. 11; and N. Mark Collins, Jeffrey A. Sayer and Timothy C. Whitmore, *Conservation Atlas of Tropical Forests: Asia & Pacific*, (Macmillan; London, 1991), p. 185–186.

6. *Southeast Asia Rainforests*, p. 34.

7. *Thailand National Report to the United Nations Conference on Environment and Development (UNCED)*, June 1992, p. 142.

8. Hoang Hoe, "The Role of Forestry for Sustainable Development in Vietnam," unpublished paper, n.d., p. 5, and Richard Pardo, "Forest Policy Foundation for Vietnam," FAO/UNDP Project VIE/82/02, August 1989, p. 3.

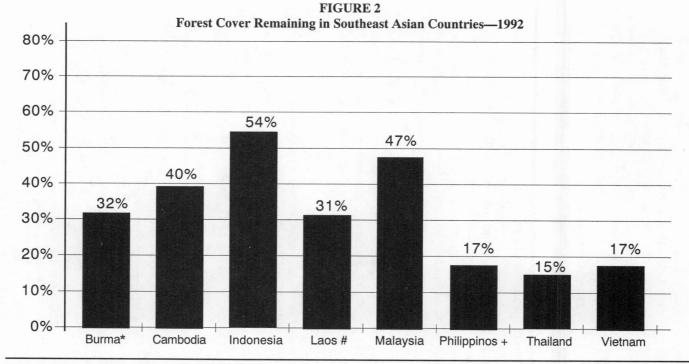

FIGURE 2
Forest Cover Remaining in Southeast Asian Countries—1992

Notes: * Burma: Range of estimates 30% to 33%.
        # Laos: Range of estimates 28% to 34%.
        + The Philippines: Range of estimates 14% to 20%.

higher).[35] But as the FAO noted in 1986, timber cutting was being carried out much faster than the forest could regenerate itself.[36] And that was before the Papua New Guinea government decided in 1993 to accelerate significantly the rate of logging.

CAUSES OF DEFORESTATION

The main causes of deforestation in every country of Southeast Asia are commercial logging, fuelwood gathering, shifting cultivation, conversion to agriculture, and other development projects (hydroelectric dams, transmigration). The importance of each of these factors varies from one country to another, but smallholder encroachment on forests, deforestation from slash and burn agriculture, and logging are always closely related to one another. Thus, assigning a certain percentage of deforestation in a given country to one or another of these factors can be misleading.

The shifting agriculture practiced by indigenous forest-dwelling peoples, which involves continuous production in a particular site for only a few years before moving on to a new site, is blamed by forestry officials throughout Southeast Asia for most of their deforestation. Indonesia's 1985 forestry plan emphasized the importance of controlling shifting cultivation in order to reduce deforestation.[37] Malaysia blames shifting cultivation for the deforestation of 4.6 million hectares in the country as a whole and 3.3 million hectares in Sarawak alone.[38] Vietnamese officials attribute the degradation of 5 million hectares of forest to shifting agriculture by ethnic minorities living in the highlands,[39] and since the late 1960s, the Philippine Forestry Ministry and logging interests have actively propagandized the idea that shifting cultivators were the main culprit in the Philippines' rapid deforestation.[40]

Vietnam and Laos, too, have aggressively sought to convert shifting cultivators to fixed crop production and tree farming. The Vietnamese government has already converted some 500,000 upland people practicing shifting cultivation and are in the process of resettling another 500,000.[41] The Lao government has set a target of resettling 900,000 shifting cultivators as permanent cultivators by the year 2000 and hopes to eliminate shifting cultivation entirely by the year 2050.[42]

There is abundant evidence, however, indicating that most slash and burn agriculture in Southeast Asia in the past has not destroyed or degraded the forests.[43] Shifting cultivation usually does not result in deforestation unless those who use it are confined to an area too small to permit adequate fallow periods. But when logging or other development projects are introduced into the forests, or population grows too large in forested areas, shifting cultivators are forced to reduce the fallow period. The danger to the forest occurs when the fallow period is too short to allow the forest to regenerate.[44]

Shifting cultivation has resulted in forest loss in the region, but the main pressures on the forests have been from lowland populations in search of agricultural land. In nearly every Southeast Asian country, high population to land ratios—exacerbated in some cases by maldistribution of land—have altered the delicate ecological balance that existed for generations in the uplands between ethnic minorities and the forests.

In the upper slopes of Northern Thailand, where ethnic minority populations have increased more rapidly than elsewhere in Southeast Asia (because of immigration from Burma, Laos, and China as well as exceptionally high birth rates), shifting cultivation has resulted in seriously degraded forests. But the main areas of deforestation in Thailand have been the Northeast, East, and Central regions, where the primary cause of deforestation has been the conversion of forest land to lowland agriculture for both commercial and subsistence production.[45]

In Vietnam's midlands (the area between the lowlands and high mountain altitudes), deforestation has been driven by increasing population density, much of which is accounted for by the resettlement or migration of some 3.5 million ethnic Vietnamese (*Kinh*) into the midlands.[46] By the 1980s, the ethnic minorities, most of which had practiced shifting cultivation in the past, were outnumbered by ethnic Vietnamese (*Kinh*) in the central highlands region for the first time.[47] Specialists at Hanoi's Institute for Social Studies estimate that 70 percent of the forest destruction has been carried out by the ethnic Vietnamese who have moved from the lowlands into forest lands with unsustainable logging and agricultural technologies.[48]

In Laos as well, most of the damage to the forest in the midlands is done by lowland farmers who have taken advantage of logging roads to move into the forest because of insufficient rice land and low yields. The shifting cultivation practiced by minorities living in the midlands has maintained ecological balance in the past, but increasing population in the midlands has tended to shorten the fallow periods, leading to deforestation.[49]

In the Philippines the ethnic minorities practicing true shifting cultivation constitute less than half the population of the upland forest zone. Most of the damage to forests is caused by relatively recent immigrants into the forests, primarily from the lowlands, who bring with them technologies inappropriate for upland agriculture, in particular the plow.[50] Despite the Forestry Department's traditional bias against shifting agriculture, the official Philippine report to the U.N. Conference on Environment and Development attributes only 8.4 percent of the country's annual deforestation to shifting cultivation.[51]

Similarly, in Indonesia, the main population pressures on the forests have not been from shifting cultivators but the massive program of transmigration from densely populated Java to the more thinly populated outer islands, where the country's tropical forests are located. The World Bank estimates that transmigration is responsible for about 30 percent of the deforestation in

Indonesia.[52] The transmigration settlement sites have been mostly either in or near forests, and after migrants try to convert the forest land to annual food crops that are inappropriate for the soils, they frequently move on to cut down more forests to begin all over again.[53]

When both its direct and indirect effects are taken into account, commercial logging operations, much of which is for export, must be considered the most important cause of deforestation in the region. Logging is the single most important factor in this lowland migration into upland forest areas. In the case of Indonesia, for example, the World Bank notes that logging contributes to deforestation indirectly through logging roads that open up the forest to smallholders and by attracting new settlers to the forest with logging jobs.[54] The Philippine government has noted that shifting agriculture destroys forests primarily in logged-over areas, where the presence of logging roads as well as the assistance of logging companies has encouraged hundreds of thousands of land-hungry farmers to seek new agricultural land.[55] In Papua New Guinea, logging accounted directly for only one-third of the forest loss in the recent past, but the logging roads have opened up the forests to agricultural expansion, which accounts for the bulk of the deforestation.[56]

In every country in the region, commercial logging has been carried out in an unsustainable manner and at an unsustainable rate. "Sustainable" production of timber is used here as defined by the International Tropical Timber Organization (ITTO): "a level [of production] that may be attained perpetually . . . [and is] consistent with a prescribed mix of other forest values."[57] In Sarawak, the maximum rate of sustainable logging was estimated by the ITTO in 1990 at 6.5 million cubic meters of timber per year. But the rate of harvesting in Sarawak (based on data from the previous year) was then estimated at 13 million cubic meters of timber per year, and it increased in 1990 to 18.8 million cubic meters per year.[58] The ITTO found that what has been called "selective logging" in Sarawak is in fact highly destructive to the forest, with bulldozers and skidders destroying about 40 percent of the area logged.[59]

In Indonesia, the period of rapid deforestation began with the assignment of large-scale concessions (ranging in size from 100,000 to 1.5 million hectares), to logging concessionaires under the Basic Forestry Act of 1967.[60] The maximum sustainable cut for timber has been estimated at about 22 million cubic meters per year, but the government already allows logging concessionaires to cut about 31 million cubic meters per year, and has allowed sawmills to be built that have a capacity of about 52 million cubic meters per year.[61] Logging practices in Indonesia damage an average of 50 percent of the forest area logged.[62]

The World Bank estimates that 800,000 hectares of forests are logged annually in Indonesia, but that only 80,000 to 150,000 hectares of forests are destroyed annually because of logging alone.[63] This estimate of 10–20 percent of forests logged over forests lost annually appears too low, given the highly destructive nature of Indonesian logging. Moreover, there is some evidence that a large proportion of the log production is going unreported to the government. The leading coalition of Indonesian environmental organizations, WALHI, estimates that the gap between official log production figures and effective demand in the wood processing industry would amount to some 284,000 hectares logged.[64] If it is assumed that the actual figure for forests logged annually is nearly 1.1 million hectares, and that 40 to 50 percent of the forests logged are destroyed, logging would be the *direct* cause of 33 to 43 percent of Indonesia's forest loss. The estimated 70,000 to 100,000 hectares of forest loss due to forest fires is also attributable primarily to destructive logging, so logging may well account for 50 percent of Indonesia's annual deforestation.[65]

In the Philippines, logging concessionaires were believed by forestry specialists to be destroying an average of 30 percent of the forest in the early 1980s.[66] The annual "allowable cut" as of 1986 was 8.3 million cubic meters, which a government task force figured would exhaust the country's commercial timber resources within a decade if continued.[67] Philippine government figures for forest losses from logging during the 1980s were absurdly low, averaging only 2,870 hectares destroyed by logging annually during the decade of the 1980s.[68] Philippine environmentalists estimate that just one logging company was destroying nearly 20,000 hectares of forests annually in Palawan province in the late 1980s.[69]

Intensive commercial logging began in Thailand with the decision in 1968 to divide nearly half the forest area of the country into more than 500 timber concessions. In the 1970s, as the military penetrated deep into forest zones, especially in the Northwest, by building strategic roads, it brought illegal logging and conversion of forest land to upland crop production.[70]

In Vietnam and Laos, state production targets have been set without regard to sustainability, thus severely degrading the forests.[71] In both countries, logging has been carried out by state enterprises rather than the private sector, but there has been relatively little central government control over logging. In Vietnam, the central government directly controls only 1.4 million hectares of forests—about a third of the country's remaining forest cover—whereas some 300 provincial forestry enterprises carry out logging on the rest.[72] Similarly, 72 percent of all forest production in Laos is carried out at the provincial level and thus beyond central government control.[73] Logging techniques in Vietnam are much less destructive than those in peninsular and insular Southeast Asia, but loggers return to cut the same forests after as little as two or three years, thus rapidly degrading the forests.[74]

Cambodia and Papua New Guinea are alike in having little or no capacity to monitor commercial logging and having turned their logging concessions over to foreign companies. The Cambodian central government has opted to give those concessions to logging companies from France, Thailand, and Indonesia.[75] The government of Papua New Guinea has allocated its logging concessions to Japanese, Korean, Malaysian, and Indonesian companies and has shown little interest in strengthening its capacity to monitoring or enforcement, which actually diminished (in terms of number of personnel assigned to monitor forests) by a third between 1972 and 1987.[76]

Systems of allocating logging concessions and taxing logging operations have contributed to the unsustainable exploitation of forest resources by making those concessions sources of windfall profits with little or no responsibility for the conservation of the forest required as a condition. Concessionaires in Indonesia, Thailand, and the Philippines have operated for years with concessions ranging from 1 to 10 years (in the pre-Martial Law Philippines) to 30 years, far shorter than the tropical forest's growing cycle of 50 to 70 years.[77] Thus, concessionaires have had no financial incentive for sustainable forest management. And the ridiculously low fees charged by governments in all three countries on logging operations have subsidized damaging logging and provided incentives for wasteful practices. They have also encouraged the accumulation by logging firms with far more concessions than they could hope to manage efficiently.[78] Indonesia has increased its share of the economic rents from logging from only 8 percent in 1989 to about 22 percent in 1993.[79]

Governments have failed to enforce legal requirements for concession, such as reforestation activities, so the concessionaires have ignored their responsibility to replant. After the ouster of the Marcos regime, 90 percent of Philippine logging concessionaires were found to be violating the terms of the lease by failing to carry out reforestation activities.[80] In Indonesia, according to a regional timber journal in 1991, only 4 percent of concession holders were conducting "proper logging practices.[81]

Logging concessions have been allocated by governments in the region in order to enrich their own families and their political and business associates. Prominent among the Indonesian timber concessionaires are close friends and family of President Suharto, who wield enormous influence over forest policy.[82] In the case of Sarawak, where timber sessions are the *main* source of wealth, the linkage between political power and logging concessions is equally blatant: the concessions are all owned by the political allies and relatives of the most powerful political figures in Sarawak.[83] In the Philippines as well, logging concessions have been allocated by the officials of the presidency and of the Forestry Department to political and business allies.[84] In Papua New Guinea the problem has been bribes to prime ministers and forestry ministers by foreign timber companies to ensure that they get lucrative logging concessions.[85]

Log and timber product exports have played a significant role in deforestation in the region. The Philippines exported between 69 and 83 percent of its timber harvest at the height of its log export boom from 1962 to 1972, before the Japanese moved on to Indonesia and Malaysia as the main sources of raw logs.[86] Malaysia increased the percentage of its log production that was exported from 44 percent in 1975 to 60 percent in the early 1980s.[87] It is now the world's largest exporter of raw logs, with 58 percent of the market worldwide. Half of the logs and sawn wood produced in Malaysia and nearly two-thirds of the plywood was exported in 1992.[88]

Indonesia, once the dominant log exporter worldwide, is now the world's largest exporter of plywood, with 40 percent of the world market. Plywood exports earn about 16 percent of the country's foreign exchange (27 percent of non-oil earnings).[89] Of Indonesia's annual production of 26.5 million cubic meters of raw logs, almost half is turned into wood products for export.[90]

Papua New Guinea decided in 1993 to raise its log export volume from 1 million cubic meters the previous year to 6.4 million cubic meters. More than 60 percent of its log production was already being exported, but it will now be exporting 90 percent of its production, and approximately 60 percent of deforestation will be from logging for export. Papua New Guinea's role as one of the few countries in the region still involved in log exports has exacerbated the long-time problem of massive corruption in the allocation of timber concessions.[91]

For the mainland Southeast Asian states, on the other hand, timber exports have been largely focused on Thailand as a market, and in the case of Burma and Cambodia, have been linked with domestic armed and political conflict. Exports of Burmese teak have been important to the survival of Burma's military regime, the State Law and Order Restoration Council (SLORC). Those exports have provided part of the financial resources needed to buy sophisticated arms from China and other countries,[92] while helping to obtain the political-diplomatic support of Thailand. Officially acknowledged log exports earned the regime an estimated $200 million as of 1989, and they have accounted for about one-third of Burma's total export earnings in 1990–92.[93]

Thai companies were awarded 40 timber concessions in Burma, including several in the area controlled by Shan state warlord Khun Sa, who receives a share of the profits, and in the area formerly controlled by the Karen insurgents.[94] Although official timber exports to Thailand are given by the SLORC as 1.2 million cubic meters, the actual level is certainly much higher. Estimates of the total volume of exports to Thailand alone have ranged from 8 million to 30 million cubic meters annually.[95] Those volumes of timber would be 50 percent and almost 200 percent, respectively, of the official volume of timber used for fuelwood in Burma in 1990.[96] And the logging being done by Thai companies, working with short contracts and no supervision, is clear-cutting rather than being in any way selective: eyewitness accounts report whole square miles of teak forest leveled, and regulations forbidding logging on steep hillsides or near streams and rivers being ignored by the Thai loggers.[97]

Some observers believe even *more* timber may be going to China than to Thailand. According to one report, some 80 to 100 timber trucks loaded with teak logs cross into China every night—far more than cross the Burmese-Thai border.[98] Even taking the low figure for the volume of exports to Thailand, therefore, it seems clear that most of the timber harvested in Burma is being exported.

The situation in Cambodia is analogous to that in Burma, in that the political regime has seen timber exports as a key means of providing the financial resources as well as diplomatic support from Thailand needed for regime survival. But logging deals with Thailand and other foreign countries have been made not only by the incumbent regime but by other armed factions as well. The Vietnamese-supported State of Cambodia (SOC) regime in Phnom Penh exported logs to Vietnam and the Soviet Union for years to repay its debts to those countries, which had reached $1.1 billion by 1989. But by the late 1980s, the SOC began to sign contracts with Thai logging firms with close relations with Thai officials. The total volume of timber exports to Vietnam, Thailand, and other countries approved by the SOC in 1991 was more than 320,000 cubic meters. Meanwhile, the Khmer Rouge faction had signed contracts with Thai companies in 1989 for extraction of up to 200,000 cubic meters of timber annually.[99] Having lost its financial support from China following the signing of the Cambodian peace agreement in October 1991, the Khmer Rouge quickly adjusted to the loss by granting a huge 62-square mile timber concession to the Thai government-owned Forestry Industry Organization. That concession would result in the export of about 250,000 cubic meters of timber annually for four years and generate about $100 million annually for the Khmer Rouge—approximately the same as the total revenue of the SOC for 1992.[100] But in early 1992 the Khmer Rouge awarded a total of 15 concessions to Thai companies to extract up to 15 million cubic meters of timber from the Khmer Rouge zone over periods of 3 to 5 years—a potential of 3 million cubic meters per year—thus increasing the revenue for the Khmer Rouge severalfold.[101]

The Sihanoukist and Son Sann (KPNLF) factions also gave concessions to Thai logging companies totalling about 175,000 cubic meters of timber annually.[102] That brought the total volume of timber exports agreed to by the four Cambodian factions to about 3.7 million cubic meters per year for a country whose sustainable level of timber extraction is generously estimated by UNDP at about 250,000 cubic meters per year.[103]

But that total does not even take into account the "illegal" exports of logs to Vietnam, Thailand, and Laos carried out by Cambodian officials at the provincial level and military deserters from both Khmer Rouge and Phnom Penh armies without the approval of the central government. Those illegal exports were estimated by UNDP at more than 450,000 cubic meters per year, which would bring the total export of Cambodian logs to nearly 4.2 million cubic meters annually. If the UNDP estimate of 6 million cubic meters of timber being used for fuelwood and industrial uses annually in Cambodia is reasonably accurate, Cambodia would have exported about 40 percent of the timber cut down in 1992.[104]

For Laos, timber exports appear to have played an important but secondary role in deforestation up to the late 1980s. The Lao government's official figure for log exports in 1986–1987 was about 10 to 15 percent of log production.[105] After 1988, however, both legal and illegal log exports increased rapidly. The Lao government's most recent figure for legal exports was 300,000 cubic meters annually, while illegal exports have been estimated at 50-100 percent of the legal figure.[106] The World Bank staff estimated total log production in 1990 at more than 530,000 cubic meters, which suggests that most of the total log production of Laos—and all of the additional log production since 1988—was being exported, legally or illegally.[107] The biggest single reason for the vast increase in log production as well as exports is almost certainly the suddenly increased hunger of Thailand for raw wood following the 1989 logging ban in Thailand.[108]

CONSEQUENCES OF DEFORESTATION

The consequences of rampant deforestation are similar throughout the region: in one Southeast Asian country after another, highly destructive flash floods that have occurred in recent years that were attributable in large part to the massive deforestation of watersheds. In Leyte Province of the Philippines in 1991, flash floods and mudslides killed an estimated 2,400 people and left tens of thousands of people homeless. The tragedy was blamed by the province governor on illegal logging in the province.[109] In November 1988 Thailand's 14 southern provinces were inundated by flash floods because of deforested hillsides. In Nakhon Si Thammarat, flash floods and mudslides in a steeply sloped area that had once been forested but had been converted to rubber and agriculture buried entire villages and farmlands under several feet of logs, trees, and sand. More than 200 people were killed.[110]

In Burma's Salween River Valley, severe erosion on denuded hillsides contributed to flash floods in August 1991 that made more than 200,000 people homeless.[111] That same month in three central provinces of Cambodia flash floods that damaged roads, reservoirs and irrigation structures were caused in part by the denuded watersheds that could no longer hold back tropical rains.[112] In the Sumatran province of Aceh, floods in 1990 destroyed several villages and prompted a call by the province governor to end logging that could have contributed to the floods.[113] Also Vietnam's northern midlands, which have been rendered barren by deforestation, now suffer regular flash floods during the monsoon season.[114]

The failure of deforested watersheds to hold back tropical rains has destroyed agricultural land and profoundly affected the climate and hydrological systems of Southeast Asia. In Vietnam, for example, topsoil lost to runoff because of deforestation is estimated at 1,000 tons per hectare per year.[115] Furthermore, Vietnam's major rivers in the north and in the central highlands have lost much of their rate of flow during the dry season—a particularly serious problem for Vietnam, which counts heavily on hydropower to meet its long-term energy needs. In many districts, the streams have dried up, and residents have had to dig deeper underground to get drinking water.[116] Similarly, the Mekong River and its tributary river, the Xe Set, in Laos now carry less water than in the past.[117] In northwestern Luzon in the Philippines, deforestation reduced rainfall and affected both the quantity and quality of crops. The volume of water for industrial, recreational, and domestic uses in watersheds has been reduced by the loss of Philippine forests.[118]

Another impact of deforestation affecting every country in the region is increased pollution of rivers, lakes, and coasts by sedimentation, with consequent reduction of fish catch. Rivers in the deforested watershed in Sarawak have become so muddy and polluted with diesel fuel that the fish catch is now only one-tenth of pre-logging levels.[119] Siltation of dams and irrigation systems, damage to agricultural crops, and threats to the livelihood and cultural survival of indigenous forest dwellers are also widespread throughout the region.[120] In Cambodia, the Tonle Sap Lake has been silting up for years as a result of deforestation, sharply reducing the productivity of fishing and farming.[121] Finally, deforestation threatens the extinction of many thousands of plant and animal species that are endemic to each Southeast Asian country.

The costs of deforestation to Southeast Asian economies are difficult to calculate but are clearly enormous. In the Philippines, the opportunity costs of lost timber alone from deforestation is estimated by the government at 35.7 billion pesos (more than $1.3 billion at 1990 exchange rates).[122] The annual loss to the Indonesian economy from deforestation is calculated, more conservatively, by the World Bank at $1.1 billion.[123] A study by the Thailand Development Research Institute of the economic effects of deforestation on agricultural production concluded that one hectare of forest loss reduced agricultural output by $155, with even greater reduction of agricultural output as deforestation grew more severe.[124]

POLICY RESPONSES OF SOUTHEAST ASIAN GOVERNMENTS

Southeast Asian governments have come under a combination of international and national pressures in recent years to take new actions to stem forest loss. Most have responded in one or both of two ways: adopting a new national forestry plan and passing some kind of ban on logging nationwide or banning log exports. A survey of these policy responses suggests that the bans have not been successful in slowing the rate of deforestation in the region, and that the forestry action plans have generally failed to address all the critical issues in the country's loss of forests.

Logging and Log Export Bans

Since the mid-1980s, all Southeast Asian countries under study, except Malaysia and Burma, have adopted some kind of ban, moratorium, or major new restrictions on logging or log exports. Whether the net result of these policy initiatives has been a slowing of logging or deforestation is not yet clear, since no figures comparing regional countries before and after the bans are available. In some cases, however, the impact of the ban does not appear to have been positive. The Thai logging ban simply shifted logging operations to neighboring countries, while the log export ban adopted by Indonesia may have speeded up logging to serve the processed wood export industry.

Thailand was the first Southeast Asian country to adopt a log export ban (in 1977).[125] It was also the first to ban logging nationwide, as a result of protests by rural villagers against destructive logging, a campaign by environmentalists over logging concessions in wildlife sanctuaries and protected forests, and public outrage at the tragic 1988 mudslide in Southern Thailand.[126] Initially the logging ban was applied in December 1988 to all timber concessions in 12 southern provinces, but it was extended to the entire country in January 1989. The Thai logging ban had loopholes allowing logging if it was approved before the ban or if it was connected with construction of roads, dams, or other development projects. Illegal logging, sometimes involving the military, is estimated to destroy 55,000 hectares of forests annually.[127] If that figure were accurate, the ban would have reduced the rate of deforestation to about 11 percent of the pre-log ban level.[128]

However, the Thai log ban simply shifted the attention of Thai logging companies to neighboring countries, especially Burma and Cambodia. Politically influential Thai military officers and civilians moved quickly after the log ban to make deals with counterparts in Burma, Cambodia, and Laos. Thai Army Commander General Chaovalit went to Burma in December 1988 and negotiated access to timber concessions for Thai timber firms with connections with the ruling Chart Thai party and its coalition partner, the Social Action Party, or with senior military officials.[129] Forty-nine timber concessions controlled by 29 Thai companies in Burma reportedly extended over 830,000 hectares of forest.[130]

Thai timber companies with connections to Thai military and civilian officials along the border with Cambodia also managed to sign concessions with all four Cambodian factions.[131] The Thai search for new timber culminated in early 1992 with the major agreement with the Khmer Rouge providing Thailand with up to 9 million cubic meters of timber annually from Western Cambodia.[132] In January 1992, Thai Prime Minister Anand Panyarachun admitted that Thai logging companies were behind the destruction of forests in Indochina and Burma, although he did not suggest any specific actions to address the problem.[133]

Indonesia adopted a log export ban in 1985, not to conserve forests but to spur the development of a forest products industry both for export and for the domestic market. Creating a higher value wood products export industry could reduce the pressure on Indonesia to export such high volumes of wood products. Because Indonesia controls 40 percent of the market for tropical hardwood products, it could slow the volume of its exports and raise prices in order to hold its export income steady. But the Indonesian government has resisted the suggestion that it might slow the rate of logging, claiming Indonesia would lose export earnings.[134]

The Indonesian log export ban has also been linked with high levels of trade protection for its wood processing industry, which has been able to get logs at lower prices than its competitors in the world market. That protection has removed the external pressure for efficiency in production.[135] As a result Indonesia's timber products industry is highly wasteful: for every 1 cubic meter of wood cut, .25 cubic meter is lost at the mill.[136]

The Philippines banned the export of raw logs in 1986, but log exports had already declined to less than 20 percent of the level of 15 years earlier.[137] More significant was the ban on exports of sawn timber in mid-1989.[138] In 1991, the Department of Environment and Natural Resources passed an administrative order banning logging in "virgin forests"—a restriction that had little meaning, since few forests are totally undisturbed by humans. In 1989, logging was banned in all provinces with less than 40 percent tree cover (65 of the 73 provinces), but it has not been enforced, and the government now estimates that 25 percent of all logging is illegal.[139] A commercial logging ban was passed by the Senate in 1991 but has never passed the House of Representatives, because of opposition by logging interests.[140]

All three Indochinese countries have adopted some kind of log export ban in the past two years, but it is unclear how effective they are. Vietnam banned log exports in 1991 and then announced a ban on all timber exports to take effect May 30, 1992, although it does not apply to the Ministry of Agriculture and Forestry, which continues to undertake such exports.[141] The ban also does not affect logs that are imported from Cambodia for transshipment to Thailand.[142]

Laos introduced a temporary ban on all logging in August 1991, asserting that the step was necessary because illegal logging had reached unacceptable levels.[143] In 1992, however, the Lao government ended the ban, awarding logging concessions to several foreign firms, including those from Thailand.[144] A Laotian forestry official claims that Laos first imposed a ban on raw log exports in early 1988.[145] But it was either rescinded or was ineffective, because in 1991 the government again announced a ban on exports of raw logs by its provinces in conjunction with the logging ban.[146] In fact the Lao government's own enterprises continued in 1992 to carry out logging and processing of timber for export as well as exporting raw logs to Thailand.[147]

Cambodia adopted a "moratorium" on log exports in September 1992 when the Supreme National Council (SNC), the national reconciliation body formed by representatives of the SOC and the Sihanoukist and Son Sann resistance factions after the UN-brokered peace agreement, agreed on the measure. The log export ban went into effect January 1, 1993, despite objections by the Khmer Rouge, who were boycotting the SNC, and was enforced by the United Nations Transitional Authority in Cambodia (UNTAC). It thus served the dual purpose of conserving Cambodia's forest resources while depriving the Khmer Rouge of financial support.[148] Dozens of violations of the ban were recorded by UNTAC in the first few weeks, mostly involving timber shipped to Thailand from Koh Kong. Moreover, the moratorium had a massive loophole: it did not cover logs processed by Cambodian sawmills, which suddenly sprang up after the moratorium, particularly in the Thai border area.[149] Finally, the ban was dependent on the questionable good will of Thailand, whose cooperation in closing the Thai-Cambodian border was necessary to prevent the massive illegal movement of logs from Cambodia.

Malaysia banned log exports from Peninsular Malaysia in 1985, in order to preserve what remained of its forest cover, but logging had already shifted to Sarawak and Sabah. In 1993, Sabah, threatened with the depletion of its timber resources within a few years, carried out a temporary ban on log exports, mainly to have enough logs to service the state's growing timber processing industry. The ban will reduce somewhat the rate of logging in Sabah.[150] That left Sarawak as the only source of raw logs for export in Malaysia.

National Forestry Plans

Another policy response by most of the Southeast Asian governments to international interest in the problem of deforestation has been to formulate "National Forestry Action Plans" aimed at both meeting forest development and conservation objectives. These plans have been drawn up in conjunction with the Tropical Forestry Action Plan, a cooperative effort involving the Food and Agriculture Organization (FAO), the United Nations Development Program (UNDP), the World Bank, and various bilateral development assistance agencies.[151] The TFAP has been widely criticized by environmentalists for having put commercial exploitation of forests above forest conservation and for its failure to give nongovernmental organizations and communities affected by the plans adequate opportunities to participate in their formulation.[152]

These forestry action plans differ in many respects, reflecting the degree of forests remaining and the current role of commercial logging in the national economy. A common denominator of the plans in the region, however, is that they seek to reconcile an increase in the availability of raw wood and a minimum of forest cover. None of these plans envisions ending or reducing to a minimum commercial logging in these forests. Instead they suggest that logging can continue on a more sustainable basis. Most of them call as well for much heavier reliance on reforestation and tree plantations in the future. And in every case, these plans pose more acute conflicts between commercial exploitation of forest or plantation land and the interests or existing forest dwellers.

The Indonesian Forestry Action Plan (IFAP), funded by the World Bank and assisted by the FAO, proposes little change in the existing system of forest management. Moreover, it was formulated through an exercise from which nongovernmental organizations and communities were effectively excluded.[153] The IFAP calls for the continued logging of much of Indonesia's forests on the basis of optimistic assumptions about sustainable logging. (The Indonesian Ministry of Forestry had asserted in a 1990 study that Indonesia could actually increase timber yields while adopting certain measures to make it more sustainable.)[154] A draft of the IFAP circulated in 1990 revealed that the objective of the plan was to "insure [sic] the adequacy of raw materials" for "industries serving the rapidly growing domestic and export markets."[155]

One of the biggest threats to Indonesian forests is the ambitious Indonesian plan to become the world's largest producer of pulp, paper, and rayon by the end 1990s. That plan involves building 56 large pulp and paper mills by 2005, with the first ten to be completed by 1995. These mills are projected to consume 9.2 million cubic meters of wood by 2000 and 25.8 million cubic meters by 2030.[156] The NFAP calls for "massive development of industrial pulpwood plantations," projecting the conversion of 4.4 million hectares of unproductive forest lands into industrial wood plantations by the year 2000. But its projections of plantation production appear to be wildly optimistic, raising the danger that pulp and paper industries will be met by high rates of natural forest destruction.[157] Moreover, government programs to encourage timber plantations provide strong financial incentives for concessionaires to get approval for clearing old-growth forests in order to establish timber plantations on them.[158]

One or the key issues in Indonesia's IFAP is what will be done to reform the terms of the timber concession regime and enforce them more effectively. The NFAP acknowledges that the present system provides windfall profits to concessionaires (estimated by the World Bank at $1.2 billion annually), but avoids a commitment to a specific solution to the problem. On other issues, such as length of contract, performance obligations, and logging methods, it calls for "meaningful change" but is again silent on what policy changes will be made, if any.[159]

Finally, the NFAP pledges to allocate 10 percent of Indonesia's land area (19.5 million hectares) to "conservation areas."[160] But the significance of this pledge is reduced by the fact that such areas have not been protected from logging in the past. There are 3.8 million hectares of legal timber concessions already located within "protection forests," with another 710,000 hectares located in "conservation forests," despite the fact that logging is supposed to be excluded by law from both types of forests.[161]

The Philippine action plan, first drafted in 1989, is called the Master Plan for Forestry Development. It is based on the assumption that logged-over forests can produce the timber needed by the Philippines on a sustainable basis if the rotation is increased to 60 years. It advocates ending the logging of "virgin" forests (a small fraction of primary forests) but would permit the cutting of up to 30 percent of the country's primary dipterocarp forests, extending logging well beyond existing concession areas. It seeks to reduce illegal logging by relying on concessionaires rather than building the capacity of the government for enforcement.[162] In short, the plan appears to reflect the position advocated by forestry ministry and logging interests rather than that of environmentalists and community groups.

Thailand's "Forestry Master Plan," on which drafting began in 1990, does not represent an entirely new exercise in forest policy, since it builds on the 1985 National Forestry Policy. The earlier policy emphasized the promotion of tree plantations to serve the Japanese with wood chips, paper, and pulp. It called for increasing "tree cover"—as distinct from "forest cover"—to 40 percent of land area, but only 15 percent of the area is to be in forests for conservation, whereas 25 percent is to be in "forests for economic purposes," meaning tree plantations. Thus, the plan called for cutting down half the forests that remained at that time.[163]

The 1985 Forestry Policy resulted in a huge increase in planting of eucalyptus plantations from 136,000 hectares in 1984 to 1.1 million hectares in 1989, with a further expansion to 3 million hectares envisioned by the government. These eucalyptus plantations replaced family farmland, communal forests, and grazing land, thus eliminating forest products and firewood for the communities. Meanwhile, eucalyptus plantations depleted the soil and monopolized water resources. In many forest-dwelling communities, villagers fought the establishment of eucalyptus plantations.[164]

So when the Thai government announced in 1990 that it would draw up a forestry master plan within the framework of the national policy and the TFAP, the Non-governmental Organization Coordinating Committee on Rural Development, representing 205 Thai development NGOs, refused to participate in the process as required by TFAP guidelines. The master plan appeared to tilt heavily toward commercial interests. It was financed by the Finnish International Development Agency, and uses the same Finnish consulting firm that had helped the Philippines draw up its forestry master plan.[165]

A discussion draft of the plan completed in 1992 calls for the resumption of logging and conversion of 3.5 million hectares of deforested land to "forestry leaseholds" allocated to villagers currently occupying the land, but transferable to commercial tree plantations. Thai NGOs argued that the plan would not only accelerate deforestation but "worsen conflicts between the industrial sector and rural communities over the control and use of forest land." They fear it will force communities to relinquish their agricultural lands and village commons for eucalyptus plantations.[166]

The Laotian Tropical Forestry Action Plan proposes for the first time to set aside 10 percent of the country's total land area as national parks and other protected areas. In contrast to the Thai forestry plan, the Laotian TFAP recognizes the need to treat plantations as cash crops rather than forests in order to emphasize that they should not "compensate for the use of natural forests." The plan also established for the first time an allowable timber cut (280,000 cubic meters annually) based on sustainability criteria.[167] But that log production limit was considered by forestry specialists from the FINNIDA, the Finnish development assistance agency, to be as much as 50 percent higher than actual sustainable yield And two years later, the government raised the "allowable cut" by 30 percent to 400,000 cubic meters annually.[168]

The Vietnamese TFAP outlines a series of targets for the forestry sector to reach in the 1991–1995 five-year period, including expanding the area of special-use forest land from the current 0.9 million hectares to around 2 million hectares and slightly expanding protection forests (protection of steep slopes and other areas requiring permanent vegetation) from 5.7 million hectares to 6 million hectares and establishing 500,000 hectares of industrial tree plantations. But it also calls for maintaining the existing level forest cover while increasing its export of forest products to $400 million annually. It does not explain how this can be done, except to "improve" logging.[169]

Papua New Guinea's Tropical Forestry Action Plan also advocated intensive exploitation of the country's forests co achieve "accelerated development." That country's forests are unique in the region in being owned almost entirely by local clans, yet the TFAP was based entirely on logging by commercial timber companies. It called for an increase in the annual cut from about 2 million cubic meters to 3.6 million cubic meters. But the government really wanted a much higher target of 6 million cubic meters—a target that it ultimately decided to exceed when it raised log export volume for 1993 to 6.4 million cubic meters.[170] The plan proposes new legislation to deal with the problem corruption, but the credibility of such legislation in the face of a system of logging concessions that invites abuse is questionable.

Malaysia, Burma, and Cambodia have not undertaken forestry plans within the framework of TFAP. In the case of Malaysia, however, authorities have had to respond to the ITTO study mission's proposal that log production be reduced to 6.5 million cubic meters annually. After more than two years of maneuvering over the issue, the government of Sarawak announced in 1993 that it would reduce its log production from 18 million cubic meters to 15 million cubic meters by 1994.[171] But that would still leave the annual rate of log production million 2 cubic meters higher than it was at the time of the ITTO mission—a level the ITTO found to be twice the level that was sustainable.

CONCLUSION

This overview of forest management in Southeast Asia shows that no state in the region has yet made the transition to sustainable management of its forests. Moves toward banning or limiting logging or log exports have been accompanied by too many loopholes and too little political will to protect the remaining forests. Viewing the interactions among forest policies of the mainland states as a single system, one must conclude that those moves have failed to slow down deforestation in that subregion.

Nor have any of the forestry action plans adopted by Thailand, the Philippines, Indonesia, Vietnam, Laos, and Papua New Guinea committed the government to a clean break with past policies of mining the forests. In retrospect, those TFAP exercises appear for the most part to have been carried out to please international agencies and industrialized country governments without altering the development path already chosen by the governments.

The two major causes of forest destruction, encroachment by lowland populations due to population pressures and commercial overexploitation of commerce pose difficult policy issues for the governments of the region. To avoid the destruction of the forests remaining governments have to adopt macroeconomic policies that provide incentives for efficiency in the timber products industry, limit logging to sustainable rates (based on strictly scientific criteria) and to appropriate types of forests, and adopt regimes for logging concessions that offer economic incentives for sustainable forest management and that enforce strict requirements for the least destructive logging techniques and reforestation.

Indonesia and Papua New Guinea are the only countries in the region that can continue to mine their forests for export revenues for more than a decade. International financial institutions—especially the World Bank—will need to take a firm position on sustainable forest management in lending to those countries. International arrangements for trade in tropical timber that reward sustainable management of forests and punish mining of the resource would also reinforce those within the two governments interested in conserving forests.

Further intensification of agriculture throughout the region, accompanied by more educated rural populations, will be required to ease pressures on the remaining forests. The longer-term aim in densely populated countries will have to be to return some of the migrants of forested upland areas to the lowlands instead of continuing to increase population densities in the uplands. International agencies and donor countries must do more to support agricultural research aimed at supplying technologies that can increase yields and are also environmentally sustainable.

Tree plantations must be part of the solution to the deforestation problem for Thailand, Vietnam, and the Philippines. But such plantations—especially eucalyptus plantations—conflict with the needs of forest-dwelling communities, and none of these states has successfully integrated those communities into its forest policy planning. Decentralization of forest management decisions must be part of any successful strategy for halting deforestation, but it has not been adopted yet by any of the Southeast Asian nations.

NOTES

The author wishes to acknowledge the assistance of Vichai Suthamtarikul in researching this paper and Mike Fallon of EESI in preparing the figures, as well as the assistance of Fred Scwartzendruber, Nels Johnson, Richard Pardo, and Mimi Kleiner in obtaining many of the documents cited.

1. World Bank, Asia Regional Office, *Indonesia, Forests, Land and Water: Issues in Sustainable Development*, Report no. 8722-IND, June 1989.

2. Mark Dillenbeck, "Forest Management in Indonesia, with Special Emphasis on Production Forests and Parks and Protected Areas," Discussion Draft, IUCN/The World Conservation Union-U.S., August 1991, p. 5.

3. Stan Sesser, "Logging the Rain Forests," *The New Yorker*, May 27, 1991, p. 46.

4. "The Teak Connection" (Red Bank, NJ: Rainforest Relief, n.d.).

5. *Network News* (Biomass Users Network), vol. 4, no. 1, January-February 1990, p. 1.

6. For Vietnam, see Arthur Westing and Carol E. Westing, "Endangered Species and Habitats of Viet Nam," *Environmental Conservation*, vol. 8, no. 1, spring 1981, pp. 59-62.

7. John MacKinnon and Kathy MacKinnon, *Review of the Protected Areas System in the Indo-Malayan Realm* (Gland: IUCN and UNEP, 1986), pp. 18-19.

8. Official Thai estimate of forest cover of 27 percent (slightly less than 15 million hectares) exaggerates the actual level of forests, because it includes rubber plantations and secondary scrub growth. Larry Lohmann, "Commercial Tree Plantations in Thailand: Deforestation by Any Other Name," *The Ecologist*, vol. 20, no. 1, January/February 1990, fn. 4, p. 16.

9. This assumes 53 percent forest cover in 1961 (27.5 million hectares) and 7.6 million hectares of forest remaining in 1988. See Martha Belcher and Angela Gennino, eds., *Southeast Asia Rainforests* (n.p.: Rainforest Action Network and World Rainforest Movement, 1993), p. 38 and Lohmann, "Commercial Tree Plantations," p. 16. An official Thai government report figures the annual rate or deforestation at 3 percent, based on 30 million hectares of forest in 1960 and 14 million hectares of forest in 1990. See *Thailand Country Report to the United Nations Conference on Environmental Development (UNCED)*, June 1992, p. 134.

10. *Thailand Country Report*, p. 134.

11. For the higher figure, see Dr. Marian delos Angeles et al., "Philippines," *Economic Policies for Sustainable Development* (Manila: Asian Development Bank, 1990), p. 191. It includes forest lands that are highly degraded and may not fulfill minimum ecological functions. For the lower estimates, see *Southeast Asia Rainforests*, p. 34.

12. Robin Broad and John Cavanagh, "Marcos's Ghost," *The Amicus Journal*, Fall 1989, p. 21.

13. Ibid., p. 66.

14. *Southeast Asia Rainforests*, p. 34.

15. The low estimate of 110,000 hectares lost annually is given in *Vietnam Tropical Forestry Action Programme Forestry Sector Review Executive Summary* (Hanoi: Ministry of Forestry, Socialist Republic of Vietnam, 1991), p. 13; a mid-range estimate of 150,000 hectares per year is given in Richard Pardo, "Forest Policy Formulation for Vietnam," FAO/IMD (Rpkect VOE/82/002), August 1989, p. 3, and in *Vietnam National Report to UNCED* (Hanoi, 1992), p. 16. A government study drawn up in 1985 cited the high estimate of 200,000 hectares per year. See National Conservation Strategy Secretariat, "National Conservation Strategy" (draft), Hanoi, June 1985, p. 12.

16. Pardo, "Forest Policy Formulation," pp. 3, 8.

17. See sources cited in note 15 above.

18. Michael D. Benge, *Cambodia: An Environmental and Agricultural Overview and Sustainable Development Strategy*, Bureau for Research and Development, Office of Environment and Natural Resources, Agency for International Development, Washington, DC, November 1991, p. 2; John V. Dennis and Gregory Woodsworth, *Report to the United Nations Conference on Environment and Development (UNCED): Environmental Priorities and Strategies for Strengthening Capacity for Sustainable Development in Cambodia*, Submitted to UNDP-Phnom Penh, April 1992, p. ii.

19. Dennis and Woodsworth, *Report to the United Nations Conference*, p. ii.

20. This is based on forested area of 7.24 million hectares (40 percent of 18.1 million hectares) as of 1992. Dennis and Woodsworth, *Report to the United Nations Conference*, p. 9.

21. The low estimate is based on Norman Myers, *Deforestation Rates in Tropical Forests and the Climatic Implications* (London: Friends of the Earth, 1989), and the mid-range of estimates of the deforestation rate (325.00 hectares per year) from *Southeast Asia Rainforests*, p. 20. The higher estimate is based on the official 1981 figure of 47 percent forest cover and the lower estimate for deforestation rate of 120,000 hectares per year from "Staff Appraisal Report: Lao People's Democratic Republic Forest Management and Conservation Project," World Bank, January 11, 1993, p. 1.

22. *Southeast Asia Rainforests*, p. 23.

23. *Southeast Asia Rainforests*, p. 20.

24. *Southeast Asia Rainforests*, p. 6.

25. "Ministry of Primary Industries, Malaysia," *Fact Sheets: Forestry and Environment*, May 1992, pp. 1, 10.

26. This calculation is based on figures in *The Tropical Timber Industry in Sarawak, Report of a Congressional Staff Study Mission to Malaysia, March 25–April 2, 1989 to the Committee on Foreign Affairs, U.S. House of Representatives*, September 1989 (Washington, DC: U.S. Government Printing Office, 1989), pp. 3, 11; *Southeast Asia Rainforests*, p. 24; N. Mark Collins, Jeffrey A. Sayer, and Timothy C. Whitmore, *Conservation Atlas of Tropical Forests: Asia and Pacific* (London: MacMillan, 1991), pp. 185–96.

27. *Southeast Asia Rainforests*, p. 24.

28. *Report Submitted to the International Tropical Timber Council by Mission Established Pursuant to Resolution I (VI "The Promotion of Sustainable Foreign Management: A Case Study in Sarawak, Malaysia [sic]*," International Tropical Timber Council, Eighth Session, Denpasar, Bali, Indonesia, May 16-23, 1990, (hereafter *A Case Study in Sarawak*), p. 35.

29. *The Tropical Timber Industry in Sarawak*, p. 11; "Logging the Rainforest," p. 47.

30. Barber, Johnson, and Hafild, *Breaking the Logjam*, p. 10; *Southeast Asia Rainforests*, p. 14.

31. Barber, Johnson, and Hafild, *Breaking the Logjam*, p. 10.

32. Environmental Defense Fund, "The National Forestry Action Plan (NFAP) for Indonesia: A Critique," July 1991 (hereafter "A Critique"), p. 15, n. 7.

33. *Indonesia, Forests, Lands and Water*, p. 4.

34. *Southeast Asia Rainforests*, p. 30.

35. Ibid., Myers, *Deforestation Rates in Tropical Forests and their Climatic Implications*, p. 40.

36. Colchester and Lohmann, *The Tropical Forestry Action Plan*, p. 61.

37. Charles Secret, "The Environmental Impact of Transmigration," *The Ecologist*, vol. 16, no. 2/3, 1986, p. 84.

38. "Fact Sheets," p. 10. Officials of the Sarawak Forestry Department conceded in meetings with the International Tropical Timber Organization study mission in 1989 that the indigenous minorities who have practiced shifting cultivation have not cut down more forests than loggers, and that the government simply arbitrarily reclassified all forest under shifting cultivation out of the category of forest land, regardless of its condition. *A Case Study in Sarawak*, p. 106.

39. Le Trong Cuc, "The Current Issues of Natural Resource Conservation in Vietnam." Paper presented to the first Conference of Asian Conservation Organizations, March 12-16, 1989, *Tiger Paper*, July–September 1989, p. 8.

40. Owen Lynch and Kirk Talbott, "Legal Responses to the Philippine Deforestation Crisis," *New York University Journal of International Law and Politics*, vol. 20, no. 3 (spring 1988), p. 683; Owen Lynch, *Whither the People? Demographic Tenurial and Agricultural Aspects of the Tropical Forestry Action Plan* (Washington, DC: World Resources Institute, 1990), p. 17, n. 6.

41. "Vietnam National Plan for Environment and Sustainable Development 1991-2000: Framework for Action," Hanoi, December 1990, p. 89.

42. World Rainforest Movement, "Notes for NGO/GEF/World Bank Consultation on 'Lao PDR: Forest Management and Conservation Project," Washington, DC, April 2, 1993," p. 9.

43. See, for example, Michael Dove, *Swidden Agriculture in Indonesia: The Subsistence Strategies of the Kalimantan Kantu'* (Berlin: Mouton Press, 1985); Harold Olasson, ed., *Adaptive Strategies and Change in Philippine Swidden-based Societies* (Los Banos: Forestry Research Institute, 1981); Terry Grandstaff, *Shifting Cultivation in Northern Thailand* (Tokyo: United Nations University, 1980).

44. See Otto Soemarwoto, "Interrelations among Population, Resources, Environment and Development," in *Environment and Development in Asia and the Pacific* (Nairobi: United Nations Environment Programme, 1982), p. 84; Government of Lao PDR, Ministry of Agriculture and Forestry, *Lao People's Democratic Republic Tropical Forestry Action Plan (First Phase)*, Executive Summary, August 1990, p. 7; "Philippines," p. 193.

45. *Sustainable Development of Natural Resources: A Study of the Concepts and Applications of His Majesty the King of Thailand* (Nairobi: United Nations Environment Program, 1988), pp. 4–13.

46. Bo Ohlsson, "Forestry and Rural Development," Forestry Sector Review Tropical Forestry Action Plan, Vietnam, VIE/88/037, Ministry of Forestry, Socialist Republic of Vietnam, UNDP and FAO, Hanoi, 1990, p. 1.

47. Gareth Porter, *Vietnam: The Politics of Bureaucratic Socialism* (Ithaca: Cornell University Press, 1993), p. 35.

48. Talbott, "Trip Report," p. 10.

49. The agricultural techniques of ethnic minorities in the higher altitude forests, on the other hand, are considered to be more damaging, since they are not based on returning to the site in later years. *Lao People's Democratic Republic Tropical Forestry Action Plan*, p. 7.

50. Lynch and Talbott, pp. 684–685; "Philippines," p. 193. Some recent studies indicate that swidden agriculture is actually becoming less common in the Philippine uplands, as more of the uplanders are practicing sedentary agriculture. Maria Concepcion Cruz, Carrie A. Meyer, Robert Repetto, and Richard Woodward, *Population Growth, Poverty and Environmental Stress: Frontier Migration in the Philippines and Costa Rica* (Washington, DC: World Resources Institute, 1992), pp. 21–22.

51. *A Report on Philippine Environment and Development: Issues and Strategies, A National*

Report for the 1992 United Nations Conference on Environment and Development, Manila, 1992, p. 2–12.

52. World Bank, *Indonesia*, pp. 2–3.
53. Charles Secret, "The Environmental Impact of Transmigration," *The Ecologist*, vol. 16, no. 2/3, 1986, pp. 77–88.
54. *Indonesia, Forests, Land and Water: Issues in Sustainable Development*, p. 3.
55. A Report on Philippine Environment and Development: Issues and Strategies, A National Report for the 1992 United Nations Conference on Environment and Development, Manila, 1992, pp. 2, 12, 13.
56. Colchester and Lohmann, *The Tropical Forestry Action Plan*, p. 56.
57. A Case Study in Sarawak, p. 27.
58. A Case Study in Sarawak, pp. 35–36; Jomo K. S., "The Continuing Pillage of Sarawak's Forests," *Logging against the Natives of Sarawak* (Kuala Lumpur, INSAN, 1992) revised edition, p. iii.
59. A Case Study in Sarawak, pp. 34–35.
60. Roger Sedjo, "Incentives and Distortions in Indonesian Forestry Policy," Report for the Environmental Division, ASTEN, The World Bank, October 23, 1987, pp. 10–11.
61. Barber, Johnson, and Hafild, *Breaking the Logjam*, p. 86; Carl H. Petrich, "Indonesia and Global Climate Change Negotiations," *Global Environmental Change*, March 1993, p. 73.
62. Barber, Johnson, and Hafild, *Breaking the Logjam*, p. 85.
63. World Bank, *Indonesia*, p. 3.
64. An official report is said to have indicated that only 30 percent of log production in Kalimantan was reported to the government in 1990. Callister, *Illegal Tropical Timber Trade*, p. 22.
65. Dillenbeck, "Forest Management in Indonesia," p. 13.
66. Gareth Porter with Delfin Ganapin, Jr., *Resources Population and the Philippines' Future* (Washington, DC: World Resources Institute, 1988), p. 25.
67. Porter and Ganapin, *Resources*, p. 24.
68. A Report on Philippine Environment and Development, table 2.5, p. 2–13.
69. Broad and Cavanagh, "Marcos's Ghost," p. 20. For a detailed study showing that the logging in Palawan by the logging firm in question is unsustainable, due to overcutting and excessive felling damage, see Philippine Integrated Area Development Program, "Logging Methods Review," Integrated Environmental Program, National Council on Integrated Area Development, Position Paper, Philippines, 1985.
70. Komon Pragtong and David E. Thomas, "Evolving Management Systems in Thailand," in Mark Poffenberger, ed., *Keepers of the Forest: Land Management Alternatives in Southeast Asia* (West Hartford, CT: Kumarian Press, 1990), pp. 172–75.
71. Pardo, "Forest Policy Formulation for Vietnam," p. 12; The World Bank, Agriculture and Natural Resources Operations Division, Country Department 1, East Asia and Pacific Regional Office, "Staff Appraisal Report: Lao People's Democratic Republic Forest Management and Conservation Project," January 11, 1993, p. 1.
72. Pardo, "Forest Policy Formulation for Vietnam," p. 12.
73. "Staff Appraisal Report," p. 2.
74. Ian Armitage, "Management of Natural Forests," Forestry Sector Review, Tropical Forestry Action Plan, Vietnam, Ministry of Forestry, Socialist Republic of Vietnam, United Nations Development Program and Food and Agriculture Organization of the United Nations, VIE/88/037, Technical Report no. 7, Hanoi, 1990, p. 28.
75. Dennis and Woodsworth, *Report to the United Nations Conference*, p. 10.
76. Colchester and Lohmann, *The Tropical Forestry Action Plan*, pp. 64–65.
77. On Indonesia, see World Bank, *Indonesia*, p. 10; on Thailand, see Theodore Panayotou, "Management of Natural Resources for Sustainable Development: Market Failures, Policy Distortions and Policy Options," Prepared for USAID/Thailand, May 1988, p. 77; on the Philippines, see Porter and Ganapin, *Resources*, p. 27.
78. See Panayotou, "Management of Natural Resources," pp. 76–77; Barber, Johnson and Hafild, *Breaking the Logjam*, pp. 87–89; Porter and Ganapin, *Resources*, p. 28.
79. Barber, Johnson, and Hafild, *Breaking the Logjam*, p. 87.
80. Porter and Ganapin, *Resources*, p. 27.

81. Debra J. Callister, *Illegal Tropical Timber Trade: Asia-Pacific* (Washington, DC: Traffic Network, 1993), p. 22.

82. Petrich, "Indonesia and Global Climate Change Negotiations," pp. 71–72.

83. "The Continuing Pillage," pp. iv–vi.

84. For the most complete account of the links between political power and timber licenses in the Philippines, see Marites Danguilan Vitug, *Power from the Forest* (Manila: Philippine Center for Investigative Journalism, 1993). Also see Porter and Ganapin, *Resources*, p. 26.

85. Colchester and Lohmann, *The Tropical Forestry Action Plan*, p. 63; *Southeast Asia Rainforests*, p. 30; Aaron Maizlish, "Papua New Guinea Logging Out of Control," *World Rainforest Report*, October–December 1993, p. 5.

86. Porter and Ganapin, *Resources*, table 3, p. 26.

87. *Logging*, p. ii.

88. *Southeast Asia Rainforests*, p. 24.

89. Ministry of Forestry of the Republic of Indonesia, *Indonesian Tropical Forestry Action Programme*, Executive Summary, vol. 1, p. 1.

90. This calculation assumes that one quarter of the volume of the logs has been lost in the milling process. See note 135. The figures for 1992 log production and timber exports are from *Southeast Asia Rainforests*, p. 14.

91. Colchester and Lohmann, *The Tropical Forestry Action Plan*, pp. 63–64.

92. Harbinson, "Burma's Forests Fall Victim to War," p. 72.

93. "Burma Trading Teak Forests for Armaments," *E-Sheet* (Vancouver), April 5, 1991, p. 1; *Far Eastern Economic Review*, August 8, 1991, p. 58; *Southeast Asia Rainforests*, p. 6.

94. Thais Lending a Big Hand in the Rape of Teak Forests," *Bangkok Post*, May 19, 1990; "Burmese Logs Spark Violent Conflicts," *The Nation* (Bangkok), February 10, 1991; "Khun Sa 'forced' to joint logging deal," *The Nation*, February 16, 1991.

95. *Southeast Asia Rainforests*, p. 6; "Burmese Logs Spark Violent Conflicts," *The Nation* (Bangkok), February 10, 1991.

96. *Southeast Asia Rainforests*, p. 6.

97. "Burma Trading Teak Forests for Armaments"; Hamish McDonald, "Partners in Plunder," *Far Eastern Economic Review*, February 22, 1990, p. 18; "Cash-Starved Regime Courts an Ecological Disaster," *Financial Times*, June 21, 1990.

98. *Far Eastern Economic Review*, August 8, 1991, p. 57.

99. Benge, "Cambodia," p. 2; Dennis and Woodsworth, "Report to the United Nations Conference," p. 12.

100. Ken Stier, "Timber Deals Boost Khmer Rouge," *Newsday*, February 1, 1993, p. 15.

101. *Far Eastern Economic Review*, January 21, 1993, pp. 15–16.

102. Dennis and Woodsworth, *Report to United Nations Conference*, p. 12.

103. Ibid.

104. Ibid.

105. Government of Laos PDR, Ministry of Agriculture and Forestry, *Lao People's Democratic Republic Tropical Forestry Action Plan (First Phase)*, Executive Summary, August 1990, p. 8; Mongkhonvilay, "Agriculture and Environment," p. 16.

106. *Southeast Asia Rainforests*, p. 20.

107. "Staff Appraisal Report," p. 1.

108. Larry Lohmann, "Lao People's Democratic Republic Tropical Forestry Action Plan (First Phase), Main Report, August 1990: A Critique," November 11, 1990.

109. *The New York Times*, November 6, 1991, and November 7, 1991.

110. Mervin E. Stevens, "Biologic Diversity—Human and Plants," unpublished paper, April 5, 1990.

111. Rod Harbison, "Burma's Forests Fall Victim to War," *The Ecologist*, vol. 22, no. 2, March–April 1992, p. 73.

112. Dennis and Woodsworth, *Report to the United Nations Conference*, p. 13.

113. *Southeast Asia Rainforests*, p. 17.

114. *Southeast Asia Rainforests*, p. 46.

115. Le Trong Cuc, "Rehabilitation of the Ecologically Degraded Midlands in Northern Vietnam," Paper for Seminar on Environment and Natural Resources and the Future Development Laos and Vietnam," May 3, 1991, p. 4.

116. Vo Quy, "Vietnam's Ecological Situation Today," unpublished paper, n.d. (1985), p. 8
117. *Lao People's Democratic Republic Tropical Forestry Action Plan (First Phase) Main Report*, August 1990, p. 67.
118. Porter and Ganapin, *Resources*, p. 25.
119. *Logging*.
120. See "Malaysia" (Annex 3), *Economic Policies for Sustainable Development*, p. 143; Le Trong Cuc, "Rehabilitation"; Porter and Ganapin, *Resources*, p. 25.
121. Bala Chandran, "Cambodia's Forests Die in Environmental 'Killing Fields,'" Inter Press Service, October 11, 1993.
122. *A Report on Philippine Environment and Development*, p. 2–15.
123. *Indonesia*, p. 4.
124. *Thailand Country Report to the United Nations Conference on Environment and Development* (UNCED), June 1992, pp. 135–36.
125. In 1977, Thailand banned exports of logs except for pines and rubberwood and banned all teak exports, although teak boards and planks were later exempted. Callister, *Illegal Tropical Timber Trade*, p. 34.
126. Larry Lohmann, "Forestry in Thailand: The Logging Ban and Its Consequences," *The Ecologist*, vol. 19, no. 2, 1989, p. 32.
127. *Southeast Asia Rainforests*, p. 42; Callister, *Illegal Tropical Timber Trade*, p. 22.
128. Based on estimate of average loss from 1961 to 1988 of 480,000 hectares. *Southeast Asia Rainforests*, p. 38.
129. McDonald, "Partners in Plunder," pp. 16–18.
130. Harbinson, "Burma's Forests Fall Victim to War," pp. 16–18; *The Teak Connection*.
131. Angela Gennino, "Cambodian Forests Feed Neighbors Timber Needs," *Phnom Penh Post*, August 7, 1992, pp. 1, 8.
132. See note 81 above.
133. *The Age* (Melbourne), January 24, 1992.
134. World Bank, *Indonesia*, p. 9.
135. Roger Sedjo, "Incentives and Distortions," p. 16.
136. EDF, "The National Forest Action Plan for Indonesia," p. 11.
137. International Institute for Environment and Development and World Resources Institute, *World Resources 1987* (New York: Basic Books, 1987), table 20.3, p. 288.
138. Ibid.
139. Callister, *Illegal Tropical Timber Trade*, p. 33; *A Report on Philippine Environment and Development*, p. 2–12.
140. Ibid.
141. Callister, *Illegal Tropical Timber Trade*, p. 34; *Wall Street Journal*, May 5, 1992, p. A10.
142. Callister, *Illegal Tropical Timber Trade*, p. 21. In January 1993 it was reported that Vietnam and Laos were both providing raw logs to Thailand under contracts that were "due to expire shortly." *Far Eastern Economic Review*, January 21, 1993, p. 15.
143. Ibid.
144. Callister, *Illegal Tropical Timber Trade*, p. 33; *Southeast Asia Rainforests*, p. 23.
145. Somphong Mongkonvilay, "Agriculture and Environment under the New Economic Policy of the Lao People's Democratic Republic." Paper for the Seminar on Environment, Natural Resources and the Future Development of Laos and Vietnam," The Indochina Institute of George Mason University and the Environment and Policy Institute of the East-West Center, May 3, 1991, p. 16.
146. *Southeast Asia Rainforests*, p. 33.
147. Angela Gennino, "Cambodian Forests Feed Neighbors Timber Needs," *Phnom Penh Post*, August 7, 1992, p. 1; Callister, *Illegal Tropical Timber Trade*, p. 21.
148. *Phnom Penh Post*, November 20–December 3, 1992.
149. *Bangkok Post Weekly Review*, February 28, 1993; *The New York Times*, May 2, 1993; *Phnom Penh Post*, January 15–28, 1993.
150. *Southeast Asia Rainforests*, p. 28.
151. For a critique of the Tropical Forestry Action Plan. see Marcus Colchester and Larry Lohmann, *The Tropical Forestry Action Plan: What Progress* (London and Penang: World Rainforest Movement and *The Ecologist*, n.d.).

152. See Marcus Colchester and Larry Lohmann, *The Tropical Forestry Action Plan: What Progress?* (London: World Rainforest Movement and *The Ecologist*, 1990); *The Tropical Forestry Action Plan: A Critique* (Washington, DC: Friends of the Earth/Environmental Policy Institute/Oceanic Society, 1989); Robert Winterbottom, *Taking Stock: The Tropical Forestry Action Plan after Five Years* (Washington, DC: World Resources Institute, 1990).

153. Barber, Johnson, and Hafild, *Breaking the Logjam*, pp. 151, 157.

154. Dillenbeck, "Forest Management in Indonesia," p. 1; "A Critique," p. 2.

155. "A Critique," pp. 1.

156. "A Critique," p 6; *Pulping the Rainforest: The Rise of Indonesia's Paper and Pulp Industry* (London: Down to Earth, 1991).

157. "A Critique," pp. 7–10.

158. Sedjo, "Incentives and Distortions," p. 14.

159. "A Critique," pp. 10–11.

160. *Indonesian Tropical Forestry Action Programme,* Executive Summary, vol. 1, p. 3.

161. Dillenbeck, "Forest Management in Indonesia," p. 7.

162. See Colchester and Lohmann, *The Tropical Forestry Action Plan,* pp. 74–83.

163. "Manifesto of 21 Non-Governmental Development Organizations Declaring Censure of the Government's National Forest Policy," April 11, 1990.

164. Larry Lohmann, "Commercial Tree Plantations in Thailand: Deforestation by Any Other Name," *The Ecologist,* vol. 20, no. 1, January-February 1990, p. 10.

165. *Bangkok Post,* May 17, 1990.

166. "Thai NGOs on Thai forestry plan," Bangkok, October 22, 1993.

167. Lao Peoples Democratic Republic, "LPDR Tropical Forestry Action Plan," pp. 9, 12, and 15.

168. *Southeast Asia Rainforests,* p. 23.

169. *Vietnam . . . Forestry Sector Review,* pp. 20–21.

170. Colchester and Lohmann, *The Tropical Timber Action Plan,* pp. 57, 61–62; Maizlish, "Papua New Guinea Logging," p. 5.

171. *Southeast Asia Rainforest,* p. 28.

10 SHOWTIME FOR SOUTHEAST ASIA: AN ECONOMIC AND POLITICAL CROSSROADS

Bernard K. Gordon

Is the title I've chosen for this chapter just too familiar? Does the word "crossroads" genuinely apply to Southeast Asia today, especially since it has been used so often before? Sure, a critic might say, there are new issues on today's agenda, but are they really as significant as some of the monumental changes the region has faced before?

For example, in the early postwar period Southeast Asia faced a basic choice between communism and the West. Most chose the West. Not long after, in the 1960s, the region faced another choice. That was the choice between accommodation and cooperation on the one hand, or regional conflict—as in Indonesia's *Konfrontasi*—on the other. Again, cooperation—or at least non-conflict—was chosen, and ASEAN was born. Later, in the wake of America's defeat in Vietnam, it was said that there was once again a choice. This time it was whether to come to terms with Hanoi, or to "stay the course." That was a rough time for some in the region. For awhile in the early and mid-1970s, it seemed that at least Thailand would revert to form, and once again bend with the wind. But that issue was resolved when Vietnam's leaders showed the other side of their Janus face. Thailand came quickly back into the fold, and ASEAN formed a united front against Hanoi. In the process, Singapore was nominally out front, but Indonesia was quietly in support of the noisy little island upstart.

After that, the 1980s was a more quiet time. ASEAN held firm against Vietnam; built its internal political cohesion; and in the process helped broker the resolution of the Cambodian crisis. The effort worked, and eventually Hanoi withdrew from Cambodia. That signalled three changes. Along with having given up the ghost in Cambodia, the Vietnamese may also have given up their long-cherished hopes for an "Indochina Federation." Not long afterwards they tacitly, but undeniably, spurned socialism. They acknowledged the superiority of the market, and cooperated with the well-known goal expressed by a Thai leader: to "turn Indochina from a battleground into a marketplace." Singapore was once again in the lead in reaching out to the Vietnamese, but it was soon joined by Thailand and Malaysia, as all in the region now concentrated on making a buck.

The 1980s was also the period of strong economic growth, almost everywhere in the region except for war-torn Cambodia and the sick and ailing Philippines. The result was that Southeast Asia's progress was so strong in the 1980s that for most outsiders it fell "off the screen." For Americans, whose attention had been so heavily focused on the region for so long, this was a welcome and happy change. But it also occasionally led Southeast Asians to wonder whether the United States had put them too low on America's agenda. That fear was first prompted by George Shultz's relative inattention to the region, and it was strongly reinforced during Mr. Baker's time. But both Mr. Shultz and Mr. Baker would have strongly disagreed—they would have said secretaries of state have to pay most attention to problem areas, and Southeast Asia happily was not among them.

In many respects, that is still true. The region is peaceful—externally and in large part internally as well—and it is now clearly a part of the global economy. As a market for American goods, for example, Southeast Asia is booming. In 1992, U.S. exports to Indonesia grew by an astounding 47 percent, by 12 percent to Malaysia, and by more than 9 percent to Singapore. And in each case big bucks were involved, as figure 1 shows.[1]

To put this performance into perspective, I have compared U.S. exports to Singapore with Brazil—America's largest market in South America (figure 2). In 1986, U.S. exports to each were roughly equal, but since then, Singapore has left Brazil in the dust.

Likewise, ASEAN's imports from *Japan* have also grown, and in recent years even more sharply than from the United States In 1992, ASEAN as a group imported almost $47 billion from Japan, and are now well above imports from the United States.

On the other side of the coin, ASEAN's *exports* to both Japan and the United States are now quite large. In 1991, Malaysia exported $5.4 billion to Japan and $7.5 billion to the United States (figure 3). In 1992, Singapore sold the United States nearly $12 billion. As those figures suggest, and as figure 4 shows, the United States is the largest market for most ASEAN members. Only Indonesia, with its large oil and gas reserves, sells more to Japan.

These trade figures have brought relative prosperity to Southeast Asia, and the evidence is worth recalling. In 1990, GDP *per capita* in Indonesia was $2,180; in the Philippines $2,300; in Thailand $3,900; in Malaysia $6,140; and in Singapore $15,580.[2] These numbers are astounding, especially in Thailand and Malaysia (and of course Singapore), and with this growth in prosperity has come a significant change in public discussions about the region's long-term economic as well as its political interests.

APEC, THE EAEC, AND AFTA

Two major issues, and a related but narrower development, have brought this to a head. The first of the two major issues was the establishment in 1989 of APEC, the acronym for "Asia Pacific Economic Cooperation." The second was ASEAN's decision, in 1991–1992, to establish and gradually implement

FIGURE 1
U.S. Exports to ASEAN, 1986–1992 ($Bns)

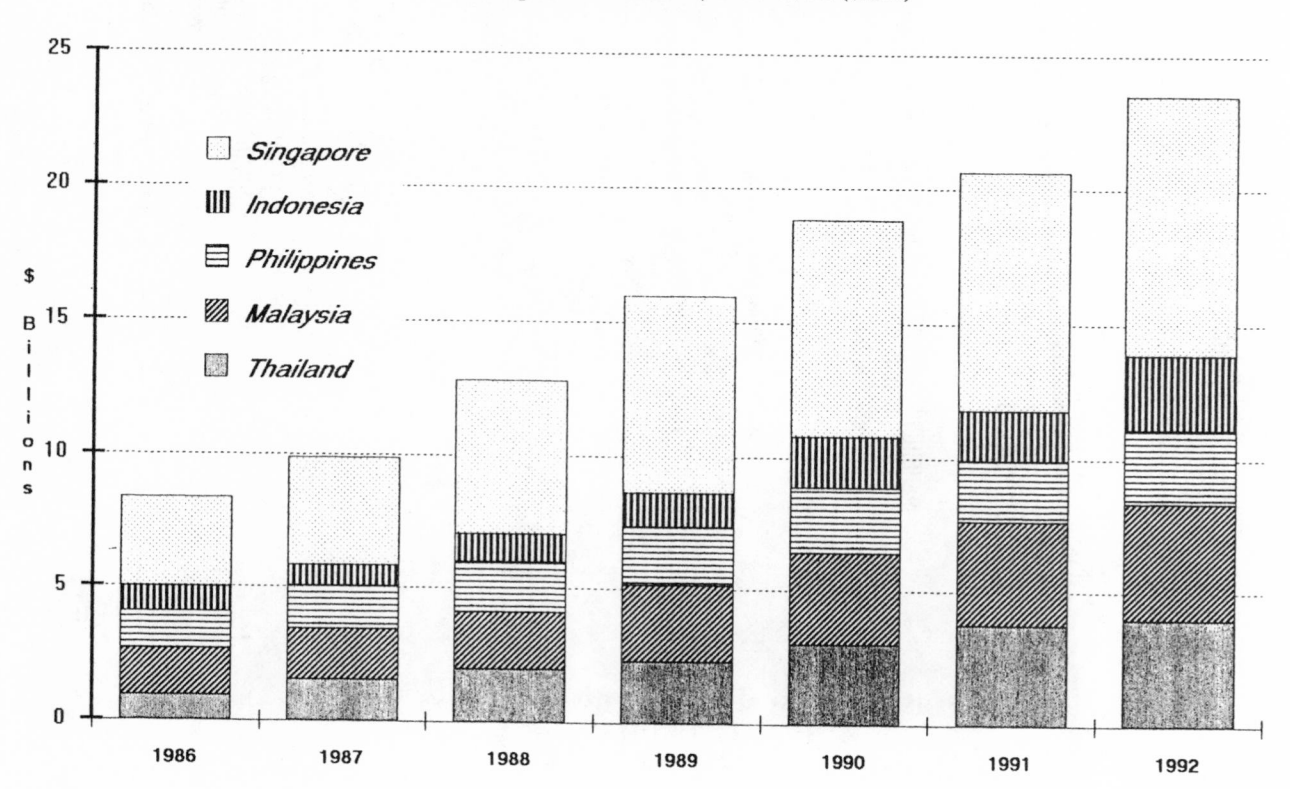

FIGURE 2
U.S. Exports to Brazil & Singapore 1986–1992 ($Bns)

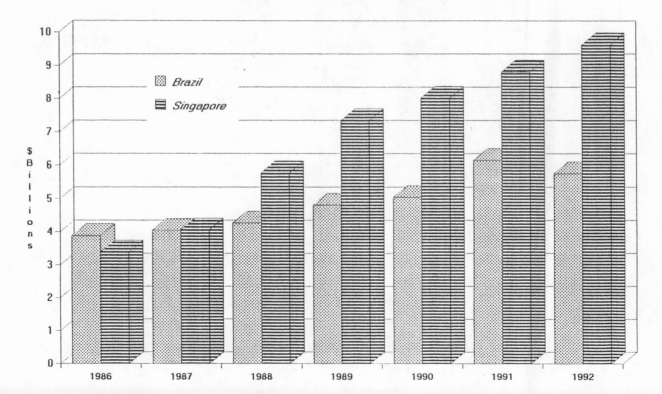

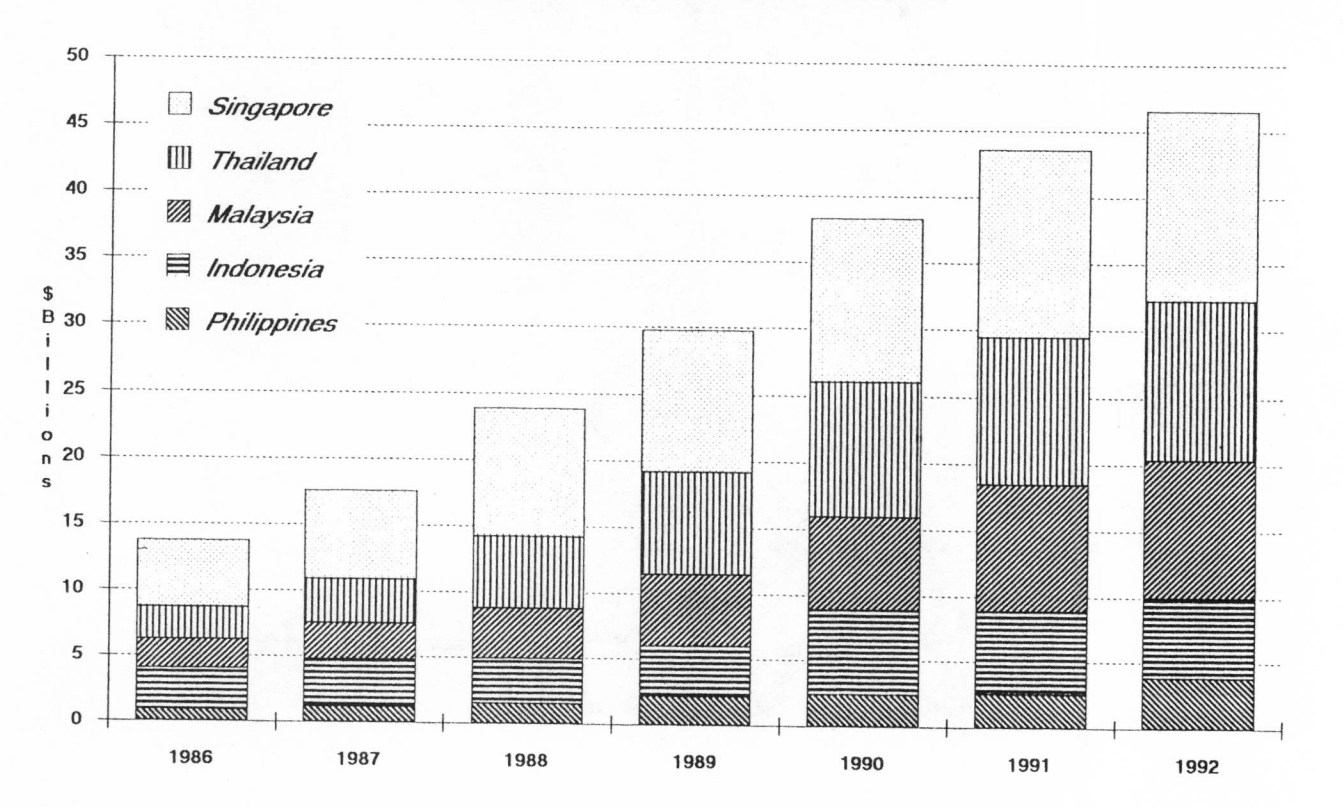

FIGURE 3
ASEAN Imports from Japan, 1986–1992 ($Bns)

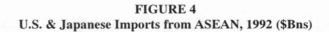

FIGURE 4
U.S. & Japanese Imports from ASEAN, 1992 ($Bns)

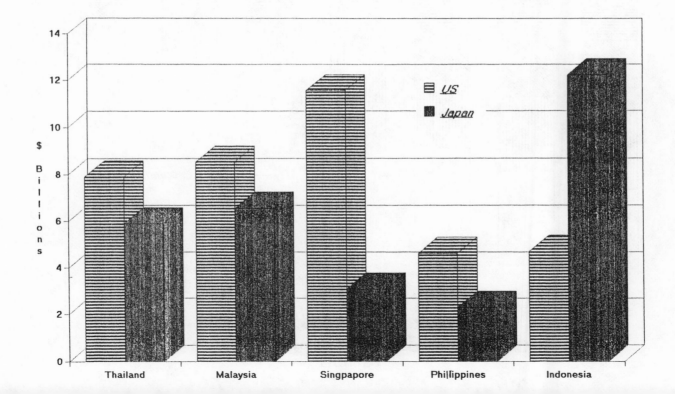

an ASEAN Free Trade Area (AFTA). Between these two formal developments, there were calls in late 1990 for a third body, an "East Asia Economic Group." It still has its champions today, though with a slight name-change, to East Asia Economic Caucus (EAEC).

A bit of history about APEC: it was initially an Australian brainchild, and in its first conception it did not include the United States. But that omission was quickly resolved, and the concept has had very strong American support ever since. Indeed at APEC's first formal meeting in Australia, the United States was represented not only by the secretary of state, but by other members of the president's cabinet as well. That high level of American interest and support was quietly maintained throughout the Bush administration. Secretary Baker once referred to APEC as "an idea whose time has come," and as we all know from the APEC meeting in Seattle in mid-November 1993, the Clinton administration has picked up that momentum and really run with the ball.

Now a second bit of history: close on the heels of APEC's first glimmerings, some in ASEAN expressed their doubts about APEC's likely direction and outcomes. They worried that their long, careful, and successful efforts to build ASEAN might be overwhelmed and/or overshadowed by APEC. The reason is straightforward: ASEAN commands a good bit of respect among Southeast Asia's leaders in business and government (it has also helped spawn a thriving industry among the region's academics). The issue was not so much that it could point to concrete material benefits, but it could point to important intangibles, of which the most important was its visibility. For example, ASEAN has created an institution known as the "post-Ministerial" meetings, which means that immediately after their foreign ministers' talks, they are joined by their counterparts from all the industrialized nations. In other words, ASEAN's "voice" has been greatly augmented in recent years, and *no ASEAN leader was willing to lose that access.*

President Suharto and his foreign minister, Ali Aletas, shared that concern, but they were upstaged by Malaysia's prime minister, Datuk Sri Dr. Mahathir Mohamed. It was his call for an East Asia Economic Group that sounded early alarms because it included only those who were ethnically and racially "East Asian." In other words it would exclude not only the United States, but Canada, Australia, and New Zealand as well. Secretary Baker took strong exception to the racial and *economic* exclusion of the United States, and depending on who you believe, so did the Japanese. I say "depending on who you believe" because there are lingering suspicions that at least some Japanese were not averse to the exclusion. Indeed there are even some thoughts that the original EAEC proposal did not come from Dr. Mahathir, but was inspired by Tokyo.[3] We are not likely soon to find out, but three points about the APEC-EAEC relationship are clear nevertheless.

The first is that Japan, like Korea, found itself between a rock and a hard place. At the 1991 APEC meetings in Seoul, both were confronted by Malaysia's insistence to establish an EAEC, and simultaneously by very strong American reservations to the Malaysian concept.[4] But in the final analysis both Japan and Korea supported APEC, partly because to give any encouragement to the EAEC was likely to be taken "as an expression of *kenbei* (dislike of America),"[5] and neither Japan nor Korea is anxious to promote that view.

Second, neither Indonesia nor Singapore fully endorsed the Mahathir proposal for an EAEC. In Singapore's case the reason was twofold: first, its commitment to a global trade regime as open as possible; second, its dislike for any approach to world trade so openly and directly opposed by the United States. That view of the United States has been shared by Indonesia, which resented Mahathir's proposal for what can best be called additional personal reasons. By that I mean President Suharto's role: in Indonesia, in ASEAN, and especially in ASEAN's history, he is now something of a godfather figure. But he has never received from Prime Minister Mahathir the degree of deference that he believes Indonesia (and perhaps himself) are owed—despite his role as leader of ASEAN's largest and most populous state.

Perhaps the explanation is that the sharp-tongued and confrontational Mahathir is simply cut from different cloth, but whatever the reason, the Malaysian prime minister has found it difficult to defer to the courtly Javanese. On top of that, Mahathir's call for an EAEC was not the first time he acted without clearing an initiative with Jakarta,[6] and that too rankled Suharto. Nevertheless, in an effort to accommodate the Malaysian proposal—and at the same time to dilute the idea—Singapore and Indonesia won ASEAN support to change its name. EAEG would be transformed from "group" to "Caucus," as in East Asia Economic *Caucus*. One wag has remarked that this would nevertheless leave it a "Caucus without the Caucasians."

The third point is that Dr. Mahathir will not go quietly. He remarked last year that he is "convinced" the EAEC "can become reality in five years or less."[7] To make his point, and allegedly to protest what he sees as eventual American domination of APEC (more about this later), he announced that he would stay away from APEC's Seattle summit. His complaint was that APEC "would be turned into a formal body to help the stronger members."[8]

None of this should allow us to be led too far from the two larger issues: APEC'S creation in 1989, and ASEAN's agreement in 1992 to establish its Free Trade Area, or AFTA. This came in Singapore in January 1992, on the occasion of the fourth ASEAN summit conference. The decision to formally create an AFTA was largely the product of the widely revered and hugely successful Anand Panyarachun, twice (and temporarily each time) Thailand's prime minister.

Again, a bit of history is relevant. In the early 1960s, as a young man,

Anand Panyarachun was the permanent secretary to Thailand's then foreign minister, Thanat Khoman. In that role, he played a very prominent part in the initial discussions that led to ASEAN's predecessor organization, the Association of Southeast Asia (ASA), established in 1961. Not long afterwards, in the wake of Indonesia's *Konfrontasi*, Anand—still working for Thanat Khoman—was among the half-dozen Thai, Malaysian, and Indonesian officials who took the steps that led to the formation of ASEAN in 1967. Anand, in other words, was "present at the creation," and it is fair to say that the goals and success of ASEAN have long been very high on his agenda, and that they remained there during his years out of government. Thus, it was only to be expected that at the near-end of his career, but now in his own right as Thailand's prime minister, Anand should press for and finally achieve a formal ASEAN commitment to establish a free trade area.

The reason for that commitment is that ASEAN has long been criticized as merely a "foreign ministers' talking shop." As a thousand critics have said, ASEAN could not point to any so-called "tangible" results of importance, and that *perception* of its insufficiency has made economic cooperation a particularly attractive goal. It was made more attractive to the extent that ASEAN's efforts in Cambodia, and its stance against Vietnam, had succeeded. In other words, while its successes in Indochina had helped bring ASEAN members close together, an agreement on economic cooperation could be just what the doctor ordered for ASEAN's next phase. Beyond that, since greater economic cooperation was the alleged reason for ASEAN's creation in the first place, improving intra-ASEAN trade could now become a proper goal in its own right.

In practice, of course, expanding intra-ASEAN trade has never been either very important nor particularly achievable, at least until very recently. The reason is that ASEAN members, aside from Singapore, largely produce similar commodities, and as they began producing manufactured goods, those too were very similar. The consequence is that ASEAN's true markets have been in the already-industrialized world—meaning mainly the United States and Japan. But by 1991, it was possible to foresee a time when patterns of production would have sufficiently developed so that an intra-ASEAN market, for at least some manufactured sectors, would become a reality. Thailand, for example, now exports more in manufactured goods than agricultural commodities, and it has entered the ranks of the "newly industrializing economies." It is in that context that the Thai prime minister could persuade his fellow leaders that a putative ASEAN "free trade area" could make sense, especially if it were phased in over a sufficiently long period of time.

The new economic agreement, signed at the 1992 ASEAN summit, called for cooperation in five sectors: trade, industry, finance and banking, transport, and communications. But its most significant element was the commitment to AFTA—the free trade area—with a 15-year timetable for full implementation. The mechanism for reaching the goal was a Common Effective Preferential Tariff, an Indonesian suggestion known as "CEPT." It called for ASEAN members to accelerate tariff-reduction on 15 groups of products in three broad categories: manufactured goods, processed agricultural items, and capital goods. At the end of the 15-year period, tariffs are expected to range between 0–5 percent. The agreement allowed for an "exclusion list" for "sensitive products"—those items that a member believed could not yet be exposed to increased competition.

There was much initial jockeying in connection with these exclusion lists. For example in October 1992, the ASEAN economic ministers agreed to put more than 3,600 products on an accelerated, or "fast track" schedule for tariff-reduction. But by December, when they met for the third AFTA council meeting, they proposed delaying reductions "on more than 3,000" of that total. Indonesia listed 1,600 items for "temporary exclusion"; the Philippines 1,100; Malaysia and Brunei about 600 each; and Thailand listed 118. Interestingly, Thai officials stressed that their 118 was the same as proposed by free-trading Singapore.[9] Indeed the whole process was one in which members were anxious *not* to be seen as too protectionist. The Thai press, for example, reported that although Thailand had been pictured as a "villain in the eyes of its ASEAN counterparts," the deputy prime minister "succeeded in persuading [them] that Thailand was more than ready to go along with AFTA."[10] Likewise, an Indonesian economist wrote that his country could not continue to rely on protectionism. AFTA would leave Indonesia "with no choice but to increase the quality of its export products."[11]

Even so, it became apparent that not all ASEAN members were prepared to implement AFTA according to its original schedule, and by late 1993 the date for implementation had been put forward by a year. The new schedule called for its implementation beginning in January 1994, but with no change from the original 15-year deadline for full implementation.[12] Singapore's new trade and industry minister, S. Dhanabalan, was very critical. He sharply suggested that ASEAN members who were backpedaling (presumably Indonesia, the Philippines, and Thailand) should not assume that "others will keep their markets open for them to export while they have their protected markets for their own." But he put the main blame squarely on ASEAN's business groups, for their "schizophrenic approach":

I never believed the . . . chambers of commerce and the private sector that if things are left to them, the whole free trade arrangement will move faster. That's not true, because they are the ones who put pressures on their own governments to go slow or erect protective barriers.[13]

The likelihood is that AFTA will begin to see implementation of its schedule for gradual tariff-reduction, though the Philippines, and to a lesser extent Indonesia, will continue to be laggards. Weak central government in the

Philippines, and the influence of a number of powerful agrarian and industrial-commercial interests, will not allow President Ramos to move ahead easily on most items of importance. By the same token, Indonesia's more centralized system, along with the commitment of President Suharto, will permit gradual and positive change. In Jakarta, the AFTA format will simply provide an additional reason to go ahead with an already-begun program of trade liberalization.

In ASEAN as a whole, the tenor of discussions during the past two years now reflects a widespread view that trade-liberalization is an objectively worthwhile goal. Discussions are frequently marked, for example, by references to "fast track" trade approaches, and the forces opposing liberalization—as in Thailand—are regularly singled out for criticism. In other words, political pluralism, based on frankly and openly competing economic interests, is on the rise in much of the region. It is characterized by a genuine trade debate, and the symbols and symptoms are quite similar to discussions of the *politics* of trade policy in the United States. In this growing debate, moreover, the burden of proof has shifted. It will now be increasingly incumbent on those who want to resist lowering trade barriers to demonstrate convincingly why they cannot do so.

APEC'S IMPACT

The APEC summit meeting held in Seattle, in November 1993, will have a profound impact on all these aspects of Southeast Asian affairs. President Clinton went to the meeting immediately following his NAFTA victory in Congress, and it is likely that we have now entered a new phase. Of course there were some ASEAN reservations about the impact of NAFTA on trade and investment in Southeast Asia, and they will continue, but ASEAN was in no way undermined in Seattle. Quite the opposite: ASEAN's program for tariff-reduction under AFTA was fully endorsed by APEC, and the decision to host the next APEC summit in Jakarta, under President Suharto's auspices, was a masterstroke. Indeed when President Clinton closed the APEC sessions, he was flanked by Japan's prime minister on one side, and President Suharto on the other. The image conveyed was precisely what Jakarta wishes: a clear recognition of Indonesia's prominence in the Asian region as a whole.

Very probably, a by-product of the discussion to have Indonesia host APEC's next summit was to put to rest—perhaps once and for all—the EAEC proposal. It has not been formally shelved, but it does not have to be; indeed APEC referred to ASEAN as a "caucus" within APEC, and the word could not have been an accident. Now it will be up to ASEAN to gracefully shelve EAEC, and Malaysia will not have much support to prevent that unless it persuades others it is being "victimized." But Prime Minister Mahathir has not covered himself with glory by boycotting the APEC sum mit, and he has done little since to improve his credibility. He has repeatedly charged that President Clinton was "manipulating" events by calling for and hosting the APEC summit, in order to impose unilaterally an American vision for the Asia-Pacific region. "We were worried that APEC would be manipulated by the big powers. Today, it has been proven that it is in fact being manipulated."[14]

Few others will share that view, which is not to say that the United States must not proceed very carefully, and it will be useful to review some specific aspects of the future U.S. role. I will first discuss the U.S. vision for APEC, and then Southeast Asia's views of American relations with Japan, with China, and with Southeast Asia itself.

From its outset in 1989–1990, the United States adopted a careful "let's not push too hard" view of APEC. But in the United States, it is virtually impossible to separate issues of foreign policy from issues of domestic politics, and as the time drew near for his hosting of the APEC summit in Seattle, it was evident that the president's interests were going to be served. That meant that if he was going to attend the meeting—and he was—APEC would have to be given a higher profile among Americans. Accordingly, last spring, a former Carter administration official, C. Fred Bergsten, was asked to chair an "Eminent Persons Group" to prepare an APEC agenda and a report for the leaders' consideration.

Bergsten of course is a very well-qualified economist, whose Institute for International Economics in Washington, DC, has established a solid reputation for its books, studies, and reports on nearly every aspect of international trade and economics. But he is not simultaneously an Asian specialist, and his forays into issues of U.S.-Japan trade have often been marked by controversy.

Both before and since the Plaza Accords in 1985, for example, he has been a leader in pressing the view that one of the main keys to improving America's trade deficits with Japan is to lower the value of the dollar in relation to the yen. There have been several devaluations since then, and when none achieved the desired results, Bergsten argued for further declines in the dollar. Most recently, he is reported to have said to Sony's Akio Morita that an "ideal" rate would be 100 yen or even less. None of this has endeared him to many Japanese economists and industrialists, who have been hard hit by the resulting *Endaka*, or "high yen." And while some Americans share Bergsten's views, or something like them, many economists do not. In their perspective, downward currency valuation for a nation like the United States is seldom a long-term cure for a trade deficit, which in any case is a phenomenon whose true significance is the subject of much disagreement.[15]

I mention this because Bergsten's choice as chair of the Eminent Persons Group was not unaccompanied by some baggage, and under his guidance APEC was presented with a "vision statement." It included recommendations for future APEC development, and it argued for a timetable under which APEC would at least begin discussing, by 1995–1996, a "framework" for something approaching an Asia-Pacific free trade regime. Not surprisingly, it was just as quickly shelved by the APEC summiteers, at least formally. Whatever some of them may think of a free trade area, the Eminent Persons' Report had the earmarks of what they feared: a seemingly heavy-handed U.S. charge leading APEC in a particular direction. The timetable, in other words, could not help but fuel suspicions that President Clinton might seek to "use" APEC's momentum to add to the pressure on the EC in the GATT-Uruguay negotiations. And while most in Asia are themselves very anxious to see a successful and early resolution of the GATT talks, they fear the increased "regionalization" of the global economy that such a tactic implies.

The result of all this is likely to be a modest brake on any quick APEC development into a more formal structure for trade and investment liberalization. That in itself should not be a discouragement for the United States, since one of the early visions for APEC—to which former Secretary of State Baker lent his support—was to develop initially along the lines of the OECD. Critics might argue that the OECD is not impressive—that it is just another "talking shop." But the OECD has greatly expanded data exchange and transparency among the economies of the industrialized nations, and helped lay the basis for some of the EC's steps toward harmonization. If APEC developed along similar lines in its still-early stages, that would not be a bad outcome.

Other Southeast Asian concerns are with America's relations with Japan and China. In Japan, the major issue has been the trade deficit, and while the APEC meeting certainly did not resolve that, President Clinton and Prime Minister Morihiro Hosokawa have made a start toward more civility in dealing with their bilateral problems. In Seattle, the president referred again, and positively, to the "framework" agreement reached in Tokyo in July 1993, and this implies that the United States is prepared to be patient, at least for a time, while Japan gets its own political house in order. In China, issues of human rights will continue to complicate the relationship, but the issue is not restricted only to China. One of the strongest Southeast Asian undercurrents in recent years has been the view that Asian democracies cannot be judged by American standards, and that view resonates most strongly in Singapore, Indonesia, and of course Malaysia.

In that light, the president's warm support for Jakarta as the site of APEC's next summit was once again reassuring. It clearly signals that Southeast Asia does not represent an obsessive U.S. human rights concern, and that only China will occupy the main attention. Southeast Asia worries that U.S.-PRC relations can come unstuck on the issue: as a result either of China's insistence on MFN without qualification, or the equally strong U.S. insistence that China must demonstrate genuine human rights improvements. The issue will sorely test Winston Lord's considerable abilities, particularly to the extent that China remains convinced that the Western nations are divided. Beijing believes it is an asymmetrical relationship: that the United States, Japan, and Southeast Asia need China more than China needs them, and in Seattle the Chinese side was publicly unyielding.

Nobody knows how this will play out, but it is a safe bet that China holds more of the winning cards. Among those cards are China's influence with North Korea on the issue of nuclear weapons; its position on the Spratly Islands; its missile deliveries to the Middle East; its ability to spark a new arms race, including one with Japan; and of course its markets. Everything considered, it is difficult to see how the United States will not have to accept less than an "ideal" solution to the China issue.

But Southeast Asia's concerns have been not only with U.S.-China relations. The region's leaders have been equally concerned to assure a continued U.S. presence in the region, both in military and economic terms. The APEC summit, with its high visibility in the United States, is promising in that respect as well. With its emphasis on the large economic opportunities in East Asia, the summit helped to provide a solid American *public* understanding for continued "forward deployments" in the Pacific. ASEAN states worried about that well before the China issue came to the forefront because they feared that Japan would eventually dominate their region once again.

This is perhaps the most ticklish issue, since America's investments in the region are no longer as dominant as they once were. From Southeast Asia's viewpoint, as Lee Kwan Yew has often said, the ideal is to have a roughly equal American and Japanese presence. But while each is a powerfully important *trade* partner for the region, the same is not true for their investments. There are troubling signs in the patterns of U.S. investment, for they tend overwhelmingly to favor Europe, Latin America, and Canada, as figures 5 and 6 illustrate.

Similar lessons are revealed by examining investments and exports in Southeast Asia, and comparing them with a region with similar U.S. investment levels. The following pairs *Thailand* with *Colombia*, *Malaysia* with *Chile*, and *Singapore*—in order to show comparable investment levels—with *Argentina and Venezuela* combined.

As figure 6a shows, closely similar levels of U.S. investment in Asia and South America are associated with very *different* levels of U.S. exports. The Singapore case is the most striking: although U.S. investments there are essentially identical with America's investments in Argentina and Venezuela combined, America's *exports to Singapore are almost $2 billion higher*. The same pattern is shown in the Thai-Colombia case: Thailand has the smaller U.S. investments, but its imports from the United States are substantially greater. Even more pronounced is the Malaysia-Chile contrast, since investments are nearly identical, but the United States exports twice as much to

FIGURE 5
U.S. Investments, 1980–1991, $Billions

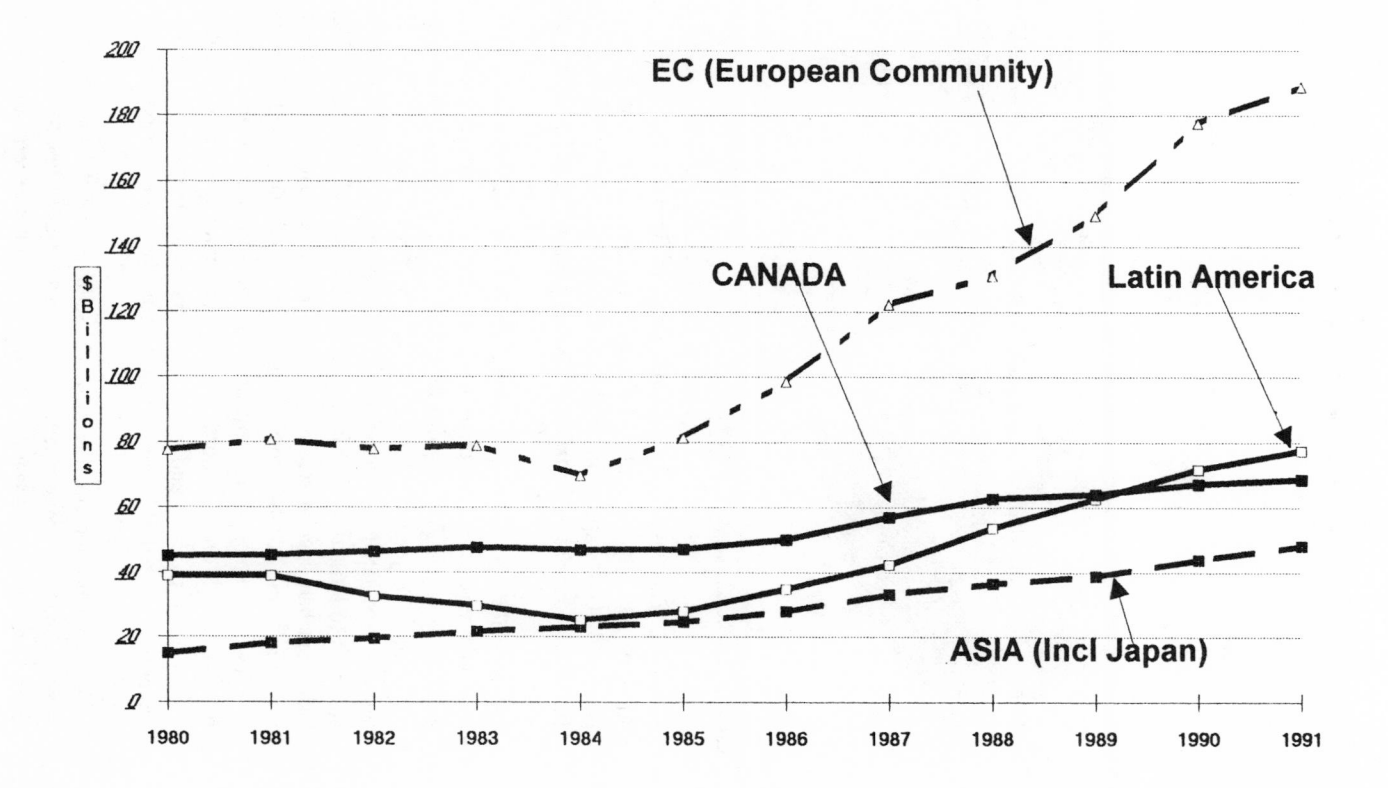

FIGURE 6
Where America Invests, 1991 (Total=$450 Bn)

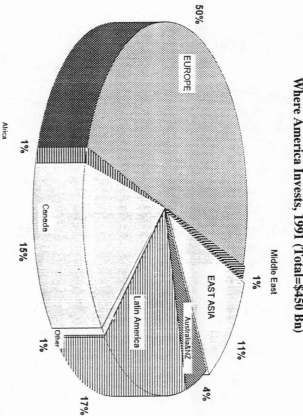

Malaysia. The result of these patterns, as figure 7 shows, is that Southeast Asia remains an attractive investment environment for the United States, and that is where APEC, with its commitment to a new investment regime, can make a major contribution. If the ASEAN states seek genuinely to preserve a U.S.-Japanese "balance" in the region, they will need to pay more attention to attracting U.S. investments. From the 1970s to the 1980s, Southeast Asia had special relative attractions for American investment (for example in terms of labor costs), and for much of that period, there was still a low level of Japanese investment with which to be compared. But today is a different era. More and more of the world's market economies now welcome the "Yankee Dollar," and Southeast Asia recognizes that there are other regions that can put U.S. investment to equally good, and possibly even more highly profitable use.

In that environment, the ASEAN states will need to work at attracting greater American investment. If Southeast Asia wishes to avoid too close a tie only to Japan, and wants instead to continue to see a strong American as

America, with 17 percent of United States global investment, took just 15 percent of U.S. exports in 1991, while East Asia—with only 10 percent of U.S. FDI—purchased nearly double that proportion (27 percent) of U.S. exports.

These illustrations help underline the importance of assuring that South-

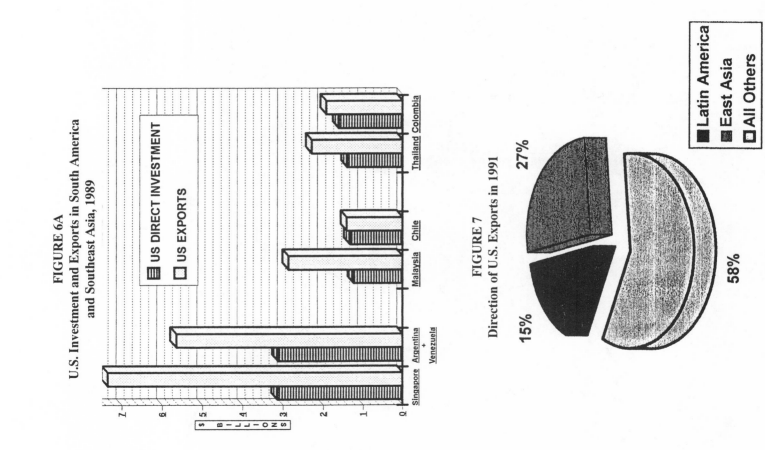

FIGURE 6A

U.S. Investment and Exports in South America
and Southeast Asia, 1989

■ US DIRECT INVESTMENT
□ US EXPORTS

$ BILLIONS

Singapore Argentina Malaysia Chile Thailand Colombia
              +
           Venezuela

FIGURE 7
Direction of U.S. Exports in 1991

27%

15%

58%

■ Latin America
▨ East Asia
□ All Others

FIGURE 8
U.S. Global Investments & U.S. Exports, 1970–1991, $Billions

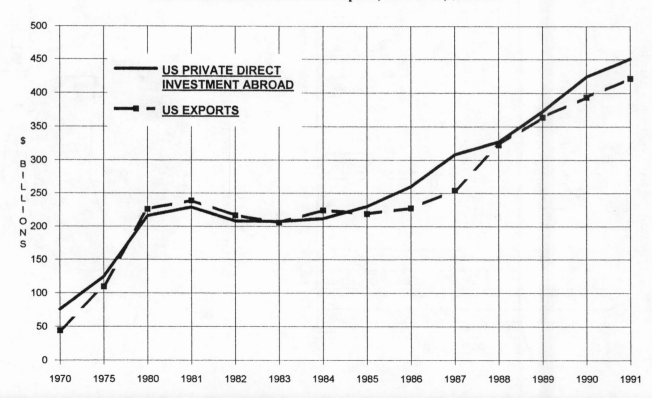

well as a Japanese presence, its member states will need to further liberalize and open their economies. That will be in their own direct interest, especially to the extent that they recognize, as figure 8 makes so clear, the historically very close relationship between U.S. investments and U.S. exports.

It is in that sense that I began this chapter by suggesting that the region is now at a crossroads. If it takes the path of genuine openness, considerable opportunities lie ahead, but if it follows the timeworn paths of protectionism, restrictions on investment, and excessive sensitivity to fears of "foreign manipulation," the future is liable to be less bright.

NOTES

1. All charts and related data in this chapter are my own, and unless otherwise specified, are calculated from two sources: U.S. Commerce Department, *Foreign Trade Highlights* (various years); and the IMF, *Directions of Trade Statistics*, annual issues, various years.

2. These data, from *The Economist*, October 30, 1993, are on a PPP (purchasing-power-parity) basis.

3. Further support to that view will be given by the recent report that "some of Tokyo's trade and foreign affairs bureaucrats favor a Mahathir-style Asian trade bloc if the GATT breaks down" (Richard D. Fisher, Heritage Foundation Asian Studies Center *Backgrounder*, November 9, 1993).

4. For a useful discussion of the conflicting pressures on Japan see the two articles in *Nihon Keizai*, November 20 and November 25, 1991, in the *Daily Summary of the Japanese Press*.

5. Yoichi Funabashi made this point in the *Asahi Evening News*, January 31, 1992.

6. For a discussion of the "seemingly frosty personal relations between the two" see M. G. G. Pillai, "Mahathir-Suharto talks augur well for ASEAN," in *Bangkok Post*, August 5, 1993, FBIS, August 6, 1993. He argues correctly that "The presumption in Kuala Lumpur is that Indonesia behaves like an elder brother, and in Jakarta that Malaysia was getting too big for her boots."

7. *Bernama* (Kuala Lumpur) January 26, 1992 in FBIS, Asia-Pacific, January 27, 1992.

8. For a report that Mahathir "slammed the United States" in connection with APEC see AFP Hong Kong in FBIS, August 4, 1993.

9. *The Nation* (Bangkok), December 10, 1992, in FBIS, Asia-Pacific, December 11, 1992.

10. *The Nation* (Bangkok), December 14, 1992, in FBIS, Asia-Pacific, December 15, 1992.

11. Heijrahman, of Gajah Mada State University, in ANTARA, January 14, 1993, FBIS, January 15, 1993.

12. The *Straits Times* (Singapore), October 8, 1993, reported that Thailand's Deputy Prime Minister (Supachai Phantichapak) made this official in October. As reported in FBIS, October 12, 1993.

13. *Business Times* (Singapore), October 2–3, 1993, in FBIS, October 5, 1993.

14. Examples of Mahathir's rhetoric are in *The New Straits Times* (Kuala Lumpur), August 4, 1993, in FBIS, August 6, 1993. He has also said that APEC would serve the interests of the "economically strong countries and not the weaker ones," and that he boycotted Seattle because Clinton's invitation was not "democratic." A useful summary of his views is in "Odd Man Out spurns Apec's US 'party'," in *Financial Times*, November 12, 1993. More recently, Prime Minister Mahathir has taken other steps that detract from his image as a serious leader: for example by cancelling contracts with British firms when London newspapers criticized the British and Malaysian governments on foreign aid, and by imposing a ban on showings of the film "Schindler's List." Old suspicions of his racism were rekindled when Mahathir argued that the movie put Germany in a bad light, and reflected only the interests of a "certain race."

15. The writings of Herbert Stein, most often in *The Wall Street Journal*, are instructive on this point.

11 THE PRC, TAIWAN, AND THE OVERSEAS CHINESE

Ralph N. Clough

The breakup of the Soviet Union and the demise of communism there and throughout most of the world has radically altered the international environment in East Asia. Even though the Chinese Communist party clings to power in mainland China, communism has lost its place as the state ideology. It is spurned by the young and by Chinese intellectuals. Even Chinese Communist cadres increasingly engage in capitalistic behavior, setting up companies and seeking profits. Pragmatism reigns; Chinese leaders stress economic modernization as the prime directive. Throughout East Asia concern with economic growth overshadows the preoccupation with military security that characterized the cold war period. Economics is in command.

During the twentieth century China has not had the economic influence on Southeast Asia that the size of its population would justify. Until World War II Southeast Asia was dominated by European powers and its trade links were mostly with Europe. During World War II the Japanese military drove out the Europeans and occupied Southeast Asia. Throughout this period China was backward, assailed by civil wars, encroachment by foreign powers and invasion by Japan.

After the establishment of the People's Republic of China in 1949, China soon allied itself with the Soviet Union and sought to influence Southeast Asia politically through backing communist parties in French Indochina, Burma, Malaysia, Indonesia, and the Philippines. Beijing had a significant political outreach, but its economic links with Southeast Asia were weak.

China's principal contacts with Southeast Asia were through the overseas Chinese, who had migrated there for 100 years or more, mainly from the south China provinces of Fujian and Guangdong. They became a major element in the business class of those countries. Many retained links with their home villages and sent money back. In the early years after the establishment of the PRC, Chinese communism had considerable appeal to the overseas Chinese in Southeast Asia, especially the young. Students flocked to Chinese universities. But after land reform, the three-anti and five-anti movement, and the anti-rightist campaign, in which many relatives of overseas Chinese were killed, jailed, or otherwise discriminated against, enthusiasm for Chinese communism cooled and the student flow and remittances dried up.

During the 1950s the Chinese communists turned inward, mainly concentrating on modernizing China after the Soviet pattern. Later China was convulsed by the Great Leap Forward, the Cultural Revolution, and the political struggles ending with the death of Mao and the overthrow of the Gang of

Four. Only after Deng Xiaoping returned to power and began his program of economic reform and opening up to the outside world did China begin to forge a place for itself as a major regional economic power. Today, with a population of 1.2 billion and a booming economy, especially in the coastal regions, China for the first time is becoming a strong contributor to the rapidly growing East Asian economy.

THE SURGING CHINESE ECONOMY

For the past 14 years China's economy has grown at nearly 9 percent annually, by far the fastest growth rate of any of the world's large economies. It is now the third largest economy in the world, drawing near to that of Japan. This rapid growth resulted primarily from the domestic economic reforms instituted in 1979 by Deng Xiaoping that freed the energies of the Chinese people from the deadening grip of centralized state planning and control. Beginning with rural reforms that tripled real income in the countryside over a period of eight years, Chinese leaders next began to dismantle the system of state-set prices throughout the economy. The result was the rapid growth of private firms and township and village enterprises controlled by units of local government. Today, state-owned enterprises produce less than half of China's industrial output and, if services are taken into account, the state's share of output is only about 25 percent.[1]

China's rapid economic growth was closely linked to an opening to the outside that encouraged foreign trade and invited foreign investment. From 1980 to 1992 the dollar value of China's foreign trade grew in nominal terms at more than 12 percent a year or more than twice as fast as world trade. Almost 80 percent of China's exports are now in manufactured goods.[2] In 1992 China had exports of $85 billion and imports of $81 billion, a total foreign trade of $166 billion. China had become the tenth largest exporter in the world.

The rapid growth of the PRC's foreign trade was made possible by radical changes in the way trading was done. Instead of continuing to limit foreign trade to a few centrally controlled agencies, the PRC permitted thousands of individual manufacturers and local trading companies to engage directly in foreign trade. It also periodically devalued its currency to keep narrow the gap between the official and black market rates and established swap markets throughout the country at which local currency could be exchanged for foreign currency. It has reduced restrictions on imports.

Foreign investment has also played a significant role in China's foreign trade and economic growth, especially in the province of Guangdong and Fujian. By 1991 cumulative direct foreign investment in China reached $22 billion in some 20,000 enterprises. During 1992 an additional $11.2 billion poured into China and during the first six months of 1993 $9.4 billion more arrived.[3] Investors have been attracted by China's continued rapid growth, by the opening of the domestic market to goods manufactured in China by foreign-invested firms, and by the opening of the service sector to foreign investment.

After Deng Xiaoping's trip to south China in early 1992, economic growth spurted even more rapidly, reaching a rate of 12.8 percent for the full year. Local officials gained greater autonomy to pursue their own plans, a 20 percent increase in state bank lending occurred, the issuance of local bonds and shares supplied still more capital, and the number of companies nearly doubled. Shortages of construction materials developed. Urban inflation mounted to an average of 13 percent and continued to rise during the first half of 1993.[4] In July 1993 Vice Premier Zhu Rongji took over the Central Bank and launched a drive to reduce lending and bring inflation under control without causing a sharp contraction in growth, such as had occurred in halting the economic overheating of 1988–1989.

A country the size of China and growing so fast cannot fail to have a profound impact on the region. A number of bottlenecks threaten to slow growth, however, including shortages of energy and transportation. These problems probably can be overcome, but potentially more serious threats, which are difficult to evaluate, are the spread of corruption, the struggle for power likely to follow the demise of 89-year-old Deng Ziaoping, and the emergence of rural unrest caused by excessive taxation and the diversion of grain purchase funds to other uses. Another uncertainty is whether economic decentralization will make impossible the effective use by the central government of macroeconomic instruments to manage the national economy.

Accepting the probability that some of the problems already referred to will slow the growth of the Chinese economy, China will still be a powerful player in East Asia throughout the rest of the decade. The economic reforms and the opening to the outside have won such strong support from interest groups within China, including influential individuals in the Chinese Communist party, that it would be almost impossible for any new leader to reverse the direction taken since Deng set the process in motion in 1979. Thus, any appraisal of economic trends in Southeast Asia will have to take account of China's probably sizeable impact.

THE EMERGENCE OF "GREATER CHINA": HONG KONG

Hong Kong's traditional role was as an entrepot for China, an excellent port that provided docks, cargo-handling and transshipping facilities, and financing of trade. Under British rule it had an orderly society, an efficient bureaucracy, a stable, convertible currency, low taxes, and a minimum of restrictions on trade and travel. It became an increasingly important port on the China coast, a magnet for commerce and tourism.

After the Chinese communists took over the China mainland and the United Nations imposed an embargo on China during the Korean War, Hong Kong turned increasingly to manufacturing. Textile manufacturers and other industrialists who had fled from Shanghai to Hong Kong made an important contribution to the colony's industrialization. The shortage of land in Hong Kong precluded the establishment of heavy or land-intensive industry; consequently Hong Kong's numerous small-scale firms produced mainly light consumer goods for export.

By the mid-1980s manufacturing had become the territory's most important economic sector and its largest employer, but another radical change in the Hong Kong economy occurred in the latter part of the decade. Manufacturing employment fell from 905,000 in 1984 (42 percent of total employment) to 655,000 in 1991 (23 percent) and its contribution to gross domestic product fell from 24 percent in 1984 to 17 percent in 1990.[5] Manufacturing had become only the second largest employer and the third largest contributor to gross domestic product, after financial and business services. The sharp drop occurred because rising wage and land costs had made many of Hong Kong's labor-intensive products noncompetitive in the international market. Hong Kong entrepreneurs by the thousands took advantage of China's opening to the outside and moved their manufacturing operations into neighboring Guangdong province. Thus began the economic merging of Hong Kong and mainland China into the first building block of "Greater China."

A gradual transformation has occurred in Hong Kong investment in China in the form of ownership, in the sector invested in, and in the geographic area involved. At first, Hong Kong entrepreneurs cautiously engaged in subcontracting to factories in China, investing little. But when the PRC liberalized its conditions for investment, many Hong Kong businessmen established wholly owned firms in Guangdong, mainly to produce goods for export. As China gradually opened its domestic market to the products of foreign-invested factories, the joint venture between Hong Kong and mainland China firms became increasingly popular. Joint ventures provided advantages to both parties in allowing access to the domestic market and extending import privileges.

Investment in China at first was limited to manufacturing, but bottlenecks in transportation and in power became substantial constraints to further industrial expansion. Hence, the Chinese government encouraged investment by foreign firms in roads, ports, and electric power generation. In 1985 a Hong Kong company entered into a joint venture with a government-owned PRC company to construct the Daya Bay nuclear power plant in Guangdong. A Hong Kong businessman, Gordon Wu, undertook to construct a freeway from Hong Kong to Guangzhou. Another, Li Ka-shing, has become a majority shareholder in a joint venture with Mitsui and Co., Kumagai-Gumi (HK), and China's state-owned shipbuilder, COSCO, to build a huge container port at Yantian, in the Shenzhen Special Economic Zone. Beijing has selected Yantian to become one of China's four main deepwater international ports. Still another Hong Kong financier, Peter Woo, the son-in-law of a shipping magnate, the late Sir Y. K. Pao, has signed letters of intent to improve port facilities in Wuhan and Chongqing and to set up a Chongqing-Shanghai freight shipping fleet.[6]

The most recent opportunities for Hong Kong-based companies came with China's opening of certain portions of its tertiary industries to foreign investment. A Japanese company based in Hong Kong, Yaohan, is building a shopping center in Shanghai. A Hong Kong department store, the Sincere Company, which originated in Shanghai, is now returning there, as is an American insurance company, the American International Group, which also got its start in Shanghai. Hong Kong is increasingly becoming a base for foreign companies that have or plan to have operations in China. During the past four years 675 international corporations established their regional headquarters in Hong Kong.[7]

Hong Kong companies, while still investing primarily in Guangdong province, are moving not only into Shanghai and its Pudong Special Economic Zone, but also inland, where cheaper land and labor beckon. Moreover, because economic activity is gaining momentum in the inner provinces, companies believe that they will gain an advantage from getting in early.

As of mid-1993, Hong Kong government officials estimated that Hong Kong provided 60 percent of China's overall foreign investment and that 80 percent of Guangdong's trade passed through Hong Kong. Entrepreneurs in Hong Kong have invested in some 30,000 enterprises in China, either wholly owned or joint ventures, that employ three million workers.[8]

Familiarity with the language and customs not only tends to direct trade and investment by Hong Kong Chinese initially to their ancestral home, but sentimental attachment to that particular corner of China sometimes induces wealthy Chinese to make philanthropic donations to promote its modernization. For example, Sir Y. K. Pao, the Hong Kong shipping magnate, who came from Ningbo in Zhejiang province, was greatly impressed with the port facilities and commercial enterprises of that city when he first returned there in 1984. Finding that Ningbo, with a population equal to that of Hong Kong, had no comprehensive university, he contributed $20 million to found one. After his death, Ningbo University continued to be funded mainly by Pao's widow and daughters and by other overseas natives of Ningbo.[9]

Investment is not only flowing from Hong Kong to China, it is also flowing in substantial volume from China to Hong Kong. In 1992 China was the leading foreign direct investor in the territory, with investments of an estimated $20 billion, surpassing Japan ($11.5 billion) and the United States ($8.5 billion).[10] Chinese enterprises are investing in factories, construction, importing and exporting, hotels, transport, banking, and real estate. At least a thousand Chinese companies operate in Hong Kong, including those run by provinces and cities. The Chinese have found that Hong Kong is a good place to make money and to avoid much of the red tape they must cope with in the PRC. Mainland corporations established in Hong Kong can borrow money from Hong Kong banks.

Many mainland companies would like to be listed on the Hong Kong Stock Exchange in order to raise money in Hong Kong, but few have been able to comply with the complicated rules for listing, which require accounting and financial behavior consistent with international standards. As of October 1993 only four mainland companies were listed, but others had purchased "shell" companies already listed and used them to float shares.[11] In October 1993 a fifth Chinese company, the Maanshan Iron and Steel Company in Anhui province, was about to be listed on the Hong Kong Exchange with a share offering of US$440 million, which it intended to use for upgrading its outdated equipment.[12] Another steel company, Shougang (Capital Iron and Steel), recently purchased 51 percent of Tung Wing Steel, a leading Hong Kong steel supplier, joining with another Hong Kong firm and a Canadian consortium to make the purchase. Shougang is on the way to becoming a transnational corporation, having bought a Peruvian iron mine and Masta Engineering Company, an American designer and manufacturer of metallurgical machinery. It has sold a rolling mill to Indonesia and has 14 overseas joint ventures with a total investment of over $300 million.[13] As yet, large companies in mainland China have not learned to be truly multinational, creating the close relationship between manufacturing and marketing that is characteristic of the Japanese and Korean conglomerates. But, as the Shougang example illustrates, some would like to become transnational and progress in that direction probably will occur during the 1990s.

The foregoing brief review mentions only a few of the economic links that are making Hong Kong and the China mainland increasingly interdependent. The flow of people, goods, capital, and information across the border in both directions grows daily. So long as the Chinese economy itself continues to grow, both its dependence on Hong Kong and its contribution to Hong Kong will continue to deepen.

On July 1, 1997, Hong Kong will cease to be a British colony and will formally become a special administrative region (SAR) of the PRC. According to the Joint Declaration of the British and Chinese governments signed in 1984 and the Basic Law promulgated by the National People's Congress in 1990, the SAR will retain Hong Kong's unique social, economic, legal, and other systems for 50 years after 1997.

In October 1992 Governor Christopher Patten advanced proposals for broadening the franchise for the 1994 and 1995 elections in order to make the Legislative Council more representative of the people of Hong Kong and more difficult for the Beijing government to manipulate. The PRC adamantly opposed the proposals and, as of November 1993, prolonged negotiations between the Hong Kong and Chinese governments had produced no agreement, despite concessions on Patten's part. The PRC threatened to hold new elections in 1997 if no agreement is reached and the Hong Kong government proceeds with the Patten proposals for the 1994 and 1995 elections. Should that happen, political uncertainty will cloud the inception of the new SAR.

The people of Hong Kong seem ambivalent about the political future. According to public opinion polls, they favor greater democracy, but they also favor good relations with Beijing and the two may be incompatible. Voter turnout has been low in past elections and few people have a clear understanding of the Basic Law or the complex Patten proposals. So far, the business community appears little affected by the political impasse. The territory is prosperous, funds continue to pour in and the stock market continues to rise. Most business people are optimistic that the growing economic integration of Hong Kong and mainland China will continue and that the transition from colony to SAR will be accompanied without serious disruption. The interests of the major Hong Kong and mainland players are seen as so closely intertwined that ways will be found to protect the territory's basic way of doing business.

THE EMERGENCE OF "GREATER CHINA": TAIWAN

Before Deng Xiaoping instituted economic reforms and opening to the outside in 1979, trade between Taiwan and mainland China was minuscule. Exports to the mainland were virtually nonexistent and imports of some $46 million in 1978 consisted almost entirely of foods and medicines of mainland China origin bought in Hong Kong. After Chiang Ching-kuo authorized travel to the PRC in 1987, trade grew rapidly, even though the Taiwan government required that the trade be indirect, via a third country. By 1992 trade between Taiwan and mainland China had increased to $7.4 billion. The pace picked up further in 1993, with two-way trade surging to $13.3 billion during the first eight months.[14]

Taiwan's trade with mainland China is closely related to investments there by Taiwan entrepreneurs. As in Hong Kong, Taiwan's rising wages, labor shortages, and the high cost of land made labor-intensive manufactures uncompetitive in the world market. Consequently, the production of such goods was shifted to the mainland, where land and labor were relatively cheap. The PRC welcomed the capital investment and the managerial, technical and marketing skills that Taiwan entrepreneurs had to offer. It established a special economic zone (SEZ) in Xiamen, Fujian, opposite Taiwan, the counterpart of the Shenzhen and Zhuhai SEZs opposite Hong Kong and Macao in Guangdong. According to the Mainland Affairs Commission in Taiwan, mainland investment by Taiwan entrepreneurs reached $11 billion by 1992 and increased by an additional $2.37 billion during the first eight months of 1993.[15]

A large proportion of the exports from Taiwan to mainland China consists of machinery, equipment, raw materials, and semiprocessed goods shipped to the factories of Taiwan entrepreneurs on the mainland that produce goods for export. A smaller but steadily increasing flow of exports from the mainland to Taiwan consists of semiprocessed materials to be finished in factories in Taiwan. Thus, the growing web of investment and trade is increasingly linking the island and the mainland together.

Taiwan's mainland China investments, which make Taiwan the second largest external investor in China, next to Hong Kong, have followed the pattern of Hong Kong's investments: from smaller to larger investments, from simpler to more sophisticated technologies, and from Guangdong and Fujian up the China coast to Shanghai and beyond and also inland, even as far as Xinjiang.

Taiwan's trade and investment in China have been driven by the complementarity of the two economies. The mainland has raw materials, cheap labor and land, and the necessary infrastructure. Taiwan has capital, experienced managers, technicians, and marketing connections overseas. Their interaction has been facilitated by the fact that they share a common language and culture.

Hong Kong has been indispensable to Taiwan's trade and investment in mainland China because the ROC government prohibits direct shipping and air travel across the Taiwan Strait. More than 3,000 Taiwan companies have established subsidiaries in the colony, mainly as a channel for making their indirect investments in the mainland.[16] Questions have been raised as to whether Taiwan's trade and travel will continue to be routed through Hong Kong after it becomes officially a part of the PRC in 1997. The government in Taiwan has declared, however, that it intends not only to maintain existing relationships with Hong Kong, but to strengthen them. A step in that direction was the opening of a branch in Hong Kong in September 1993 by the Hua Nan Commercial Bank, the first Taiwan bank to set up a branch in the colony. Taiwan's largest bank, the Bank of Taiwan, with a capitalization of $44 billion, has received permission from the Hong Kong government to open a branch in Hong Kong and expects to do so early in 1994.[17] Even if the ROC should change its policy and authorize direct trade and travel, Hong Kong probably would still play an important role for most Taiwan entrepreneurs because of its proximity to Guangdong, its extensive web of connections with other parts of China, and its unequaled port facilities, financing capability, and other resources for conducting business in mainland China.

Economic interaction between Taiwan and the mainland has been more constrained by political factors than that between Hong Kong and the PRC.

The ROC government not only has prohibited direct trade and travel, it is also concerned lest Taiwan's economy become too dependent on mainland products or markets or that important industries in Taiwan be "hollowed out" by the transfer of too large a proportion to the mainland. Hence, it opposes very large investments, such as the $7 billion petrochemical complex, once contemplated by Formosa Plastics for Fujian and more recently being considered for a Yangtze river site. It prohibits mainland investment in Taiwan, bans the import or export of a substantial range of commodities, and warns against investment in high technology plants on the mainland.

Although ROC government leaders declare that they favor the eventual political unification of Taiwan with mainland China, they demand that mainland China first become a democratic, free-market system and that its leaders recognize Taiwan as an equal political entity, stop interfering with its international position, and cease threatening the use of force against it. Since the PRC is unlikely to fulfill these conditions in the foreseeable future, the significant degree of economic integration that has occurred between the two areas will not lead to political integration anytime soon.

The term "Greater China" can be misleading, as it implies not only trade and investment relationships such as may exist between any two countries, but also a degree of political cooperation or integration. Some enthusiasts have forecast that the increasing economic integration of mainland China, Hong Kong, and Taiwan will lead to the establishment of a free trade area or common market. They argue that the European Economic Community (EEC) and the proposed North American Free Trade Agreement (NAFTA) will intensify regional protectionism and that only by adopting similar institutional arrangements can the three Chinese territories protect their economies and continue their rapid development. As previously indicated, however, the political obstacles to any such development are great. It is difficult to imagine Taiwan and the PRC agreeing on a plan comparable to NAFTA to eliminate tariffs between them or deciding to adopt a common currency, as the EEC proposes to do.

Moreover, Hong Kong must retain its status as a free port if it is to continue to prosper and contribute as it has in the past to the economic development of both mainland China and Taiwan. It can maintain and strengthen economic relations with both these places, but cannot be incorporated into a larger political unit subject to the many regulations and restrictions on economic activity that prevail in mainland China and Taiwan without losing its unique character. Thus, the economic links between Southeast Asian countries and the three culturally Chinese territories will continue to consist for the most part of discrete bilateral arrangements rather than ties with some hypothetical institutionalized "Greater China." Nevertheless, even though the economic integration among the three areas has its limitations, much scope still exists for heightened interaction, so long as economic growth continues strongly on the mainland, and this heightened interaction will serve as an economic stimulus to Southeast Asia.

MAINLAND CHINA AND SOUTHEAST ASIA

Individual ASEAN countries are not among the PRC's largest trading partners, such as the United States, Japan, or Hong Kong, but collectively their two-way trade with China in 1991 was $8 billion or 5.9 percent of China's total foreign trade, somewhat more than Taiwan's trade with China of $5.8 billion or 4.4 percent. Thus, the volume of trade between ASEAN and China is significant and increasing rapidly, as is Taiwan's trade with mainland China. It reflects the growing magnitude and sophistication of the PRC's industrial production as well as the opening of its domestic market to goods produced by foreign-owned companies. Border trade with Vietnam and Myanmar is also increasing, as the border provinces of Guangxi and Yunnan have been granted wider authority to conduct foreign trade.

Entrepreneurs in Southeast Asia, most of them overseas Chinese, have joined the parade of investors seeking to profit from China's rapid economic growth. Many invest in the part of China from which their ancestors originally came. For example, Mochtar Riady, whose parents migrated from Fujian to Indonesia and who heads the Lippo Group, one of Indonesia's largest conglomerates, plans to develop a power plant, port, and industrial park in Putian, Fujian. Four Singapore government corporations also have a contract to develop an industrial park in Fujian.[18] Thailand's Charoen Pokphand (CP) Group, whose founders left Shantou, Guangdong in 1919, is one of the largest investors in China, with assets estimated at $1.3 billion. It has agribusinesses in Shenzhen and other parts of China and motorcycle plants in Shanghai and Luoyang. It has announced a $2 billion development plan for a site in Shanghai's Pudong special economic zone.[19]

Overseas Chinese have advantages over other overseas investors in China. They often speak the local language and have personal and family connections at the investment site. They are familiar with Chinese ways of doing business, relying more on *kuanxi* (personal relations) than on formal institutional and legal relationships. Their family-based firms are adept at taking advantage of the legal uncertainties and unpredictability of China's current economic condition. As a Hong Kong businessman put it: "We thrive in chaotic marketplaces. It allows precisely for the kind of manipulation of circumstances that the Chinese business style encourages and for which it is designed."[20]

HONG KONG AND SOUTHEAST ASIA

Hong Kong's economic linkage to Southeast Asia is growing steadily stronger. For example, in 1989–1990 the growth in domestic exports to

ASEAN countries began to outpace growth in Hong Kong's exports to its traditional markets in Europe and North America. Hong Kong is also an important entrepot for goods shipped to and from Southeast Asia, particularly for Southeast Asian trade with China. Between 1985 and 1989 Hong Kong's imports from ASEAN countries increased at an average rate of 23.8 percent. Singapore was the colony's principal supplier of petroleum products, Thailand of rice, Malaysia of rubber, and Indonesia of plywood. Hong Kong is one of the leading investors in Southeast Asian countries.[21]

Another important activity of Hong Kong-based companies, one that is not reflected in official trade statistics, is so-called "triangular trade," in which products are purchased abroad and sold in a third country, not passing through Hong Kong. A 1991 survey estimated that such exports by Hong Kong companies would add 35 percent to those reflected in Hong Kong's official trade statistics. According to this calculation, triangular trade carried on by Hong Kong companies amounted to $38 billion in 1991. There was no breakdown as to how much of this triangular trade involved Southeast Asian countries, but it seems probable that they would account for a sizeable amount.[22]

Ten years ago the United States and Europe were the main sources of tourists visiting Hong Kong. Today the majority come from Japan, Taiwan, and Thailand. By 1989 visitors from ASEAN countries numbered 710,000, or 13 percent of Hong Kong's total visitors, and an equal number of Hong Kong residents visited Southeast Asian countries. Some 100,000 domestics reside in Hong Kong, principally from the Philippines. Cathay Pacific flies to all ASEAN countries and ASEAN-based airlines fly to Hong Kong. Fourteen licensed banks of ASEAN countries operate in Hong Kong and Hong Kong-based banks operate in all ASEAN countries.[23]

TAIWAN AND SOUTHEAST ASIA

Four ASEAN countries—Singapore, Indonesia, Thailand, and the Philippines—are among Taiwan's nine largest trading partners. Together they accounted for 5.9 percent of Taiwan's imports and 8.1 percent of its exports in 1992. As a market, they are less important than the United States (29 percent), Hong Kong (19 percent), or Japan (11 percent), and as a supplier they rank far below Japan (30 percent) and the United States (22 percent). Still, over the past 10 years, trade with these countries has gradually increased as a percentage of Taiwan's foreign trade.[24]

In recent years Taiwan has been an important investor in Southeast Asia. The same factors that encouraged Taiwan entrepreneurs to move their labor-intensive operations to mainland China have caused many to establish plants in Southeast Asia. The ROC government, concerned that its rapidly rising investments in mainland China might provide the Beijing authorities with political leverage on Taiwan, has urged businessmen to invest instead in Southeast Asia. According to statistics published in Taiwan, cumulative investments in Southeast Asia by Taiwan entrepreneurs totaled more than $15 billion between 1959 and June 1993, as shown in table 1.[25]

Overseas Chinese have also made substantial investments in Taiwan. Between 1952 and 1992 approved investments totaled $2.4 billion. About one-third of this amount came from overseas Chinese in Hong Kong and Japan. Much of the remainder probably came from overseas Chinese in Southeast Asia, although the data do not provide this breakdown.[26]

According to official statistics of the Overseas Chinese Affairs Commission in Taiwan, as of 1991 some 34 million Chinese lived outside mainland China and Taiwan. Of this number, 6 million lived in Hong Kong and 24 million in Southeast Asia. The ROC government in Taiwan works energetically to strengthen cultural and political bonds with the Southeast Asian overseas Chinese, subsidizing Chinese language schools, newspapers, radio and television broadcasts, art festivals, conferences, and overseas Chinese organizations. During 1991, 4,300 overseas Chinese students studied in Taiwan.[27]

CONCLUSION

Having reviewed briefly the economic relationships among China, Taiwan, Hong Kong, and Southeast Asia, it will be useful to step back and take a broader look at East Asia in terms of big power relationships in the region, now that the cold war is over and the Soviet Union has disintegrated. Clearly, for the remainder of this decade, the two most influential powers in the region will be China and Japan, for it will take considerably longer for Russia to reorganize itself politically and economically and develop a capability to exert influence in East Asia, in a period in which economic power will be more salient than military power.

The Chinese, for the first time in more than a century, can foresee the day, not too distant, when China can play a role in the world befitting its size and population. In order to reach that stage it must devote the remainder of the century to pursuing economic development. China's relations with Japan make an important contribution to achieving that goal. Japan is China's chief trading partner, its largest aid donor, and, since 1991, its third largest investor, after Hong Kong and Taiwan. For Japan, China offers raw materials, a huge market and workers to man Japanese-invested factories for which labor is no longer available in Japan. The Japanese are also acutely conscious of the fact that China is a nuclear power with a gradually modernizing conventional force and that the Chinese have unhappy memories of Japanese aggression. Hence, they have a strong compulsion to build a solid base through economic interaction for a long-term friendly relationship.

TABLE 1

Taiwan's Investments in Southeast Asia, 1959–1993

	Total Investment	Ranking among Investors
Malaysia	$5.6 billion	Second
Thailand	4.3 billion	Fourth
Indonesia	4.0 billion	Third
Vietnam	1.4 billion	First
Philippines	440 million	Fifth
Singapore	90 million	Thirteenth

In 1992 total foreign trade of the three culturally Chinese areas—China, Hong Kong, and Taiwan—was almost equal to Japan's foreign trade.[28] "Greater China" and Japan will play growing roles in Southeast Asia, both as traders and as investors. Japan is currently in a recession, but even when it recovers it will probably be outpaced by mainland China in economic growth. Thus, "Greater China's" importance to Southeast Asia probably will increase relative to Japan's. It has the advantage of the personal and family connections and cultural affinities with the 24 million overseas Chinese who hold so strong a position in the economies of the Southeast Asian countries. The Japanese have the advantage of more advanced technology, large and experienced banks and trading companies, and established footholds in Southeast Asian countries.

There will be some competitiveness in the relationships of "Greater China" and Japan with Southeast Asia, but their economic activities will also be complementary, for they have different things to offer. The overseas Chinese in Southeast Asia will not interact exclusively with the territories of "Greater China." While ties of language and culture incline them in that direction, they will be moved primarily by the profit motive, and where the Japanese have more to offer they will work with the Japanese.

The critical uncertainty in the equation is how fast the economy of mainland China will grow, which will depend on its political stability during the succession period, the continuation and success of the economic reform program, and the determination of China's leaders to improve China's investment climate and to open it even further to foreign economic involvement. If China continues to grow fairly rapidly, the size of its economy will ensure the absorption of very large amounts of capital from outside, especially from Hong Kong, Taiwan, and Japan. China will be competing with Southeast Asia for capital investment, but the experience of the past few years suggests that substantial amounts will flow to both areas. The Chinese practice of saving a large proportion of income is likely to persist for at least another generation or two, making available an enormous supply of capital.[29]

Although economic motivations will probably dominate the international relations of East Asia during the remainder of the decade, the competing claims of China and Southeast Asian countries, especially Vietnam, to the Spratly Islands in the South China Sea may present a disruptive security problem. As China's economic stature grows, national pride and a determination to defend territories considered Chinese will become stronger. Chinese and Vietnamese military forces have clashed in the Spratlys in the past and each is strengthening the positions it occupies in the archipelago.[30] The Chinese doubtless will continue to strengthen their positions and improve the blue water capability of their navy during the rest of the decade, but the proposal advanced by Premier Li Peng in Singapore in August 1990 indicates that Beijing prefers not to force a military resolution of the competing claims. Li proposed joint exploitation of the seabed and marine resources of the islands, putting aside the sovereignty issue and withdrawing military forces.[31]

Another and potentially more seriously disruptive security issue would be a clash between Beijing and Taipei provoked by the establishment of a "Republic of Taiwan" by the independence-minded opposition party, the Democratic Progressive party, should the latter wrest power from the ruling Kuomintang during the next few years. The people of Taiwan are fundamentally conservative, however, and it seems improbable in the increasingly democratic system on the island that they would back an action that would imperil Taiwan's security and jeopardize the developing economic interrelationship of Taiwan, Hong Kong, and mainland China.

NOTES

1. *Economist*, November 28, 1992, p. 8.
2. *Economist*, November 28, 1992, p. 13.
3. *China Briefing*, United States-China Business Council, October 1993, p. 11.
4. Remarks by the director, East Asian Analysis, CIA, to the Joint Economic Committee of Congress, July 1993, pp. 5–7.
5. Hong Kong Government Information Services, *Hong Kong: The Facts "Manufacturing Industries,"* July 1992.
6. *South China Morning Post*, October 6, 1993.
7. Excerpt from Governor Patten's speech October 6, 1993, British Information Services, New York, October 7, 1993.
8. Interview, Hong Kong Trade and Development Council, October 1993.
9. *Beijing Review*, September 27–October 3, 1993, pp. 20–23.
10. *South China Morning Post*, October 8, 1993.
11. Interviews, Department of Trade and Industry, Hong Kong government and Hong Kong Trade and Development Council, October 1993.
12. *Far Eastern Economic Review*, October 28, 1993, pp. 78–79.
13. *Beijing Review*, October 4–10, 1993, pp. 17–22.
14. Republic of China, Ministry of Economic Affairs, quoted in *Free China Journal*, October 15, 1993.
15. *Free China Journal*, October 15, 1993.
16. Philip Liu, "Mixed Diagnosis for Mainland Fever," *Free China Review*, September 1993, p. 43.
17. *Free China Journal*, October 15, 1993.

18. *Time*, May 10, 1993, pp. 28–30.

19. *Far Eastern Economic Review*, October 21, 1993, pp. 66–70.

20. Andrew B. Brick, *The Emergence of the Greater China: The Diaspora Ascendant* (Washington, DC: The Heritage Lectures, no. 411, The Heritage Foundation, September 9, 1992).

21. Statistics from Hong Kong Trade Department, "ASEAN Countries and Hong Kong," January 1991.

22. Hong Kong Development Council, *Survey on Hong Kong Domestic Exports, Re-exports and Triangular Trade*, November 1991, pp. 9–10.

23. "ASEAN Countries and Hong Kong."

24. Republic of China, Council for Economic Planning and Development, *Taiwan Statistical Data Book, 1993*, pp. 200–204.

25. *Free China Journal*, August 27, 1993.

26. *Taiwan Statistical Data Book, 1993*, p. 245.

27. Government Information Office, *Republic of China Yearbook, 1993*, pp. 187–197.

28. Japan's was $573 billion, "Greater China's" was $560 billion. Some double-counting is involved here, as the same goods are counted as Chinese exports to Hong Kong and then as Hong Kong exports when they are re-exported. Nevertheless, the figure accurately reflects the enormous volume of goods handled by the port of Hong Kong.

29. Taiwan has over $80 billion in official foreign exchange reserves, rivaling Japan and Germany for first place in the world. The chairman of one of Taiwan's largest conglomerates, the Tuntex Group, told the author in August 1993 that he estimated that Taiwan firms probably held about the same amount in private foreign exchange reserves available for investment.

30. John Garver, "China's Push Through the South China Sea: The Interaction of Bureaucratic and National Interests," *China Quarterly*, no. 132 (December 1992), pp. 999–1028.

31. Garver, pp. 1015–16.

12 SOUTHEAST ASIAN ECONOMIC EXPERIENCE AND PROSPECTS: A SUMMARY

Ben Barber

There is widespread agreement that the world's most successful developing countries have been those of the Association of Southeast Asian Nations (ASEAN) and some of its East Asian neighbors in the 1980s. Following in the footsteps of postwar Japan and then Korea, the broad bases of the populations of Thailand, Malaysia, Indonesia, Singapore, Hong Kong, and, to a lesser extent, the Philippines, have made enormous strides in income, industrial and agricultural production, exports, education, health, nutrition, consumption, and other development indicators.

Economists, political scientists, anthropologists, journalists, and geographers have all sought to explain the phenomenal growth of the region. In early December 1993, The American Council on Asian and Pacific Affairs and Seoul National University sponsored a conference in Washington, DC, that brought together political scientists, economists, other academics, officials of the U.S. and Asian governments, and representatives of the multilateral banks to analyze Asia's extraordinary growth. The main question addressed by the papers delivered at the conference as well as the ensuing debates focused on the following: Is the success of the 1980s and early 1990s a permanent part of the world's economic landscape? Or must investors and political planners be prepared for a changing of the old guard, a loss of regional cooperation, an intensification of rivalry over access to Western and Japanese markets, and a new, possibly ethnic-based, nationalism? How will this region react to the growth of China's vast productive capacity and to the faltering of Japan's economy? What will be the effect of a U.S. military disengagement caused by domestic budgetary concerns and the end of the cold war? Will North Korea's pursuit of nuclear arms dampen enthusiasm for cooperation and drive Japan and China into more militaristic postures? Can the conferees pit China against Vietnam again?

Throughout the two days of meetings, a few significant and highly contentious themes kept cropping up. The first was the role of the overseas ethnic Chinese communities in fostering economic growth in Indonesia, Thailand, and Malaysia. The conferees voiced concern that ascribing too much importance to the Chinese role has in the past sparked resentment and repression of this energetic community. And political scientists and economists were hesitant to wade into the question of "culture" as a factor in the success of the region. Yet the ethnic Chinese networking across national borders, ability to operate in a frontier environment lacking strong laws to enforce written contracts, and devotion to hard work and high savings rates did play a vital role in the region's growth.

Another recurrent theme was the emergence of China as the fastest growing and largest economic power in the region. Some participants said China was soaking up so much foreign investment that ASEAN was in danger of being left high and dry. Others said the smaller neighbors of China must follow the path of Korea and Japan by shifting rapidly to high technology exports.

Coming soon after the Seattle meeting of the heads of state of the Asia Pacific Economic Conference (APEC), the Washington participants debated the merits of that meeting, the rift between Malaysia and the rest of APEC, especially Australia, that grew from the conference, and the wisdom of an ever-broadening concept of a Pacific-wide grouping that would reach as far as Chile. As part of that issue and within discussions on the future of Indochina, the role of the U.S. military and U.S. security guarantees was discussed. Although little attention was given to the likelihood of Japan ever replacing the United States as a guarantor of security, there was debate over future relations between Japan and China as well as the Korea question.

Finally, several speakers said that one common feature that separated the successful economies from others in the developing world was the existence of a responsive and educated bureaucracy that lent legitimacy to otherwise largely authoritarian governments. However the question as to why—why did these societies evolve in this direction and produce civil servants who were honest and wise enough to hold down inflation, insist on stable, convertible currencies, invest in education, and adopt other pro-growth policies—that question remained somewhat a mystery, relegated to the category of culture, which, it was agreed, would not be broached in the conference.

The balance sheet of Southeast Asia reassures Westerners that hard work plus free markets and trade can lift all boats in a shared prosperity. Internal income distribution within the tigers—Korea, Taiwan, Hong Kong, and Singapore—and the tiger cubs—Thailand, Malaysia, and Indonesia—has been far more equitable than in the rest of the developing world. Motorbikes, televisions, universal education, and other benefits of modernity have penetrated to the furthest villages. But the world has changed since the fall of the Berlin Wall, unleashing Chinese economic rivalry and a nascent Vietnamese capacity to compete with already established and high labor cost markets in ASEAN. Observers are already asking if this will set ASEAN's members against each other in some areas, especially as they vie for capital to follow Korea and Japan into higher-technology export production. While some wish to forecast the future, others wish to dissect the near past to know why the countries of Southeast Asia—excluding Burma and Indochina—have "taken off" in such a profound and obvious manner while countries in Africa and Latin America, which began at roughly the same level of development some

30 years ago, remain mired in poverty or enjoy growth only in limited economic and social sectors.

Indeed on a visit to Nigeria recently, resident diplomats warned a foreign expert not to compare the country to Indonesia because "it infuriates the Nigerians." And yet, after a few weeks in the country, one cannot help but compare it to Indonesia, where the oil income was funneled into social and economic development in a way that has not been the case in Nigeria. And in any number of countries such as Venezuela, Haiti, and Senegal, one wishes the planners and bureaucrats and politicians might be able to visit Southeast Asia and copy some of the methods, technologies, and inspiration that have improved the lives of hundreds of millions of people while creating political stability and an expanding ability to share in the world economy.

In determining the roots of Southeast Asian success at development, the political scientist probably looks first to the role of government and the regional security situation. The economist looks at macro and micro economic policies, low inflation rates, and the role of export trade. Anthropologists look at the role of culture. And geographers examine resources, demographics, and climate.

To some observers, who keep their eyes focused on the key indicators of economic development such as growth in GNP and levels of foreign investment, Southeast Asia has already reached its peak of economic growth, influence, and success. They say that what lies before them is the path downwards, inevitably, because of the declining levels of investment in recent years and months as the explosive South China economy increasingly absorbs the available capital. Downwards unless the tiger cubs—Malaysia, Thailand, and Indonesia—can rapidly upgrade their skills and move into production of higher level export items with greater value added such as computers. Or unless external factors favor Southeast Asia, such as disruptions in China or in China's ability to engage in foreign trade such as a U.S. cancellation of the most favored nation trading status that could threaten the $22 billion trade surplus Beijing enjoys with Washington. Cancellation of China's MFN could come over the human rights issue, Tibet, or trade practices such as blocking U.S. imports, dumping, and mislabeling. A break in U.S.-China trade could cancel out this rival for investment capital. Right now, however, Southeast Asians might well shudder at one investor who commented that "essentially, in China the cost of labor is zero."

But before predicting and planning a future for this region, and before attempting to codify and export to less-developed countries some of the techniques and patterns that led to the growth of the 1980s, there remains a need to agree on what caused the success. This has not been easy since the economic policies adopted by these economic tigers and cubs is wide ranging.

DIFFERING APPROACHES TO DEVELOPMENT

Hong Kong, for example, achieved success through flagrant, unchecked capitalism of the sort that would please Milton Friedman—little government interference and guidance. But Hong Kong had two other advantages that are not duplicated elsewhere: due to British and international communications and banking ties, it became a headquarters for Western firms investing, purchasing, or selling in the region; and it became a gateway for China, serving as the port of trade for 80 percent of its exports and banker for a nation of one billion.

Singapore, like Hong Kong, enjoyed the advantages of being a city-state. Lacking a rural extension, both countries could effectively implement pricing and other policies without worrying how they might impact on farmers, fishermen, and others with whose interests conflict with urban society. And when everyone is close to home, the central government can more easily enforce its will, unlike Thailand, for example, where distant military and political leaders feel themselves immune from Bangkok's authority, especially on issues such as drugs, timber, refugees, and smuggling.

Yet Singapore chose a different route to success than Hong Kong's laissez-faire capitalism: the route of government control. Even social policy was directed by the government, which required that people buy their apartments and live in racially mixed housing. Singapore also pioneered the shift to export-oriented, free-trade strategy, followed by Malaysia. But then Singapore's government remained strongly involved, intervening to maintain the pre-eminence of exports and pushing increasingly towards increasingly higher levels of technology in services and value-added production.

One conference participant questioned the rush to privatization being urged on the region, calling it "an American fad" and an "ideology" that would divide countries between workers and elites and redefine the state. Another suggested that while the World Bank and U.S. ideal models include totally private and free markets, there are other systems that have worked well in Asia. Some state companies, such as Singapore Airlines for example, could be better run than some private companies. And while Japan had blocked foreign competition, internal competition was strong enough to provide incentive. Finally, it was mentioned that while the rush to privatize in Eastern Europe led to economic collapse, Thailand had followed a different model and let state firms slowly die out. One participant raised that ultimate question about selling off government assets: does a country sell its roads and schools too?

In addition to differing approaches to economic development, the region's ethnic and geographic diversity would seem to defy broad characterizations that might help one to draw up a pattern to explain the success of Southeast Asia. Indonesia is a petroleum exporter; Thailand leads the world in rice exports and maintains a strong agricultural base; Malaysia inherited the organization of the colonial plantation system; the Philippines has close educational and cultural ties to its former colonial master, Washington; Thailand had ethnic and linguistic homogeneity; Malaysia struggled to unite Malay, Chinese, and Indian interests; Indonesia is spread across thousands of miles on many islands; and so on.

COMMON THREADS

In the search for common threads, what stands out is that all nations in the region had stable governments. While Africa and Latin America saw frequent coups that led to abrupt changes in policies, disrupting development schemes, and frightening investors away, the statesmen and the bureaucrats at the head of Southeast Asian societies remained largely unchanged or unchallenged. Even Thailand, which saw many coups before, and one coup after the nineyear government of Prem Tinsulanond in the 1980s, remained stable insofar as the government's bureaucracy and its economic policies are concerned. Indeed its king, Bhumibol Adulyadej, although a constitutionally limited monarch, played a stabilizing role that is mirrored by other king-like figures across the region such as Suharto, Mahathir, Le Kuan Yew, Ne Win, and the recently restored King Sihanouk. But we see from this list that stability alone is not enough for success.

Indeed, not only did the tigers and the cubs have stable governments, one participant said they had "soft authoritarian" governments. The most democratic country in the immediate postwar period was the Philippines, which subsequently lagged behind in development. It would be impertinent and condescending to imply that economic development in the region came because powerful leaders and elites wisely limited the scope of free and therefore divisive expression and self-government. This flies in the face of the traditional American and Western belief that democratic systems and free economies go hand in hand in unleashing the dynamic creativity of man. Especially in the current post-cold war period, hailed as the triumph of democratic ideals over authoritarianism and central planning, it is difficult to admit that the Southeast Asian miracle grew out of authoritarian roots. But Singapore is a one-party state that suppresses press critics; in Thailand, the military has controlled all but the present government and it remains powerful; in Indonesia, one man has held power for nearly three decades; Malaysia is essentially another one-party state; and Hong Kong is a British colony struggling against pressure from China—which takes over in 1997—to install its first democratic council.

But if authoritarianism has gone hand-in-hand with economic development, the most extreme examples of it have been the basket cases of the region: Burma, Vietnam, Cambodia, and Laos. Some may argue that it is the mild form of authoritarianism akin to paternalism that works best in newly industrializing countries. But clearly this, too, while a common thread, is not sufficient to assure prosperity.

Another participant said that pragmatism was the key to success—that all the nations in the region had a distrust of ideology that Thai colleagues described as a preference for the "middle way" of Buddhism. But several participants said there was no real explanation—not even in the oft-mentioned World Bank report on East Asian economic development known as "the miracle study," issued a few weeks prior to the conference—why the authoritarian governments in the region allowed the technocrats to make economic policy. One has only to recall that when the Thai military staged a coup in 1991, within hours it announced, in what may have been its first press release after announcing the takeover, that the Bank of Thailand would continue to set fiscal policy without interference by the new military government. Several participants cited "unknown reasons" that caused powerful leaders to cede fiscal and economic decision-making authority to technocrats. There was no denigration of this paternalistic relationship and indeed a sense of awe that it had taken place and was at the root of the economic boom that swept the region.

COMMITTED BUREAUCRACIES

Therefore, one looks beyond the power of government and finds that the administration of that power has been tempered by another common factor: high quality, committed bureaucracies that are relatively free of graft. James Clad, a former reporter for the *Far Eastern Economic Review*, tells the apocryphal story of an American economist who visits a Thai colleague living in luxury in Bangkok and asks how he did it. "See that power plant?" says the Thai. "Ten percent." When the American next visits a Filipino colleague living in even greater wealth and splendor he asks the same question. The Filipino says, "See that power plant?" The American looks out the window and sees nothing. "One hundred percent," says the Filipino.

That story may elicit knowing smiles and may hurt some feelings but it illustrates what is perhaps the deepest divide between the explosively successful economies of Asia and the failures. Japan and Korea inherited a tradition of the civil service as a meritocracy. This goes back to ancient China and ancient Vietnam although there is evidence that currently the administration in those countries is vetted by political processes and weakened by corruption to the extent that it cancels out the positive impact of a more strict meritocracy. It is true that in the tiger cubs, where the best and the brightest have been allowed to study abroad and implement new policies that seemed strange to their elders, the bureaucrats have been drawn from a selective elite. But they have somehow been imbued with a sense of responsibility to produce policies that work to the benefit of the broad mass of the society. Whereas in Nigeria, Venezuela, and other developing countries the elites have become ever more independent through private security forces, cellular phones, and personal electric generators, in Bangkok and other cubs the public phones work, the electricity is for all, and everyone goes to school.

The conference participants several times mentioned the theme of education, agreeing that it was one of the major factors in the advancement of the region after World War II. Education was a common factor among the tigers and cubs—both strong primary education as well as national universities set up to train bureaucrats. The universal primary education of girls has also contributed to the spread of family planning and reduction in family size that is a sign of economic development. Meanwhile bureaucrats, trained at publicly supported national universities, were given a charge by the leaderships to make economic development the primary goal of their policies.

Those policies have not been uniform. Korea and Taiwan started by protecting infant industries as they launched ventures in international trade. The United States still objects to what it calls Japanese protectionism of its domestic markets and there are regular complaints by United States and European businessmen that Japanese firms, with Japanese government assistance, unfairly compete with Western firms. To avoid this image and to reduce the cost of production at home, many Japanese firms as well as firms from Taiwan and Hong Kong shifted some production facilities to Southeast Asia. This shift, whether it was simply to take advantage of cheap labor and entry quotas to U.S. markets, or involved a real transfer of technology, led to improved working conditions and expectations in the cubs. And in Thailand, where Japanese firms such as Yanmar and Kubota were assembling diesel motors for the Thai market, government policies required that gradually all the parts should be produced in Thailand as well.

In general, Southeast Asian countries have traditionally shown support for conservative macroeconomic management. But the support of the state for business is itself both a complex and a challenged issue that saw participants debating whether it helps or hinders economic growth and better income distribution; and whether it can be controlled. In ethnically homogeneous states such as Japan and Korea, said one participant, such state-business ties can have a nationalistic aspect that energizes the economy, making diverse interest groups such as labor and consumers more willing to sacrifice for the growth of the country and their companies' market shares. Another participant asserted, however, that in other cases such state-business ties maintain cronyism that saps the vitality out of true competition. However, defenders of these relationships say it is simply a new, Asian version of the adage "What's good for General Motors is good for the U.S.A." Yet once government and business get so close, it is hard to separate them and to control that relationship. A reluctance or inability to restrain business has led to abuses in Southeast Asia such as deforestation, destruction of national parks, pollution of drinking water, sale of harmful pesticides and chemicals, and land use that caused flooding or the diversion of traditional water flows needed for rice cultivation.

Some participants said, however, that the real cause of environmental damage was expanding population in the rural areas. Farmers from the fertile plains are expanding up into the forested hillsides and water-catchment areas. In this they are aided by governments who build roads that conveniently aid loggers to get wood out and farmers to exploit the logged-over areas.

UNDER THE U.S. UMBRELLA

As ASEAN followed in the footsteps of Japan and Korea, it did so with a great sense of security and a great savings in military expenditures due to the U.S. military umbrella in the region, another factor that is not easily duplicated elsewhere in the world. U.S. forces are currently deployed in Japan, the remnants of the vast force that occupied the country after World War II and installed a model democracy. Some 35,000 U.S. troops are also still deployed in South Korea, left over from the force that fought the Korean War in 1950–1953 against the communist North and communist Chinese "volunteers." Until 1991, the United States maintained two giant bases in the Philippines—Subic and Clark. And after sending millions of U.S. troops to fight in Vietnam, Laos, and Cambodia during the Vietnam War from 1965–1972, the last 50,000 men on the Southeast Asian mainland were withdrawn from Thailand in 1976 at Bangkok's request. But a small U.S. advisory presence remains in JUSMAG Thailand and there are regular Cobra Gold training exercises with the Thai military. To partially replace the lost Subic Bay Naval Base and Clark Air Force Base, Singapore has offered to host a U.S. military mission. Other ASEAN nations as well as Australia are openly vying to host U.S. military exercises and ship and aircraft repairs or visits.

This U.S. umbrella since 1945 has, in addition to reducing the cost of security to ASEAN, given confidence to the foreign investors who discovered the region in the 1980s. The relationship between this security and prosperity is, however, a two-way street. The U.S. military was unable to prevent the fall of South Vietnam, Cambodia, and Laos to Communists. But the communists did not continue on to conquer the region as U.S. analysts and proponents of the domino theory had predicted. Instead, ASEAN nations banded together in support of free markets as an alternative to communism. While Vietnam bogged down in Cambodia, fought with China, lost its Soviet backers, and crumbled into poverty, ASEAN countries prospered and retained their independence. Some say that the flow of Thai and Singapore-produced consumer goods smuggled into Saigon and Hanoi did more to blunt the aggressive expansionism of Vietnamese communism than the U.S. military.

Indeed, even Thailand, with its Cambodian border occupied by hundreds of thousands of Vietnamese troops and Cambodian and Lao refugees and guerrillas, never fielded more than a relatively small force for a nation of 60 million, yet it has peacefully developed in the very shadow of war. One may argue it was the presence of the U.S. umbrella just over the horizon that facilitated that to happen.

But the presence of the U.S. military has been an even more direct spur to economic development. The postwar prosperity of Japan was ignited when it became the logistics base for the U.S./UN forces in the 1950–1953 Korean War. Similarly, Thailand benefitted from straight and well-built roads built high above the flood plain by the United States in order to truck bombs to the five airfields used to bomb Vietnam during the Vietnam War. When the war ended, those roads were powerful engines of development.

DEVELOPMENT'S AFTERMATH

Thus, the policies most clearly identified by the participants at the conference as crucial to ASEAN's success are government stability, investment in primary education, pushing exports of manufactured goods rather than primary products, pragmatism, some form of minimal government intervention, keeping inflation to an average 8 percent, and an optimistic approach to the problems of development.

But once the development takes root, a change sweeps society that has not been easy to cope with. Pollution, urban slums, crime, prostitution, and the pervasive links between businessmen and government have all grown up in what had been rather sheltered societies. Unions emerged in Korea as powerful players. The exposure to Western thought and values through newspapers and television has profoundly affected the Asian societies and created a huge gap between the generations. This is leading to pressure for more democracy and political instability. The business-political coalitions that led the way to double digit growth in the late 1980s are now challenged to share their power and to clean up the environmental and social problems created by rapid urbanization and unchecked growth. At the same time, it is not clear that the business-political team is going to be able to bring the cubs up from being a low-level platform for producing textiles and assembling electronics to the second stage of higher-value added, capital intensive production that could turn a Thailand into a Korea much as Korea is turning into a Japan.

Outlooks for the economic future of Southeast Asia are bright with expectations of a continuation, though perhaps at a slower rate, of its economic growth. Even the Philippines is expected to advance. Vietnam is starting to come on line despite the continuing U.S. embargo due to the residual emotional damage left over by the Vietnam War. Recent decisions to allow multinational bank loans to go forward and allow U.S. groups to join in projects funded by those banks are bound to spur confidence by investors from Japan, France, Australia, and other countries not hindered by any embargo.

But the region is cooling down a bit as foreign investment slows down. Now domestic consumption and investment is responsible for most economic growth. This is partly due to the awakening of a powerful neighbor to the north as a player in the world trade market.

CHINA TAKES OFF WHILE VIETNAM WARMS UP

The need to adapt internal policies to move up to the next level of technology and to develop domestic markets and sources of investment has become clear by the emergence of a new development giant in the region—China. From 1990 to 1992 China's GDP growth rate more than doubled from 5 to 13 percent, passing Malaysia, Thailand, Indonesia, and Korea. Some say if one simply took the region around Guangdong, where economic liberalization has gone on the longest and received the largest foreign investment and technology, the growth rate could be 20 percent. By 1991, foreign investment into China reached $22 billion. In 1992, another $11 billion arrived, and in the first six months of 1993, some $9.4 billion more was invested. There are disturbing signs that some of this investment has come at the expense of ASEAN, which is seeing its first decline in several years in foreign investment.

Hong Kong and Taiwan investors have led the way and become deeply involved with China, moving from smaller to larger investments and moving from Guangdong up the coast to Shanghai and then inland. This has created what some say is "Greater China"—a concept that could increase the tension between ethnic Chinese minorities and the majority ethnic groups in Malaysia, Indonesia, and, to a lesser extent, Thailand.

ETHNIC CHINESE

There was great interest in the discussions over the existence and the role of a "Greater China"—an economic, cultural, and possibly political arrangement linking mainland and overseas Chinese. Indeed, it was agreed that it is a very sensitive topic. It is evident to all observers of the region and yet proves politically incorrect to address squarely: Just how important is the role of Confucian influences and the ethnic Chinese subculture in the economic development of Southeast Asia? Clearly the ethnic Chinese have prospered to the extent that it appears they energize if not dominate the economies of several nations. They pursue a common work ethic, a sense of duty to one's elders and society—what we might call in America the Protestant ethic. From Japan to Singapore, this East Asian ethic holds that the family and the society is held paramount while individualism—that bedrock of Western culture—is downplayed. Some 30 years ago analysts scorned this groupism as an obstacle to breaking out of rural poverty. They admired the ability to diligently apply the innovative technologies invented by the more individualistic and creative scientists of America but doubted it would lead to very much. Now analysts are awed by the brilliant applications of industrial technology that have built—in an environment of hard work plus high savings rates—the economic miracle of the postwar period: U.S. trade with Asia has surpassed that with America's ancestral homelands in Europe and stands to widen that gap.

But just as Americans and the British were shocked to realize that Japan could produce deadly fighter planes as well as tinny toys, the hard-working and prosperous ethnic Chinese of Southeast Asia have alarmed and created jealousy in the majority societies around them. Indeed, in Southeast Asia we face one of the great cultural watersheds on the planet as the Japanese-Han-Confucian values that place the community first run into the Thai-Indian-Buddhist values that place self-realization and enjoyment first. This conflict is part of the ancient hatred between the Khmer and the Vietnamese. And it has had tragic and violent consequences in other Southeast Asian cultures that value dance and pleasure as ethnic Chinese minorities prosper through hard work and self-discipline.

Clearly there is a fear to offend the sensibilities of ethnic Thais, Malays, and others in the region by ascribing economic success to their ethnic Chinese minorities. Yet clearly they have been the powerhouse behind the Thai, Malaysian, and Indonesian economic miracles. Already ethnic Chinese from Taiwan, Hong Kong, Singapore, and Thailand are spearheading the development of Cambodia, Vietnam, and Laos now that investment barriers are gone and the still-communist governments are welcoming foreign capital and know-how.

The ethnic Chinese have been called the Jews of Asia, serving as valuable links in the economy and between neighboring economies but always held at arms length by the somewhat resentful non-Chinese majority. Thailand forced its Chinese to assimilate in the 1920s and 1930s, leading to widespread intermarriage and a sharp reduction in conflict with the majority ethnic Thai. But Indonesia massacred thousands of Chinese in a failed revolution in 1965 and Malaysia has also known anti-Chinese riots. Vietnam expelled many of its Chinese to China while others fled by boat. Burma has also suppressed its Chinese minority. Hence, the reluctance to offend non-Chinese majorities by ascribing too much importance to the role of the ethnic Chinese in the economy.

One participant said that in developing countries, the rule of law is at best sketchy. Powerful and socially prominent individuals are likely to prevail in commercial conflicts. This weakens confidence in the structures that govern business such as contracts. Ethnic Chinese, however, by sealing deals with a handshake rather than a written contract, and by relying on reputation, trust, family ties, and recommendations, have been able to flourish in this frontier environment. But regardless of the importance of the ethnic Chinese—if they are 10 percent or 40 percent responsible for Southeast Asian success—within the macro environment in each nation and in the region they have been instrumental in the development that has propelled so many families from the water buffalo and bamboo hut to motorbikes and universities in one breathless generation.

NEW REGIONAL ALLIANCES: GROWTH CIRCLES

Now the transnational business ties that the ethnic-Chinese have pioneered in Southeast Asia are changing, growing, and taking a unique form that some have called "growth circles." These are regions that include parts of adjacent countries, which have become intertwined in trade to an extent that surpasses national interests. For example, there is the circle formed by Taiwan, Hong Kong, and Eastern China. Then there is Laos, Vietnam, China, and Hong Kong. In addition, there is Thailand, Burma, China, and Laos. Each of these areas is building a network of roads and interdependent trading patterns. In the future, the dominant business groups setting the pace for development in these regions may come into conflict with the central governments over any number of issues such as efforts to curtail drugs in the Golden Triangle, to preserve forests in Cambodia, Laos, and Burma, to return taxes to the center, and to control border movements.

Another issue is that of the Asia Pacific Economic Conference. Bill Clinton met with the APEC leaders in Seattle, except for Malaysia's Mahathir, in an effort to forge an understanding with America's biggest trading partners. But many Asians felt it was opportunistic for the United States to try and keep one leg in the North American Free Trade Association while the other is in APEC. What the attention APEC has drawn to Asian issues revealed is the new competition for access to higher technology.

To some experts, the results of the East Asian and Southeast Asian economic development story produce no clear standards for success. By prospering despite having little natural resources, they proved that human resources matter most. The superior policies that they adopted were to emphasize exports, human capital, investment, and macro control that clamped down on inflation yet spurred growth. Cultural factors led to high savings rates. But there was a wide range of industrial policy ranging from none to highly structured. Even the United States is considering whether to learn from East Asia's experience in the matter of industrial policy. Perhaps the final analysis is that even if subsidies are given to launch industries, they should be given for a short period of time. Indonesia prospered only after it got rid of its industrial policy, while Thailand never had one, relying on foreign direct investment.

So the lessons for the rest of the world are that most countries will lose if they gamble on intervention. Another lesson is that of pragmatism—policymakers should be willing and able to reverse course when they see it is necessary. Policy must never be dictated by ideology. But in order to reverse failing policies, there must be enough openness, scrutiny, and review to conduct an objective analysis. In addition, there must be a unified bureaucracy attuned to common goals and political support for bureaucrats who act on behalf of those goals.

As the conference ended, a series of questions for future debate were tabled. One participant asked for ways to measure economic reforms in Vietnam and China and to measure the informal economies of the region. He also asked where would the tiger cubs go next—whether they would transfer to full industrialization. Another asked for study of legal systems in Southeast Asia, especially in the way China and Japan do business without resorting to courts.

Another question was to review how Southeast Asian countries viewed future multilateral security arrangements and their attitudes towards major powers such as the United States and Japan. Another participant asked to study the region's ability and interest in reaching out to Africa and Central Asia. And one asked for deeper study of changing social systems—demography, family patterns, gender issues—as well as the new political pressure groups such as nongovernmental organizations.

A future session on Indochina was suggested, since it is the Wild West of the region, and a review of Australia's place and role in the region. And a study of the area's mass media was also proposed, including how Asian and Western media see each other's regions. One participant wants a study of the Mekong River, which links so many nations in the region. And another asked for study of transnational links in the area with respect to NGOs, private sector, trade and tourism, family contacts, energy supply and consumption, and border issues.

UNANSWERED QUESTION

In the end one may ask why did these bureaucrats and the elites who gave them their direction decide to follow a relatively selfless path, to take 10 percent but leave 90? To chart an economic course that led to a majority prospering? Some say the economic vision shared by these bureaucracies was chosen with a view to history. There is also a national pride factor involved—while Thais and Malaysians and Indonesians sometimes seem prickly when lectured to by Westerners on copyright infringement, human rights, drugs, and the environment, that prickliness is also part of a sense of pride in their country. Many of those officials would be ashamed that their people would be hungry and sick, lacking the benefits of modernity. This undefinable cultural heritage, combined with the regional flows of capital, know-how, and security, appear to be the vital ingredients that have made the miracle of Southeast Asia.

Contributors

Ben Barber is a journalist and consultant. He writes for several publications, including The *Christian Science Monitor, The Washington Post,* and *The New York Times.*

Frederick Z. Brown directs the Henry Luce Foundation program in Southeast Asian Studies at The Johns Hopkins University Paul H. Nitze School of Advanced International Studies in Washington, DC, where he is also a fellow of the JHU Foreign Policy Institute. A former foreign service officer and former professional staff member on the U.S. Senate Foreign Relations Committee, Mr. Brown is author of Second Chance: The United States and Indochina in the 1990s.

Ralph N. Clough is a professorial lecturer and coordinator of the SAIS China Forum at the Paul H. Nitze School of Advanced International Studies, The Johns Hopkins University, Washington, DC. He is a retired foreign service officer, having served in China, Hong Kong, and Taiwan. Dr. Clough's most recent book is *Reaching Across the Taiwan Strait: People-to-People Diplomacy.*

Bernard Gordon is professor of political science at the University of New Hampshire, Durham. His most recent book is *New Directions for American Policy in Asia.*

Llewellyn D. Howell is professor and chair of the Department of International Studies, The American Graduate School of International Management (Thunderbird), Glendale, Arizona.

Young C. Kim is chairman of The American Council on Asian and Pacific Affairs and Director of The Gaston Sigur Center for East Asian Studies and professor of political science and international affairs at The George Washington University, Washington, DC. He is also coeditor of the *Journal of Northeast Asian Studies.* Dr. Kim's publications include *Japanese Journalists and Their World.*

Bruce M Koppel is vice-president for research and education at the East-West Center in Honolulu, HI. His most recent books focus on the politics of Japan's foreign aid, institutional and technological change in Asian agriculture, and employment issues in rural Asia.

Anwar Nasution is professor of economics at the University of Indonesia, Jakarta. Dr. Nasution is also economic consultant to several organizations, including the Ministry of Cooperatives and Small Scale Enterprises of Indonesia, the UN-ESCAP, Bangkok, Development Planning and Industrial Division, and the OECD Development Centre, Paris.

Ronald D. F. Palmer is Baker professor and diplomatic consultant-in-residence in the Elliott School of International Affairs, The George Washington University, Washington, DC. During his career in the foreign service, he served as U.S. ambassador to Togo, Malaysia, and Mauritius.

Stephen Parker is currently serving as the chief economist for The Asia Foundation and its Center for Asian Pacific Affairs. He has served as a consultant for many projects, including the United Nations Development Program in Indonesia.

Gareth Porter is director of the International Program for the Environmental and Energy Study Institute, Washington, DC. His most recent book is *Vietnam: The Politics of Bureaucratic Socialism*. Dr. Porter has been on the faculties of the School of Advanced International Studies of The Johns Hopkins University, the City College of New York, and The American University.

Hak K. Pyo is a professor in the Department of International Economics, Seoul National University, Seoul. He previously served as visiting professor at the International Monetary Fund.

Daniel Unger is an assistant professor of government at Georgetown University. Dr. Unger's publications include *Japan's Emerging Global Role* (author and editor).

Win Tin is the minister of the Ministry of Finance of Myanmar, Yangon.

Index

Africa, 163, 173n. 6, 144–45, 247, 255
AFTA, 170, 208, 213–17
AIDs, 97, 98, 155
APEC, 18, 170, 174n. 16, 208, 213–20, 222, 244, 254
ASEAN, 47, 85, 127, 143, 159, 162–65, 169–70, 172n. 1, 174n. 18, 207, 209 fig. 1, 211 fig. 3, 212 fig. 4, 213–17, 222, 236–37, 243, 244, 250–51, 252
authoritarianism, 1, 6, 11, 12, 29, 40, 43, 99, 247–48; soft, 128, 134, 247

balance of payments, 163; in South Korea, 2
Burma. *See* Myanmar
Buddhism, 42, 248, 253

Cambodia, 96–97; economic development in, 162; deforestation in, 186–87, 190, 191; forest cover in, 178–79; infrastructure in, 97; Khmer Rouge, 85, 96, 97, 189, 193, 194, 253; population of, 85; Norodom Sihanouk, 96

Canada, 11
CEPT, 216
Chile, 11, 18–19
China, 169, 171, 188, 189, 218, 219, 236, 239, 243, 252; Chinese Communist party, 227; Deng Xiaoping, 228, 229, 233; economic growth in, 228–29; Gang of Four, 227–28; human rights in, 219–20; Li Peng, 240; Mao, 227; Zhu Rongji, 229
communism, 148, 207, 250, 253; anti–, 135n. 12; in China, 227; in Malaysia, 24, 41; threat of, 128
corruption, 128
currency devaluation, 218, 228; of baht, 146, 152, 163–64

debt service, 168
deforestation, 197, 198, 250; causes of, 183–90; consequences of, 190–91
democratization, 1–2, 6–9, 12, 13, 105–9, 126–28, 129–33, 135n. 12, 154; democratic consolidation, 116–18; and economic development, 109–13; and foreign aid, 121–31; and security, 118–19
deregulation, 64–65, 169
domestic investment, 171
duty drawback systems, 165

EAEC, 18, 213–14, 217
economic growth, 168–72, 244–45, 249
economic integration, 169, 170, 234–36, 240, 254

education, 2, 17, 249, 251
exports, 159–60, 164, 168, 170, 208, 215, 228, 230, 233, 245; of rice, 140, 148
European Economic Community, 235
European Community, 164, 169, 219

FAO, 183
foreign aid, 130, 163, 238
foreign investment, 159, 160–66, 171–72, 173n. 5, 173n. 9; European, 171; North American, 171, 173n. 5
foreign trade, 160–66

GATT, 164, 169–70, 173n. 6, 219

Hong Kong, 164, 165, 169, 171, 174n. 11, 229–33, 236–37, 246, 252; Governor Christopher Patten, 232–33; Sir Y. K. Pao, 231
human rights, 18, 126, 131, 133

IMF, 90, 93, 95, 145
Indonesia, deforestation in, 50–51; deregulation in, 50–51; development financing in, 54–61; economic development in, 47–49, 50 table 2, 161, 162; exporter of plywood, 188; FDI in, 60–61; forest cover in, 178–81; Konfrontasi in, 207, 215; ODA in, 59–60, 65; President Suharto, 187, 213, 214, 217, 247; public investment in, 61–63
Infrastructure, 165
ITTO, 181, 185

Japan, 11, 60–61, 138, 152, 159, 163, 164, 169, 170, 171, 173n. 5, 187, 188, 196, 208, 213, 217, 218, 219, 222, 227, 231, 232, 237, 238, 239, 243, 244, 249, 251; endaka, 218; Keidanren, 150; Prime Minister Morihiro Hosokawa, 219

Laos, 94–96; deforestation in, 184, 186, 190, 191; economic development in, 95, 162; forest cover in, 178–78; population of, 85
Latin America, 163, 173n. 6, 174n. 12, 208, 220, 221 fig. 5, 222 fig. 6, 223 fig. 6A, 244–45, 247

Malaysia, Deputy Prime Minister Musa Hitam, 35; economic development in, 15–18, 161; exporter of raw logs, 19, 188; exports of, 19–20; forest cover in, 178–81; history of, 20–24; Hussein Onn, 33; Jaffar

Onn, 33; Look East policy in, 17, 28; Minister of Finance Daim Zainuddin, 34, 36; Minister of Finance Tengku Razaleigh, 33, 34, 35, 36; Prime Minister Mahathir Mohamed, 17, 18, 28, 30–31, 33, 35, 36–37, 38, 40, 43, 44, 213–14, 217–18, 225n. 14, 247, 254; risk assessment of, 38–43; stability in, 30; Tun Abdul Razak, 33; Tunku Abdul Rahman, 32, 33; UMNO leadership in, 31–38

MFN, 100, 245
Middle East, 42, 220
Myanmar, agriculture in, 72–74; balance of payments in, 70–71; deforestation in, 190; economic and financial reforms in, 67–69; economic development in, 162; energy in, 82–83; foreign exchange liberalization in, 69–70; forest cover in, 178–79; forestry in, 74; industry in, 77–78; livestock and fisheries in, 76; mining in, 78–79; population of, 67; SLORC in, 67; tourism in, 81–82; trade in, 79–81

NAFTA, 217, 235, 254
NGO, 113–16, 121, 123–26, 129, 134n. 9 and 10, 194–95, 196–97, 255
NIE, 8, 17, 18, 38, 60, 164, 215, 248
non-tariff barriers, 166
North Korea, 3, 9, 220, 243, 250
Northeast Asia, 138, 140, 163–64, 169

OEDC, 65, 219
open regionalism, 170
overseas Chinese, 15–16, 17, 25, 26, 31, 32, 37, 38, 43, 147–50, 157n. 41, 166–67, 169, 174n. 13 and 14, 227, 236, 238, 239, 243, 252–54

Pakistan, 135n. 12
Papua New Guinea, 197–98; deforestation in, 185, 186–87, 188; forest cover in, 181–83
People's Republic of China. See China
Philippines, 2, 135n. 12 and 14, 139, 140, 162, 163, 166, 168, 171–72, 172n. 1, 174n. 18, 178, 196, 207, 216–17, 237, 243, 247, 250, 251; deforestation in, 183, 184, 185, 186, 187–88, 190, 191, 198, 199; forest cover in, 179; President Marcos, 134n. 6, 139; President Ramos, 217
Plaza Accord, 58, 159, 163, 218
political pluralism, 217
protectionism, 141, 235, 249

security, 118–19, 133–34, 240, 244, 250–51, 255
Singapore, 11; economic development in, 161, 162, 246; Prime Minister Lee Kuan Yew,

27, 98, 99; S. Dhanabalan, 216
South Korea, 138, 139, 153, 159, 163, 164, 169, 171, 173n. 7, 187, 213–14, 232, 243, 244, 249, 250, 251; 1960 elections in, 2; cost of democratic transition in, 12; Dae-Jung Kim, 3; economic dependence in, 7–8; income distribution in, 7; indicators of structural change in, 8; industrialization in, 4; Justice Department in, 9; KCIA, 4; military/capitalist alliance in, 11; President Doo-Hwan Chun, 1, 5, 10; President Kim, 2, 5, 9, 10, 12; President Park, 1, 3, 4, 5, 12; President Rhee, 2, 3; President Roh, 1, 5–6, 10; Prime Minister Chang, 3; "Restoration System," 3; stock price index in, 11; tensions with North Korea, 9; U.S. exports to, 7; U.S. forces in, 4; wealth distribution in, 12
Soviet Union, 86, 93, 96, 99, 189, 227, 238
standard of living, 172; in Singapore, 165
subsidies, 170

Taiwan, 138, 139, 153, 159, 163, 164, 165, 169, 171, 173n. 7, 174n. 11 and 15, 233–36, 237–38, 252; Chiang Ching-kuo, 233; Democratic Progressive party, 240

Thailand, 1960s economic growth, 138; Anand Panyarachul, 141, 142, 144, 146, 149, 154, 193, 214–15; Chart party, 150, 155, 192; Chatichai government, 142, 144, 149, 150, 151, 152 table 5, 154, 155, 158n. 71; Chuan Leekpai, 146, 151, 154; deforestation in, 184, 190, 191, 192, 199n. 9; economic development in, 161; forest cover in, 178–79; King Bhumibol Adulyadej, 247; Kriangsak, 154; political participation in, 149; Prem Tinsulanonda, 142, 146, 149, 150, 152 table 5, 154, 158n. 71, 247; role of military in, 151–52, 154; Sarit Thanarat, 141, 143, 147–49, 152 table 5, 154; Social Action party, 192; state in economy, 142–47; tariffs in, 142, 144 table; Thanat Khoman, 215; Thanin, 154; triangular trade, 237

United Kingdom, 11
UNTAC, in Cambodia, 127
United States, 11, 164, 165, 169, 174n. 16, 219 9, 174n. 11, 208, 221 fig. 5, 222 fig. 6, 223 fig. 6A and fig. 7, 224 fig. 8, 225, 231, 250–51, 253; President Bill Clinton, 213, 217, 218, 219, 225n. 14, 254; President George Bush, 90, 213; President James Carter, 4; in APEC, 213–14, 218–20;

Secretary of State George Shultz, 208;
Secretary of State James Baker, 208, 213,
219; Winston Lord, 220

Vavilov Centers, 178
Vietnam, 86–94, 240, 250, 251; deforestation
in, 184, 186, 190–91; economic
development in, 88–90, 162; external
assistance in, 92, 93; forest cover in, 178–
79; petroleum in, 91–92; population of,
85; U.S. embargo in, 90

West Germany, 11
West Indies, 1
World Bank, 15, 29, 38, 47, 49, 64, 90, 93, 95,
145, 181, 184, 185, 190, 191, 194, 195,
198, 246, 248